Farther Afield

in the Study of Nature-Oriented Literature

Farther Afield in the Study of Nature-Oriented Literature

Patrick D. Murphy

UNIVERSITY PRESS   OF VIRGINIA

Charlottesville and London

The University Press of Virginia
© 2000 by the Rector and Visitors of the University of Virginia
All rights reserved
Printed in the United States of America

First published in 2000

☉ The paper used in this publication meets the minimum requirements
of the American National Standard for Information Sciences—
Permanence of Paper for Printed Library Materials, ANSI Z39.48-1984.

Library of Congress Cataloging-in-Publication Data

Murphy, Patrick D., 1951–
    Farther afield in the study of nature-oriented literature /
    Patrick D. Murphy.
        p.   cm.
    Includes bibliographical references (p.) and index.
    ISBN 0-8139-1905-3. — ISBN 0-8139-1906-1 (pbk.)
    1. Nature in literature. 2. Ecology in literature.
    3. Environmental protection in literature. 4. Environmental
    literature—History and criticism—Theory, etc. 5. Literature—
    History and criticism—Theory, etc. I. Title.
    PN48.M87 2000
    809'.9336—dc21   99-37418
                                                              CIP

For the graduate students at Indiana University of Pennsylvania who have taught me more than can be contained in any book.

Contents

Preface—
By Way of Memoir

In 1969 I took my Mustang on a two-thousand-mile trail run from Wilmington, Illinois, southwest across the Mississippi, through the Ozarks, down into the southwestern desert, across mountain ranges, some snowcapped, down into the blistering heat of the Mojave, and on to the Pacific Ocean. The Mustang, of course, was a 1965 Ford with my luggage for college in the trunk and my bass-guitar amplifier in the backseat. The trail was concrete and asphalt from start to finish, dotted with gas stations, bars, restaurants, and air-conditioned motels. My father (who would die in the fall of 1997) rode along and paid most of the bills. I paid little attention to the land through which we traveled, focusing instead on arriving at UCLA, where I would begin my university studies and leave behind—or so I thought—the Midwest and its small towns, and my father and many of his values. Having divorced my father, my mother would remarry while we were on the road, and I saw myself, as well, divorcing the past of my childhood and its parochial education. Marriage to anyone or anything was not yet on my mind, however.

Besides looking for sex, with the unreal expectations that many eighteen-year-old males had of the days of free love, when V.D. was something only Vietnam vets brought home with them, I was, as much of the rock music of the day persuaded me to do, looking for some kind of adventure.

Earth Day was on the horizon and environmental activism was growing, but none of that caught my attention. Rather, the antiwar movement became my attraction as I attempted to wed literary analysis with antiwar activism. When the invasion of Cambodia took place in the spring of 1970 and students were murdered at Jackson State and Kent State—although only the white students garnered international media attention—I skipped classes and participated in the UCLA student strike. Eventually, the campus calmed down and I returned to my early English literature survey to find that my professor demanded that I complete a rather lengthy research paper to avoid failing class. Edmund Spenser's allegory was my chosen subject, but as to why I have no recollection. That summer my father stopped funding my education once my brother, who was in the navy and stationed at Da Nang, revealed to him that I was involved in antiwar protests. I had to sell the Mustang to raise tuition money and ended up missing the fall quarter, which caused me to lose my student military deferment—a handy loophole when protesting a war.

People asked me why I was majoring in English, and my stock reply was based on a belief that literature could change consciousness, that individual ways of thinking and the direction of human lives could be altered and redirected for the collective benefit of humanity. When people found out I had been in a Catholic seminary for a year in high school, that answer seemed no more plausible but far more understandable. But by sophomore year, as my political involvement gradually increased, my doubts about that argument developed until one day, when I was attending a course on Menippéan satire, the whole literary-criticism game became transparently irrelevant to events in the world. As I stood up to leave the seminar room, the professor asked where I was going. "To change my major," I replied, and walked over to the history department.

Southeast Asian history became my focus for the completion of my B.A. I knew more about the mountains of Laos than the Alleghenies, where I now live. Although I was accepted to graduate school in history and actually took classes at a couple of schools, in the seven years after completing my undergraduate degree (in 1973) I devoted myself to full-time political activism, including running a marxist bookstore in Los Angeles for a few years. In those days, the marxist lens precluded serious attention to the global environmental crisis and the ways in which imperialism was not only oppressing and exploiting the masses but also exploiting the earth. World War III was the only global crisis that seemed imminent. Yet I frequently took issue with those in my own Maoist party and others frequenting the bookstore who portrayed socialism and communism as unfettered consumption and endless distribution. Simplification, utility, and an end to artificially induced consumer desires were at least a small part of my vision for the future.

After leaving such activism, I tried once again to return to graduate school to study history, but I couldn't muster the enthusiasm. While we were working in a supermarket, my future wife encouraged me to again return to school. Initially thinking I would take a few creative-writing classes to improve the quality of my verse, I ended up with an M.A. and experience teaching. Teaching seemed like a better career than supermarket management, and school was not only relatively easy for me but much more stimulating than doing four thousand price changes every weekend. While working on my M.A., I had encountered a visiting professor from Humboldt State who taught a class on the modern American novel at California State University, Northridge, and he introduced me to Jack Kerouac's *Dharma Bums*, which in turn introduced me to Gary Snyder. Somewhere along the way I also picked up Wendell Berry's poetry, which reminded me in very positive ways of the agrarian aspects of my childhood. Suddenly, literary study no longer seemed so "transparently irrelevant." These authors were highly involved in the world, initiating daily practices that amazingly integrated art and life, and they caused me to reflect on my own impulses to write in order to interact with readers critically and creatively.

While I ended up writing my Ph.D. dissertation on the modern American long poem, I continued to work on Snyder and Berry and gradually increased my attention to ecological literary issues. Although I was concerned early on with gendered images of the earth, my attention to ecofeminism would come later, after I overcame my initially strong resistance to any form of feminism.

Due to my background in history, I tended to lean toward context and themes in literary analysis, reinforced by postmarxist-class and nation-state analysis. The dissertation led me to develop a strong attentiveness to prob-

lems of genre and the implications of structural analysis. Mikhail Bakhtin's
dialogics has replaced Mao's dialectics as a philosophical method, but context and theme remain of crucial concern, as they must for anyone engaged
in ecological criticism. Yet, after seemingly getting away from structural and
generic analysis in the early 1990s, I find myself returning to it as part of a
developing and ongoing argument about the culture of nature writing, nature literature, ecofiction, environmental literature, and whatever other
terms critics use to label literary attention to the relationship of humanity
to the rest of nature.

And so, in the chapters that follow, I begin with a provisional taxonomy
that attempts to address the issues of mode and genre as they pertain to the
categorization of literature concerned with nature and human–rest-of-nature interaction. This taxonomy will provide an introduction to the genre
and mode structure of the subject I am addressing throughout this book.
While my introduction treats the structure of the field through a taxonomy
of literary production, my conclusion addresses the structure of the field
that analyzes such literature. It raises questions about the integration of ecological literacy into interdisciplinary studies and the implications of interdisciplinary studies for the future of English departments.

The rest of the chapters can be divided into three sections. The early
chapters (1–4) primarily expand on, develop from, and address tangentially
the concerns raised by the introductory taxonomy. They do so first by elab-
orating my views on issues within the field of ecological criticism—*ecocrit-
icsm* for short—particularly its nonfictional bias, and by addressing the illusion of nonfictionality along with the distinction between nature
literature and environmental literature. Second, they address both the relationship of ecofeminism to postmodernism and how ecocritical analysis,
particularly ecofeminism, is founded upon and presumes the possibility of
human agency in culture as well as in nature—in contrast to the lack of
agency often posited within postmodernist theories. And third, the entire
issue of genre, mode, and critical orientation is resituated through attention
to the multicultural and international dimensions of nature-sensitive and
environmentally concerned literary production around the world.

The middle chapters (5–10) emphasize discussions of specific literary
works, sometimes in groups and sometimes individually, particularly but not

exclusively those by women. These chapters illustrate various claims made in the earlier chapters. Attention is given to multicultural diversity and its relation to biological diversity, as well as to the particular insights of women writers, in terms of nature appreciation and also in terms of how creative work extends and critiques theoretical work. The relationship of cultural diversity to biological diversity, of multiculturalism to environmentalism, is particularly developed through an extended analysis of the prose and poetry of Pat Mora. I also include some consideration of nature-oriented literature in translation, treating both a variety of nature-oriented fiction and the works of the Japanese writer Ishimure Michiko.

The final chapters (11 and 12) of the book shift the focus somewhat from literary criticism to the related terrains of literary persuasiveness, literary pedagogy, the language that shapes our perceptions, and the possibility of perceptions that require new language. Although becoming more frequent, such a departure from a strictly theoretical or strictly applied-criticism focus in a book remains unusual. I have made the decision to include these chapters quite deliberately. Just as I do not think theory should be separated from application unless utterly unavoidable, neither do I believe that theory and applied criticism should be separated from pedagogy, institutional analysis, or a critique of the discourses and languages that shape our very ability to think about theories and critical interpretations. Each of these domains is part of a larger interpretive system, and I think all critical readers of literature benefit from such a reminder. It is also very much the case that my theorizing and interpretations arise primarily from books that I have taught and ideas that I have reflected on after questions or comments from students.

For those readers of this book who may not be teachers, I think it is worth observing that critical reading is a form of self-teaching that has its own kind of pedagogy, and that most readers talk about the books they read to other individuals, frequently much more for purposes of persuasion than for providing information. Persuasion, too, I believe is a type of teaching, and the ways in which readers use their reading to educate others have a pedagogy underlying them, although it is almost always an unarticulated one.

Many of these chapters began as conference presentations or lectures.

I have sought to maintain the sound of that performative orality not only because I think it makes for easier, clearer, and more relaxed reading, but also because I hope that such an oral dimension will evoke a sense of time-liness and engagement. I want to encourage readers to pick up where I leave off, to set the book down and set to work in myriad ways on changing hearts and minds, so that we can answer with theories and practices the question posed by Linda Hogan in *Dwellings*: "How do we learn to trust ourselves enough to hear the chanting of earth?"

Acknowledgments

FIRST let me thank those who have initiated or contributed to the fruition of various chapters. Katsunori Yamazato of the University of the Ryukyus helped make me believe that a trip to Japan was possible and that there would be some interest in remarks that I might wish to make there. My week in Okinawa in May 1996 provided me with the opportunity to become culturally and spatially grounded, as well as to talk to a very receptive audience about multiculturalism. Professor Yamazato and all of the faculty members I met at the University of the Ryukyus went out of their way to make me feel welcome and comfortable. I was also most fortunate to have the assistance of Ikue Kina, my student in the United States and a colleague of Professor Yamazato, who helped me prepare for the trip and was most gracious to me and my family, providing us, among many other things, with the privilege of meeting her mother.

The United States Information Service in Japan assisted me in many ways, most importantly through funding, first on a trip to Japan in 1996 and then on a lecture-research Fulbright Senior Fellowship to the University of the Ryukyus, Okinawa, in 1997–98, which included assistance with lectures given at Hiroshima, Kyōto, Nagoya, and Sendai. Professor Shoko Itoh of Hiroshima University worked tirelessly to arrange two talks for me to present in 1996, one at her campus and one to the Chu-Shikoku literary society, and another presentation in 1997. Without her efforts and suggestions,

I would never have written the chapter on ecofeminism and postmodernism.

In Tokyo in 1996 I had the good fortune of being in the hands of Professor Kenichi Takada of Aoyama Gakuin University, who extended me every courtesy and then some. And to Professor Kenichi Noda, President of the Association for the Study of Literature and Environment (ASLE)—Japan, I owe a special thanks for providing me with a platform from which to speak and for suggesting topics both provocative and challenging in 1996 and in 1998. For the first part of this book I am deeply indebted to all of my Japanese colleagues.

But my indebtedness does not stop there. Charlotte Zoe Walker's help was also very beneficial. As the indefatigable organizer of the Sharp Eyes II conference at SUNY Oneonta, Charlotte arranged for me to make the address that became chapter 3 and allowed me to present a short paper on Hogan, Escamill, and Yamashita as well; this eventually became chapter 10.

Various colleagues around the United States have also influenced and encouraged my work, and I hesitate to name any for fear of inadvertently omitting someone. Greta Gaard, however, cannot go unthanked, since her collaboration with me on other ventures has been an inspiration and has encouraged me to continue to think through more thoroughly the various issues of ecofeminist criticism that concern me. The comments of Cheryll Glotfelty, who served as an external reviewer of this manuscript, have helped me to improve it, particularly by challenging me to write more explicitly about international nature-oriented literature. Without her suggestions, I would not have written chapters 5 and 8. Three British colleagues deserve mention: Terry Gifford for his witty charm and rock-climbing agility, both literally and figuratively, who has challenged my thinking with his own brilliant *Green Voices*; Richard Kerridge, who invited my participation in one of his ventures and caused me to think through the relationship of multiculturality and inhabitation more deeply than I might otherwise have done; and Greg Garrard, who invited me to Swansea to speak at the first U.K. conference devoted to ecocriticism.

The doctoral students at IUP have been invaluable to the creation of this book. For one, many of them have encouraged me by quoting from my book *Literature, Nature, and Other* in papers and dissertations. They have helped me through various dialogues, often demonstrating that I was mistaken in thinking I had succeeded in making clear to others a theoretical construct. Several of them have read and commented on versions of the chapters herein, among them Jeff Bartone, Michelle Toohey, Joseph Register, Jia-yi Cheng-Levine, Ikue Kina, Mayumi Toyosato, Dong-oh Choi, and Yong-ki Kang. Donelle Dreese has read the entire manuscript, helping me to improve it at many points. Bonnie and Mariko, *tsuma to musume*, graciously provided time and space for me to work. In particular, Bonnie has always helped me to overcome various setbacks that otherwise might have discouraged me from completing this project.

Of course, since this book, like all my other critical work, stands as a participatory foray into the world of reading and critiquing nature-oriented literature, it becomes another part of my "once occurrent event of being," as Bakhtin would put it. And for that I have no alibi, but assume responsibility for it from start to finish, including its errors, omissions, weaknesses, and shortcomings. May these not interfere with the pleasures and challenges of the reading.

Finally, let me acknowledge the journals and books in which portions and variants of the following chapters have appeared or are forthcoming. Chapter 2, "Environmental Literature: Beyond Nature Writing and the Fiction of Nonfictionality," was originally delivered at the annual meeting of the Association for the Study of Literature and Environment—Japan (May 1996), with a Japanese translation of portions of it appearing in the *ASLE—JAPAN Newsletter*, fall 1996. The "Location, Location, Location" section of chapter 3 is based on my introduction to *The Literature of Nature: An International Sourcebook* (London: Fitzroy Dearborn Publishing, 1998) and is reprinted by permission of the press; the untitled poem in that chapter that begins "Step out onto the Planet" is reprinted from Lew Welch, *Ring of Bone*, © 1979, by permission of Grey Fox Press. A slightly different version of chapter 4, "Ecofeminism and Postmodernism: Agency, Transformation, and Future Possibilities," appeared in a special issue on ecology, women, and development of the *Journal of the National Women's Studies Association*, vol. 9, no. 3 (1997), and is reprinted here by permission of Indiana University Press. Chapter 5 is a revised version of "Anotherness and Inhabitation in Recent Multicultural American Literature," which appears in *Writing and the Environment*, edited by Richard Kerridge and Neil Sammells (London: Zed Books, 1998), and is reprinted with permission of Zed Books; quotations from "Toward Spider Springs" and "The Significance of a Veteran's Day" are used with the permission of the author: Permission granted by Simon J. Ortiz. "Toward Spider Springs" and "The Significance of a Veteran's Day" originally published in *Woven Stone*, University of Arizona Press, Tucson, AZ, 1992. A version of chapter 7 originally appeared in *MELUS* vol. 21, no. 1 (1996), copyright 1996 *MELUS*, the Society for the Study of the Multi-Ethnic Literature of the United States, and is reprinted with permission; quotations from the following poems by Pat Mora are reprinted by permission of the Arte Público Press: "Bribe," "Bruja: Witch," "Plot," and "Curandera" from *Chants;* "Echoes," "Tomás Rivera," "Miss Doc at Eighty," and "Secrets" from *Borders;* "Divisadero Street" and "Don Jaime" from *Communion.* Chapter 9 is adapted, with significant changes, from "'The Women Are Speaking': Using Women's Literature to Extend and Critique Ecofeminism," which appears in *Ecofeminist Literary Criticism: Theory, Interpretation, Pedagogy*, edited by Greta Gaard and myself (Urbana and Chicago: University of Illinois Press, 1998), and is reprinted by permission of the University of Illinois Press; excerpts from "Fish in Air" and "Reclaiming Slashburns" are taken from *Cultivating Excess* by Lori Anderson (Portland, OR: The Eighth Mountain Press, 1992) © 1992 by Lori Anderson; reprinted by permission of the author and publisher. A slightly different version of chapter 10, "Commodification, Resistance, Inhabitation, and Identity: The Novels of Linda Hogan, Edna Escamill, and Karen Tei Yamashita," originally appeared in *Phoebe: A Journal of Feminist Scholarship, Theory and Aesthetics*, vol. 9, no. 1 (1997), and is reprinted by permission. "Noonday Slumber of a Faun" and portions of "Wind-Sheared Tree" are quoted here from *The Night Watchman* by Yu Kwang-chung (Chiu Ko Publishing Co., Ltd., Taipei, copyright 1992) by permission of the author.

Introduction

Toward a Taxonomy of American Nature-Oriented Literature

s the early chapters in *Farther Afield in the Study of Nature-Oriented Literature* will demonstrate, the determination of genre and consideration of mode as well as genealogies of literary influence and traditions have generated conflict and confusion about what constitutes the American literature of nature. I will show first the need to distinguish between the terrain of ecological criticism—criticism that arises from and is oriented toward a concern with human and nonhuman interaction and interrelationship—and the distinct terrain of the literature itself. Ecocriticism can be employed in studying any literary work insofar as that work reveals or reflects something about nature and humanity's place in, with, or against it. But that does not automatically make any work that can be fruitfully interpreted by means of ecocriticism a type of nature-oriented literature. Nature-oriented literature is limited to having either nonhuman nature itself as a subject, character, or major component of the setting, or to a text that says something about human-nonhuman interaction, human philosophies about nature, or the possibility of engaging nature by means of or in spite of human culture.

Difficulties begin to arise in part when individuals take a particular subset of nature-oriented literature, such as the nonfiction prose essay of nature writing, and define that genre as the starting point for the rest of the literature. Such a move establishes prescriptive criteria for evaluating the authenticity or quality of forms of literature that do not descend from that lineage but arise from other generic or cultural literary expressions. Certainly no one would argue that Chinese T'ang Dynasty poetry or Japanese haiku and its international variations descends from the natural-history essay. But what seems apparent from an international perspective seems often invisible from an American-centered perspective.

There are many ways of representing human engagement with the rest of nature in literary forms that do not descend from natural history, that are not written in prose, that are not nonfiction, that are not rhetorically structured as essays, but that are authentic works of literature addressing nature. In an attempt to sort out some of those diverse literary forms within U.S. literature, and in order to introduce such American literature to Japanese undergraduate students, I developed a rudimentary, provisional taxonomy that I would like to present here, along with my initial reasoning, as a heuristic device. Various implications that flow from this taxonomic orientation are developed in the next few chapters

Background

From the earliest diaries, journals, exploration narratives, and travel stories, we learn that the nature of the New World was important to European explorers and settlers. The nature of this same "Old World" for Native Americans was also an integral part of their stories and songs. Each culture—the Puritans, Catholics, and Quakers, the Spanish, French, and Russians—and the various tribes viewed this nature differently as a result of religious beliefs, economic values, and goals relating to exploration and settlement. Each European group viewed the native peoples of this world differently as well, tending to associate them more with nature than with culture.[1]

To speak, then, of an American nature-oriented literature, we must recognize that ancient oral, tribal forms of such storytelling continue to exist and influence contemporary literary production, particularly but not exclusively by Native American authors. Chicano/a authors, for example, are increasingly drawing on their Native American cultural heritage in their writings, while many Euro-American writers have been influenced by Native American oral and written artistic traditions. Such writers range from Henry David Thoreau in the mid-nineteenth century to Mary Austin in the early twentieth century to Jerome Rothenberg in recent decades. We must also recognize that, into the nineteenth century, the European versions of American nature-oriented literature—*American* in the sense of being based on North American land, although aesthetically and ideologically mediated by cultures from other places—were recited, sung, and written in a variety of languages. Traces of some of these other languages, particularly Spanish and French, can be found in the literature written in English today, with the Spanish influences even more diverse as a result of the various nationalities and cultures using that language. There also exists a many-tongued, twentieth-century immigrant literature that remains largely unexplored.

As a result of the importance of nature in the daily lives of all of these people, native and immigrant alike, we find many descriptions of nature and its role in the literature that is produced. Focusing just on English-language texts, we can consider the importance of nature in the works of early colonial American writers. The idea of nature writing as a self-consciously practiced literary genre of nonfiction—natural history–based and often rhetorically rather than narratively structured prose, but more imaginative, aesthetic, and subjective than scientific natural history classifications—grew up with the nation itself and was firmly established by the time of such writers as Thoreau and Susan Fenimore Cooper, with whom the genre is often initially identified. There is also a fictional nature writing, drawing on but not limited to direct personal experience, which uses the same forms and strategies as the nonfiction variant, making it extremely difficult to distinguish from nonfiction nature writing by a close reading of the text alone (the distinction became a major dispute in the "nature fakers" controversy at the end of the nineteenth century).[2] Many works in this category are actually a mixture of nonfiction and fiction, combined in an effort to enrich the author's perception of truth or his or her depiction of reality.

There is also a distinct nature literature in the American tradition of aesthetically and narratively structured writing, which we can see in such Puritan and early republic poets as Anne Bradstreet, William Cullen Bryant, and later in Walt Whitman. For nineteenth-century fiction writers nature is often more than a setting; it is also a force or even a character, as with James Fenimore Cooper, Herman Melville, and Sarah Orne Jewett. Works such as theirs are not rhetorically structured, but aesthetically and narratively structured, and neither the poetry nor the fiction is concerned with the distinction between factual description and imaginative description.

As I will demonstrate in chapter 2, such nature writing and nature literature continue to be written and are more popular than ever, at least since the early 1900s. Such works are often read in opposition to modernist and postmodernist sensibilities and aesthetics, since they are frequently perceived as addressing the real and the organic in the world rather than the simulated and the artificial.[3] I would not, however, suggest a necessary opposition between nature writing–nature literature and modernist-postmodernist sensibilities and cultural periods. Rather, I would say that some nature-oriented literature rejects such sensibilities within the periods in which modernist and postmodernist aesthetics and philosophies predominate, while others embrace, adapt, or engage such sensibilities in their efforts to represent the relationship of humanity and culture to the rest of the world.

In addition to the mode of nature literature that I would define as including nature writing, there is also a mode that I call environmental literature that includes environmental writing. By mode I mean a philosophical or conceptual orientation rather than a style or structure (which are what constitute a genre)—the pastoral, for example, is a mode through which authors write poems, plays, novels, and essays. Nature literature and environmental literature use the same genres of poetry and fiction, for instance, but they approach their use differently.

Environmental writing often uses the essay form and various styles associated with journalism and scientific field notes, and it, too, tends to be heavily dominated by works labeled as nonfiction, while other works are fiction, and still others a mixture of the two. Unlike nature writing, however, environmental writing does not stop at describing the natural history of an area, but instead, or in addition, discusses the ways in which pollution, urbanization, and other forms of human intervention have altered the land and environment. It treats human actions in defense of, or on behalf of, wild and endangered nature. While George Perkins Marsh can certainly be labeled a nineteenth-century environmental writer, most authors who fit this categorization are ones writing in the twentieth century, especially after World War II, when a deeper scientific understanding of ecology developed and when more individuals sensed that natural environments are deeply and possibly irrevocably threatened by human activity. It may be the case, however, that the works that remain in print or have been brought back into print from the nineteenth century, and are preferred reading today, are precisely those that have more of an environmental-writing orientation than do their forgotten counterparts.

Environmental literature often begins with some of the same features as nature literature but departs from it in terms of authorial self-consciousness about environmental issues and problems. It is concerned more with the depiction of agrarian values than the plot of agrarian life, for example. In terms of fiction, environmental literature is more likely to produce a novel of ideas than a novel of action; it is more driven by theme than plot. In poetry, the concern is more often the intrinsic value of other animals' existence than what encounters with other animals mean to people.

Distinctions

Throughout the preceding section I have distinguished between works that I label as writing and ones that I label as literature. This distinction is not hierarchical. It has to do with the development of a tradition of literary analysis and with the expectations that readers tend to bring to works in terms of information and entertainment, facts and fictions, rhetoric and narration. Creative writers themselves are under no obligation to attend to or abide by this distinction.

The inclusion of writing as distinct from literature in the subject matter of English courses, particularly literature courses, has been a long process within literary studies. The field of ecocriticism really began with teachers calling for, and including in their own courses, critical attention to works of nonfiction, which, they thought, had literary merit. Until the past few decades such material would probably have been referred to as nonliterary and treated as ancillary. Currently one hears such terms as literary nonfiction and creative nonfiction. The former is certainly more accurate than the latter, but neither explicitly addresses the relationship between the literary or the creative and the nonfictionality of the text.

Rather than trying to label a work as fiction or nonfiction based on some quantitative evaluation of the degree to which it is factually accurate, literal, and representative of a direct experience by the author, I prefer to categorize works, at least in the case of prose, along the lines of whether the narrative dimension drives the selection of details and facts, or whether the narrative functions in the service of the delivery of information.

Since it is relatively noncontroversial to say that any prose literary work functions to generate a message between the author and reader, then the message component of a text cannot be the dividing line between fiction and nonfiction. Nor does the rhetorical structure itself serve this purpose, since fiction can mimic any form of human verbal communication. While factualness might seem to provide a mechanism for distinguishing fiction and nonfiction, a reader runs into the problem, on the one hand, of historical novels that contain copious amounts of factual information embedded in an invented story, such as Kiana Davenport's *Shark Dialogues* or Linda Hogan's *Mean Spirit*; on the other hand are nonfiction narratives that contain a significant amount of narrative framing, context providing, and personal musing that cannot be strictly delimited as factual or nonfactual yet are distinct from the kind of information conveyed by factual detail.

Pete Dunne's *Before the Echo: Essays on Nature*, which I will discuss again from a different angle in chapter 2, is a case in point. Cataloged as natural history, nature, and nature conservation, these essays often contain far more commentary and speculation than they do natural facts. Why? Because Dunne is primarily interested in promoting an environmental ethic rather than providing factual details about such topics as skunk hibernation. He emphasizes this point in the preface: "Many of these essays were written to impart understanding; others to point out flaws in our species' regard for the environment. A few are flights of fancy, essays that use nature to explore situations that are very human."[4] By his own admission his collection labeled nonfiction by the publisher contains more commentary and speculation than information and detail, as when he assumes the point of view of a deer trying to cross a highway.

When narrative and its various aesthetic dimensions drive the writing of a text, I would prefer to label the text a fiction, regardless of the quantity of information that constructs the message. Hence, I would label Thoreau's *Walden* fiction because of the aesthetically driven narrative strategy of condensing and rearranging more than two years of experiences into a single year. Also, the historical record indicates that Thoreau spent years reworking the original nonfictional journal entries into an artistic whole, with various speculative vignettes positioned because of their philosophical and plot effects rather than their accurately representing factual events.[5] Kent C. Ryden notes, for instance, that

> The remote forest pond that Thoreau portrays is a self-conscious literary construction that ignores the fact that, by 1850, the town of Concord had been a busy site of commerce and agriculture for two hundred years and was about only 10 percent forested. . . . Thoreau's cabin was itself surrounded by fields, woodlots, and second-growth forests, as well as by the cellar holes and overgrown orchards of a small past settlement of former slaves, petty artisans, drunkards, and other seeming outcasts from Concord society. Thoreau . . . leaves most evidence of local settlement and past and present landscape use out of his book, describing instead a largely unspoiled landscape much more in keeping with the goals of his literary project.

These remarks support my contention that *Walden* is better labeled a work of fiction than nonfiction, because they show how narrative and aesthetic criteria drove Thoreau's decisions about the inclusion of details and the image of the world he portrays. Readers are accustomed to accepting authorial manipulation of historical information and factual description for the sake of telling a good story—realizing "the goals of his literary project"—but they are not accustomed to accepting the same manipulation in a work they consider to be nonfiction.

In like manner, much of the selection and arrangement of Gary Snyder's *The Practice of the Wild* is driven by the work's poetic structure and the aesthetic and emotive affects that the narrative strategies evoke. Snyder records much that is factually accurate, but it may very well be the case that his own poetics, his aesthetic strategy for writing, is guided more by an East Asian affective-expressive poetics—one that emphasizes the author's expression of a sensibility in order to generate an emotional or intellectual response from the reader—than by a mimetic-realist poetics—the kind of strategy that is based on holding up a mirror to the world and allegedly reporting what is reflected there. While neither poetics rejects the idea that the world is real beyond human consciousness, the criteria for evaluating the truthfulness of representation is quite distinct. As Earl Miner, a pre-eminent comparatist scholar contends, "the fictional/real distinction is so very western," meaning that the fiction-nonfiction distinction generating so much debate in ecocritical circles may not be much of an issue in circles outside the United States.[7] And, as I am arguing here, the labeling of a work as fiction or nonfiction may not be determinable simply on the basis of how the author handles facts and fabrications within a text. Is omitting details any less a form of fictionalization than adding details that have happened in the world but not to the author-narrator of the work (i.e., the case of a narrator who identifies himself as the author in order to erase any sense the reader may have of difference between the author as person and the narrator as character)?

When, in contrast to the examples just given, the narrative and its various aesthetic dimensions are placed in the service of the provision of information, so that the narrative is broken or its aesthetic quality downplayed in order to foreground facts and verifiable information, then I prefer to label the text a nonfiction, regardless of the degree of afactual—that is, nonverifiable or abstract—detail and language to be found in it. Hence, I would label Richard Manning's *A Good House* or Roger A. Caras's *The Forest* non-fiction. In both, the narrative is often interrupted for the sake of detailed factual information. Such interruptions are particularly noticeable in *The Forest* because of the attention that Caras gives to his rhythmic, almost poetic, descriptive language and to maintaining a narrative that contains suspense, action, and climaxes.

Many of the works that would appear on any list of nonfiction nature writing are actually fictions, if someone uses the distinction between narrative as drive and narrative as service in terms of how decisions are made between aesthetic emphasis and factual reportage. Such a recognition enables readers to better appreciate the vision, concern, and zeal of writers that they admire. Many of them were copious note takers and journal keepers. And after an adventure ended, looking through their notes and entries written in the midst of rafting the Colorado River, climbing Mount Shasta, or backpacking across Alaska, they realized that the raw, nonfiction, factually accurate notes they were reviewing would not in and of themselves successfully convey the truth of their experience. So they reworked those notes, knowing that truth is perceived often more according to the telling than to what is being told. At that point they were in the mode of fiction to render facts more palpable, more affective in the same sense as that term is used in Miner's notion of affective-expressive poetics.

Sometimes such writers move back and forth between the modes of fiction and nonfiction within the same work. Such a variation is likely to be found more often in nature-writing narratives than in many other literary forms because such books are often collections of essays and stories written over an extended period of time and for different initial places of publication. David James Duncan's *River Teeth: Stories and Writings* is a case in point. Duncan does not identify which chapters fit the category of stories and which the category of writings, and a reviewer in the *Los Angeles Times Book Review* commented that "whether he is inventing or remembering, Duncan's prose is both inventive and memorable." In clarifying his distinction of categories, Duncan remarks that "there are many things worth telling that are not quite narrative."[8]

Heated debates continue over the degree to which a book's nonfiction factual accuracy can be subordinated to, or altered for the benefit of, the literary qualities of the text. The point at which a work ceases to be nonfiction—because of the amount of tinkering with the facts, the inclusion of things that happened to someone else but not to the author or narrator, or the degree to which the actually occurring events have been arranged and rearranged, with some events being omitted and others being foregrounded, for the benefit of the plot—remains a highly contested yet very dimly perceived swamp of presuppositions, biases, and unstated agendas. Today, that emphasis on nonfiction in many courses, in the delineation of the literary tradition, and in critical analyses threatens to exclude from critical consideration and reader attention a large body of literature that reveals ecological sensibilities and nature sensitivities. As a result, it is important to understand nature writing as one part of a larger body of literary production that could be labeled nature-oriented literature, which would include nature writing, nature literature, environmental writing, and environmental literature without any kind of value hierarchy imposed on these subcategories in terms of their thematic or informational value.

Taxonomy Table

The following table is a schematic version of the preceding taxonomy with some particular details highlighted. The types of works listed under "Modes and Genres" are meant to be illustrative rather than exhaustive. My decision about where to locate an individual work, as I will indicate in later chapters, is more a reflection of whether it is nature-focused or environmental-focused than whether it is fiction or nonfiction, rhetorically structured or narratively structured. Hence, sometimes I substitute *writing* for the category of *nonfiction*.[9]

Although this table has critical limitations and could be more detailed, and though other taxonomies that are far more refined for the relatively narrow field of nature writing exist (see, for example, Tom Lyon's excellent work in *This Incomperable Lande*), it is unique to my knowledge: no one else has developed this kind of more inclusive taxonomy for American literature. One for world literature would represent an even more daunting project in terms of the sublime magnitude of its diversity.

Modes and Genres	Structural Features
Nature Writing	
Natural history essays Rambles and meditations Wilderness living Travel and adventure Agrarian and ranch life Philosophizing	Rhetorical and narrative Often nonfiction Frequently personal First-person narration
Nature Literature	

Poetry
Observations
Pastoral odes
Agrarian and rural elegies
Domestic and garden life
Interaction with animals
Fiction
Sport stories
Animal stories and fables
Regionalism
Wilderness living
Travel and adventure
Agrarian and ranch life
Science fiction and fantasy
	Fictionality, imagery, and plot
	Fiction often based heavily on
	   experience, historical events, and
	   autobiography
	Various points of view

Environmental Writing	
Environmental degradation Community activism Wilderness defense Recreational responsibility Sustainable agriculture and grazing Environmental ethics Inhabitation	Rhetorical and narrative Polemical and ethical Deals with politics and social change Often labeled nonfiction
Environmental Literature	
Poetry Observation of crisis Agrarian values Alternative lifestyles Encountering the other *Fiction* Environmental crisis and resolution Wilderness defense Destruction of agrarian life Cultural conservation Dystopias, utopias, and fabulations	Fictionality, imagery, and plot Transformational themes Self-consciousness Advocates political and ethical values

1

When the Land Is More Than a Scape

Ecocriticism and Environmental Fiction

The Scape and the Script

IN LATE 1994 Sony ran a TV ad for one of their televisions. It shows a boy calling his parents over to look at the Grand Canyon. As they come over the camera pans out so that the viewer sees this family staring at a television image of the Grand Canyon while standing directly in front of that actual Grand Canyon scape. A visual, nontactile representation is not only depicted as being as good as the real thing, but actually as more vivid than the reality that they are ignoring. The further irony is that Sony is attempting to create a real-versus-virtual-image contrast by using an artificially established scenic overlook, which has become an official viewpoint for enjoying the Grand Canyon as scenery.[1]

This advertisement epitomizes the point that Paul T. Bryant makes in "Nature as Picture/Nature as Milieu": "We are detached and isolated from the natural world. Nature becomes static, remote, a museum piece, and we tend to treat it as such by assuming that we can preserve small bits of it in isolated reserves (parks) and then ignore it in our daily surroundings. . . .

Nature is a picture, and we don't know that we are in that picture, too."[2] I would add that nature is also a story in the sense of an unfolding series of events with various forms of causality and coincidence, and far too many people either don't know or don't want to admit that we are in that story. But we are in that story, and nature is also in every story humans tell, although not treated in the same way from one to another.

The pun in this chapter's title plays off of the archaic word *scape*, which was an alternate form of *escape*, and the suffix *-scape* attached to words to create *landscape*, *cityscape*, *seascape*, and the like. That suffix is defined in various dictionaries as meaning a specific kind of view or scene. I think that for far too many Americans, the archaic word and the suffix are synonymous. Wilderness, woods, and uninhabited or sparsely inhabited places are viewed as escapes from the urban world, from the daily violence of the contemporary global village, from the chaos and frenzy of two-career couples and sometimes even two-career individuals. Hence, one sees the phenomenon not of suburbanites but of exurbanites, such as people living in the Potomac hook of West Virginia who commute to work in Washington, D.C. There are rural counties of southeastern Pennsylvania that have been included in the U.S. government's definition of the New York Standard Metropolitan Statistical Area because so many of the residents work in New York City!

Yet the view of the nonurban as escape is precisely a *scape*, a viewpoint of where the world stands in relation to human beings—or rather, where human beings stand when they consider their relationship to the rest of the world. The idea of the land as scape establishes place, whether woods or lake or mountain range, as something separate from human culture.

And yet we are in the world, in nature, all the time, because we are ourselves natural—eating and being eaten (although usually in very small pieces), participating in symbiosis and parasitism, and replicating DNA—like myriad other creatures with varying numbers of cells. In fact, scientists have only recently agreed to expand the basic branches of life from two categories to three. One category consists of bacteria; another consists of archaea, the newest distinct designation: microbes living at the extremes of the planet that may account for as much as 30 percent of the biomass on earth. The third category, eukaryotes, consists of plants and animals, including humans, which means that at the fundamental level of cellular structure we are lumped in with virtually all of the rest of the visible life forms on the planet.

Further, the very systemic entity called a culture is also inextricably ennatured. Cultures are developed in place, not in the abstract; place shapes culture even as any culture alters the environment in which it is situated—particularly when the culture is transplanted from one kind of place to another. Many novelists buy into the scape mentality, and so their novels represent the environment as a static background for dynamic human action, much in the manner of certain types of landscape painting. But there are many others who attempt to reject such an economy in search of an ecology that can make culture and its human agents part of the big story rather than the whole story.

In this light, I am interested in novels that reveal and develop themes around and about the environments of their fictions, because they simultaneously make unfamiliar the reader's home environment and render it more noticeable and, sometimes, even more palpable. The natural and constructed environment in which people live often exists so ubiquitously that we do not notice the amazing diversity of its participants. Rather than being continuously felt, much of the natural world that pervades our daily lives goes unnoticed and is not even experienced as proximate, much less integral and synergistic to our every breathing moment.

Environmental novels, in contrast, help to remind us of that proximity; at the same time they pose problems and solutions regarding contemporary humanity's relationship with the rest of nature.

Introducing a discussion of environmental ethics, Don E. Marietta Jr. makes the following point: "People are beginning to think about the natural environment more than they used to, and they think about it differently. Old notions about the environment are giving place to very different beliefs, and new attitudes are becoming widespread."[3] His thoughts are equally applicable to a discussion of literature. The rapidly increasing number of published aesthetic texts concerned with nature, environmental issues, ecology, place, regionalism, and inhabitation has gained sufficient critical mass to generate an entire field of ecologically influenced literary studies—ecocriticism.

This phenomenon bears a striking resemblance to the generating of New Criticism by modernist literature on the one hand, and the generating of feminist criticism out of the women's movement on the other. A cursory review of the field reveals that most ecocriticism has focused on nonfiction prose, mainly the nature essay, and certain kinds of poetry. Relatively little has been said about fiction, whether long or short. There are reasons for such a focus, but I see no lasting benefit from continuing to slight the modern novel, particularly in its contemporary forms. It continues to be the genre of the greatest stylistic and thematic innovations and variations in contemporary aesthetic writing. Let me provide a brief introduction to ecocriticism based on my own perspective. Quotes and references to some critics who have helped to define the field quite clearly in recent years will give an indication of the variety of voices speaking on this subject. Then I will make a case for why the novel has been slighted.

Ecocriticism

In a 1992 essay appearing in *Western American Literature*, Glen A. Love concisely sketched a new field of literary criticism: "This ecological-environmental perspective, worldly in the most literal sense, has been called 'ecocriticism.' The term has come to summarize the response of literary study and analysis to the ecological consciousness of the last two decades and to the recognition that human culture is inextricably involved with, and ultimately subordinate to, the physical, natural world. The word 'ecocriticism' was originally coined in 1978 by William L. Rueckert, in his important essay, 'Literature and Ecology: An Experiment in Ecocriticism.'" Love, however, names an earlier work as the first full-length ecocritical study: Joseph Meeker's *The Comedy of Survival: Studies in Literary Ecology*, originally published in 1974 (a third revised edition was released in 1997 with a new subtitle by Meeker—"Literary Ecology and a Play Ethic"), and he cites Meeker as providing "a continuingly relevant explanation and justification of the practice" of ecocriticism, which I quote here:[4]

> If the creation of literature is an important characteristic of the human species, it should be examined carefully and honestly to discover its influence upon human behavior and the natural environment, and to determine what role, if any, it plays in the welfare and survival of humanity, and what insight it offers into human relationships with

other species and with the world around us. Is it an activity that adapts us better to life on Earth, or one that sometimes estranges us from life? From the unforgiving perspective of evolution and natural selection, does literature contribute more to our survival than it does to our extinction?[5]

That last question by Meeker indicates a critical approach that would subject all literary works to ecocritical scrutiny, even if one does not agree that the most important question is survival or extinction.

A reader has a right to expect that a general critical orientation would be applicable, at least to some extent, to every literary work. Indeed, Love and many others have claimed that ecocriticism is just such an approach. Michael Branch believes that it is poised on the verge of sweeping through literary criticism like a wind-fed firestorm through drought-ridden California hills:

The recent acceleration of scholarly activity in the areas of environmental ethics, environmental history, ecofeminism, and ecotheology provides a clear indication that environmental consciousness is increasingly being reflected in both academic discourse and the institutional structures which underwrite that discourse. Environmental scholarship has finally infiltrated the discipline of literary studies, where it variously appears under the rubric of nature writing, environmental literature, nature/culture theory, place studies, ecofeminism, and a number of other subdisciplines which may be constelled around the term "ecocriticism." The green writing is now on the wall—or, more precisely, the palimpsest—of literary studies, and today's burgeoning ecocritical scholarship will be tomorrow's curricular reform.[6]

There may be a certain hyperbole to Branch's remark, part euphoria at being in the midst of a vital, blossoming movement, and part creating a phenomenon through claiming to describe it, in good early modernist fashion. Nevertheless, his depiction echoes Marietta's observation. Ecological awareness is in the process of permeating American life, even the academy, and it appears in the writings of both creative and critical authors.

Ecocriticism is very much a movement, however, rather than a method. In this sense, it has already begun to replicate the history of academic feminist theory and criticism, as Cheryll Glotfelty notes in "Introduction: Literary Studies in an Age of Environmental Crisis."[7] Like feminism, ecocriticism has engaged in, and continues to encourage the practice of, recovering neglected and forgotten literary works that display an ecological or protoecological awareness, such as the stories of Charlotte Perkins Gilman. Canonical works and the entire literary tradition, from *The Epic of Gilgamesh* through John Milton to Toni Morrison, are being subjected to ecocritiques. Ecocritics have picked out and argued over major figures for a green tradition and canon, such as Henry David Thoreau, Gilbert White, John Muir, Mary Austin, Aldo Leopold, Gary Snyder, and Annie Dillard. They have disputed what should or can qualify as nonfiction nature writing, and they have contested the relationship of literature to the social activism of conservation, environmentalism, and various environmental ethics. Ecocriticism has been faulted for ignoring the contributions and specific characteristics of minority writers, particularly by those who further the environmental-justice movement or promote multiculturalism, and has begun to respond to that criticism. The role of gender has been debated by ecofeminist and deep-ecology philosophers and literary critics. And the role of theory has generated its own knotty arguments, with much of the first wave of ecocriticism seen by newer practitioners as antitheoretical and naively realist.

Glotfelty in 1991 named two premises for ecocriticism:

1. There is a material world, and
2. Human culture is connected to the material world, affecting it and affected by it. Ecocriticism takes as its subject the interconnections between the material world and human culture, specifically the cultural artifacts language and literature. As a critical stance, it has one foot in literature and the other on land; as a theoretical discourse, it negotiates between text and terra firma.[8]

Many ecocritical essays and analyses, however, display little working knowledge of contemporary critical and literary theories and tend to downplay the degree to which any literary criticism constitutes a theoretical discourse. Frequently, the authors represent themselves as being antitheoretical because they oppose abstraction. Such claims tend to ignore or minimize the problems of critically writing about reality, the material world, and the concrete by means of language-based texts about other language-based texts. But the feminist poet and activist Adrienne Rich made a useful distinction in 1984 that should be recalled here: "Abstractions severed from the doings of living people, fed back to the people as slogans. Theory—the seeing of patterns, showing the forest as well as the trees—theory can be a dew that rises from the earth and collects in the raincloud and returns to the earth, over and over."[9]

The widespread appeal of nonfiction writing and traditional realism in ecocriticism may in part result from a desire to accept the referentiality of such texts as a given rather than a problem. Such a given would free critics from the burden of analyzing the textuality, aesthetics, and rhetoric of such accounts of the real world. SueEllen Campbell, in an essay now famous in ecocritical circles, "The Land and Language of Desire: Where Deep Ecology and Post-Structuralism Meet," expresses the contention between theory and practice in ecocriticism, and also the recognition that theory must necessarily contribute to the maturation of the field: "Theory helps me to step back from myself, to *think* about desire, to see how it changes shape but still stays the same, to try to understand with my mind. . . . It is theory that teaches me how to argue that all desire is not human, that we belong not only to networks of language and culture but also to the networks of the land. But it is in nature writing—perhaps almost as much as in the wilderness itself—that I learn to recognize the shape and force of my own desire to be at home on the earth."[10]

I see my theorizing and that of dozens of others as work necessary to define a critical field. We intend to provide an articulation of the field that will enable others to join the conversation. Most of the theorizing in ecocriticism, done in the same spirit as those quoted here, has been conducted to establish a base camp, a convergence of points, and a divergence of opinions. Such theorizing is intended to enable a dialogue through evaluating our critical practice. And that practice does not primarily consist of writing about ecocriticism but writing about something called variously nature writing, nature literature, the literature of nature, and environmental literature, the definition of which remains a problem in the theory.

The Neglect of the Environmental Novel

As Glen Love's title "*Et in Arcadia Ego*: Pastoral Theory Meets Ecocriticism" indicates, pastoral literature forms one of the traditions preceding and influencing the development of environmental literature. But the pastoral has primarily been a mode of representation in poetry and drama, rather than in fiction. It can be argued that there is a good deal of pastoralism in first-person nonfictional nature writing, mainly in terms of a nostalgia for and romantic idealization of some golden age of uncomplicated individual life in the wild, or in terms of some evocation of rural simplicity and order in opposition to urban complexity and chaos, as Don Scheese has argued in *Nature Writing: The Pastoral Impulse in America*. (Certainly, it must be noted that this kind of pastoralism remains a mainstay of American cultural beliefs, as witnessed in 1996 by the Republican presidential candidate Bob Dole's nomination-acceptance speech in which he referred to having lived at one time in a better America.) As Love notes, "pastoral works upon the principle of harmony and reconciliation."[11]

Bill Broder speaks to this sort of feeling in *The Sacred Hoop: A Cycle of Earth Tales* when he remarks that "because I found the community oppressive and hypocritical, I fled it. Nature provided refuge. . . . By using nature as a refuge, I did it little honor; and, in return, the comfort nature afforded proved to be fleeting."[12] At that point in Broder's life, nature was just an escape. But later he came to realize that "the wilderness existed not as an empty refuge, but as a generator of all life, including human life and consciousness."[13] Such a perception of integration runs counter to the alienation and nostalgia that provide the basis for the dominant tradition of pastoralism as a literary mode.

Terry Gifford in *Green Voices* makes a strong case for rethinking the influence of the pastoral and the popularity of the antipastoral in modern British environmental poetry. Nature poetry tends, however, to be mainly analyzed in terms of nineteenth-century British romanticism and American transcendentalism, both idealist philosophies about human-nonhuman

natural relationships that arose from strong reactions against the mecha-
nistic and allegedly objective rationality of the Enlightenment.

Nonfiction prose, most often a naturalist essay or personal observation-
meditation, in contrast, tends to be defined as originating in the Enlightenment and the scientific–classification movement, with the eighteenth-
century botanist Carl von Linné serving as the patron saint of such accurate
observation and dissection. In this view, White and Thoreau serve as the
British and American fathers of modern nature writing, although all three
of these figures have their predecessors. I have no quarrel with the use of
such a genealogy as a general historical survey of tendencies, but I do worry
when the description begins to be used prescriptively for defining the parameters of nature writing or environmental literature as genres or modes of
representation. And such a maneuver does seem to be occurring all too frequently, even if entirely unintentionally, particularly in the construction of
anthologies.

There is an additional problem with the emphasis on science and natural history, in that it privileges written discourses practiced far more by
men, who have been extensively educated into them, than ones practiced by
women. Even when the form is one practiced equally by men and women
or more so by women, such as the personal diary, the naturalist criteria that
privileges scientific objective description over domestic subjective description still favors the men (see chapter 12 for a critique of these terms). As
Lorraine Anderson notes in her preface to *Sisters of the Earth*, "the canon of
nature writing, like the literary canon in general, has been male-centered,
both a reflection and a reinforcement of a culture that once defined only
men's experience as important and only men's voices as authoritative."[14]

The plethora of anthologies published in the past few years indicates
the increasing attention on college campuses to literature that addresses
nature and environmental issues. These texts are, after all, largely edited
and printed for use in classrooms and designed to meet the needs of certain
kinds of courses. The problem lies in the degree to which the anthologies
by default define a tradition and create a canon of commonly taught and
recognized works. Such anthologies will, as a result of their very structure
and production necessities, slight long narrative poems and novels, even
when the selection criteria do not justify such an omission. And in their fre-

quent structures of representative, historical coverage, they will emphasize white male authors, who have been the main definers and practitioners of nature writing—indeed, men have been even more exclusively emphasized in the categories of literary influence and foundational thinking than they have been in the category of practitioners of the genre. Rachel Carson is recognized as a major figure in environmental writing because of *Silent Spring*, but she is not discussed in terms of defining or developing the genre in the way that Thoreau (primarily *Walden*), Aldo Leopold (*A Sand County Almanac and Sketches Here and There*), and Edward Abbey (*Desert Solitaire*) are so treated.

Nature-writing or environmental-literature courses tend, then, to have an anthology that foregrounds essays and poetry (and to a much lesser extent short stories), and may or may not have a novel or two as separate, and apparently supplementary, reading. Thus, the textbook-publishing industry and its exigencies are one problem that readers and critics face when trying to figure out just what constitutes nature-oriented literature.

Another problem is what I have labeled the nonfictional prejudice, which constitutes the more significant reason for the critical neglect of environmental fiction. With poetry, the idea of truth has never been too closely aligned with the idea of fact. Poetry is largely defined as figurative, aesthetic language. It is a literary form that emphasizes the way an idea is expressed, not the idea itself, and the affective power of that expression. William Wordsworth in the preface to *Lyrical Ballads*, for example, claims of his own poems that "the feeling therein developed gives importance to the action and situation, and not the action and situation to the feeling." He then contends that the main aim of his poems is to increase the reader's mental sensitivity; he therefore selects subjects to the degree to which they will excite "certain inherent and indestructible qualities of the human mind."[15]

All too often, when an adjective such as *political, environmental, sentimental,* or *lesbian* is placed in front of the word *poetry*, it serves to define such literature as a minor field or deviation from the tradition, rather than serving as a topical or thematic description. Much more so than the essay or the novel, poetry, like drama, is linked with beliefs in the idealistic notion of *universal values*. In contrast, prose is more often associated with factuality, description, and observation. A large amount of contemporary nature writing consists of journalistic articles in organizationally sponsored and specialty magazines, such as *Orion, Wilderness, Outside, Harper's,* and the *New Yorker*; or else scientific, historical, and anthropological articles published in the scholarly and popular journals of those respective disciplines.

In *This Incomperable Lande: A Book of American Nature Writing,* editor Thomas J. Lyon provides a general preface and then an introduction to nature writing followed by a selection of twenty-two authors. Lyon's preface shows some of the difficulties of trying to define nature writing as being based on the naturalist essay but not quite limited to that. Lyon remarks that "most of these materials emphasize in one way or another what seems to me the crucial point about nature writing, the awakening of perception to an ecological way of seeing. 'Ecological' here is meant to characterize the capacity to notice pattern in nature, and community, and to recognize that the patterns observed ultimately radiate outward to include the human observer."[16] I find this statement at once very helpful and very muddled.

If the determination of a literary work as nature writing is based on the representation of an "awakening of perception," then could it not be represented by a variety of genres, such as poetry, drama, and fiction, rather than exclusively the essay? Lyon seems to answer this type of question by emphasizing not indications or symbolizations of the "capacity to notice pattern in nature," but the textual depiction and recording of such notices as scientific observation or personal experience. Such a claim appears to rest on the belief that nature writing consists of literal, referential language that is not fundamentally aesthetic. "I have limited this book to essays on natural history and experiences in nature," he writes, "believing that in fiction and poetry, though there are often beautiful descriptions of nature, other themes and intentions tend to predominate." At the same time, Lyon recognizes the limitations of such a decision when he notes that "many nature essays use fictional techniques of narration and characterization."[17]

Struggling with the intractable problem of limiting the contents of any anthology through developing a criteria of selection that often serves better to justify excluding items than including them, Lyon forthrightly admits: "I have arbitrarily confined this book to materials I consider nonfictional."[18] Okay, but why should we consider the best literature about nature to be that which casts the author as an "observer," rather than a full participant, physically or imaginatively?

Lyon's anthology suggests that "nature writing" is a relatively narrowly defined, "nonfictional" genre of a much larger mode of aesthetic writing: environmental literature or nature literature, a point that John Elder has come to emphasize in recent years, such as in his June 1996 keynote address at the Sharp Eyes II conference in Oneonta, New York, which honored John Burroughs, the nature-writing tradition, and new multicultural nature writing. In the introduction to *American Nature Writers*, a massive two-volume set he edited, Elder makes a crucial point: "In order to acknowledge how much vital literature of the earth is left out of the usual definition of 'nature writing,' and to encourage attention to a wider variety of ethnic, linguistic, and generic approaches, this book thus includes a section of 'General Subject Essays.' Rather than looking for the traditional nature essay where it has simply not been the preferred form, the pieces in this section take a broader perspective."[19]

Elder's remarks here no doubt reflect the development of his own thinking and of the field of ecocriticism since he and Robert Finch edited *The Norton Book of Nature Writing* (published 1990). Editing this volume at the same time that Lyon published *This Incomperable Lande*, Finch and Elder converged on the same narrow definition of nature writing as "nonfictional prose" but immediately complained that it ought to be recognized "as a literary form in its own right." But with their emphasis on Linné and scientific classification, it is unclear whether they are using the word *form* to distinguish nature writing generically by means of literary or rhetorical strategies. I believe this distinction is important because it will help determine whether the conception of nature writing enunciated in this particular anthology is based on its being a literary or an analytical form of writing. But this distinction that people often make between literary texts—as, say, narrative, lyric, or dramatic—and rhetorical texts—as, say, reports, newspaper articles, and scientific essays—is not clearly addressed. Finch and Elder claim that "to a distinctive degree, nature writing fulfills the essay's purpose of *connection*. It fuses literature's attention to style, form, and the inevitable ironies of expression with a scientific concern for palpable fact."[20]

But, certainly, "attention to style, form and . . . ironies of expression" are not exclusively the province of literature.

Also, Finch and Elder echo Lyon in claiming that "the purposes of fiction differ sufficiently from those of nonfiction that, with a few unabashed exceptions, we have chosen to exclude excerpts from novels."[21] I do not think that any universal claim can successfully be made for aesthetically differentiating literary nonfiction from literary fiction, except one cast in terms of degree of attention to certain issues. Much fiction serves as the source of factual information on all kinds of natural, social, and cultural phenomena, and this is particularly true in environmental fiction. Reading Kiana Davenport's novel *Shark Dialogues*, for example, provided me with more historical information about Hawai'i than I had ever seen in any American history text. Much nonfiction relies on such figurative devices as simile, metaphor, and analogy to generate that sense of "connection" so important to "the essay's purpose," particularly in magazine essays.

Ona Siporin, interviewing Terry Tempest Williams in spring 1996, raised the sticky issue of the fine line between fiction and nonfiction in relation to reader trust. Williams provided a fairly long reply in which she remarked: "I think the component of all art—literature, nonfiction . . . allows the writer the leeway to not let the truth get in the way of the truth. . . . [I]t gives us that kind of flexibility to create a story, to create an atmosphere so that the reader can settle in and be bathed in images, bathed in ideas." Further, Williams commented that "people always ask me when I'm telling stories . . . : 'Is that a true story?' And I say, 'Yes it is, but it isn't. . . . In the realm of art and the imagination, it is true. . . . In the realm of art anything is possible and probable and allows us those leaps of the imagination, those acts of faith that ultimately transform us and the culture that we're a part of."[22] Williams shifts here from defining nonfiction to defining storytelling, I think. In regard to the former she emphasizes the creative dimension of nonfiction as lying in selection and arrangement, omission and narrative structuring, but not necessarily including any fabrication. In regard to the latter, she includes the possibility of truthful, although not factual, fabrications and imaginative speculations. Yet, both answers are in response to the same question about nonfiction and trustworthiness in a way that suggests that the label *nonfiction* may frequently be applied by critics and publishers rather than by writers to their work.

David James Duncan in the summer of 1996 went beyond Williams's blurring of the dividing lines between nonfiction and storytelling in an article he titled "Nonfiction = Fiction," published in *Orion*. Duncan contends, and I concur, that "the kind of imaginative writing known as 'nonfiction' is, by any name, inextricably entangled in the kind of imaginative writing we call 'fiction,' and vice versa, and those who like their categories clean may as well start wringing their hands."[23]

Let me return to *The Norton Book of Nature Writing* for a moment. At the end of their introduction, Finch and Elder make the following claim:

> In the two centuries since the publication of *A Natural History of Selborne*, nature writers have undertaken excursions away from the dominant literary and scientific models, returning with their testimony about how human beings respond to what is nonhuman, and how individuals and society may achieve more significant and rewarding integration with the earth that sustains them. All literature, by illuminating the full nature of human existence, asks a single question: how shall we live? In our age that question has taken its most urgent form in relation to the natural environment. Because it has never been more necessary, the voice of nature writing has never been stronger than it is today.[24]

I want to emphasize that if all literature "asks a single question: how shall we live," then a significant number of texts also attempt to answer that question. Literature does so at times by depicting what we need to know in order to live a certain way. This kind of answer is often best provided by nonfictional prose, but not always. Fiction, particularly in the extended form of the novel, can generate a story that provides intellectual equipment for living and display the effect that such information can have on human lives as represented by fictional characters.

Literature also answers the question by constructing narratives of how various individuals have learned, or failed to learn, how to live in ecologically sensitive ways. Sometimes nonfictional prose can successfully render such stories, less frequently in a single essay than in a collection of essays or a continuous philosophical-experiential meditation. But a reader is often less likely to resist a novel's themes than those of a nonfictional work that is more overtly didactic than a novel. To some extent this distinction reflects the ongoing preference that Henry James emphasized a century ago—show the audience how to live; don't tell them. The work of multigenre authors such as Wendell Berry, including the decisions they make about which issues and stories will appear in which generic forms, suggests that environmentally concerned writers consider fiction just as truthful, and often as factual, as nonfiction, and the novel or short story more appropriate for some narratives and themes than the essay.

Berry has written some eight novels and story collections, twelve volumes of poetry, a dozen essay collections, and one biography. What is most striking about these many books is the gaps when Berry moves from one genre to the next. In the fiction, such as *The Memory of Old Jack*, religion is nonexistent; in the nonfiction it is thematically developed but not a topic in itself, as in *The Gift of Good Land;* in the poetry one can witness a spiritual movement away from Christianity toward pantheism and then back toward a biblical theology, as in *A Timbered Choir: The Sabbath Poems 1979–1997.* For Berry, certain themes and purposes evoke a specific embodiment. He usually reserves his polemics for essays, which he rhetorically structures and logically argues with few narrative digressions. In such cases, Berry works toward truth more than wisdom, but truth defined as a moral response to information. The more narrative the nonfiction, the less immediate is the concern, usually, and one can see here the relationship between narration in the nonfiction essays and narration in the novels.

The novels are about individual lives worked out in community. Except for the early parts of *Remembering*, the fiction is free of polemic and little concerned with facts, although heavily concerned with providing detailed depictions of the natural context of cultural action. Much would be lost if critics and readers affected by a nonfictional prejudice focused only on Berry's essay collections in order to learn about nature and environmental issues and ignored the rest of his writing. Yet overall his fiction has been slighted by critics, who tend to define him as either an essayist or a poet rather than a multigenre author.[25]

This nonfictional prejudice arises in part from a defensive posture in which those critics who love nonfictional prose feel constantly compelled to justify its literary merits to their colleagues who have frequently been schooled in various kinds of formalist and critical habits. It also arises from the idea that fiction somehow is incapable of conveying facts and real experience. Yet, often an environmental fiction consists of no more aesthetic reorganizing and imaginative embellishing of a lived experience than that in which Thoreau engaged when revising his journals years after the events in order to create *Walden*. Then again, sometimes a fiction is all imaginative embellishing—but what is the source material for embellishment and imagination? I see no reason to conclude that such a fiction precludes the representation of "an awakening perception" or a recognition of "the capacity to notice pattern in nature."

For this reason it is ironic that Abbey thought he was writing a novel when he created *The Monkey Wrench Gang*, but many readers treated it as a manifesto and guide for ecological sabotage; that is, they treated it as a rhetorical rather than a literary text. And I find it disappointing that, in an otherwise strong collection, *Being in the World*, editors Scott H. Slovic and Terrell F. Dixon engage in a moment of definitional correction that may arise out of nonfictional prejudice. In the headnote to Larry Littlebird's "The Hunter," the editors call the piece an "essay" despite noting that "Littlebird refers to it as a 'story.'" They go on to say, "Littlebird later recorded this and other stories. . . ."[26] Why set up this contradiction between Littlebird's label and their own, particularly when they use Littlebird's label later in the same paragraph? If this need to place an academic label on a factual story by a Native American author does not stem from nonfictional prejudice, perhaps it is the result of the editors' need to have the book conform to faculty expectations of what such a reader ought to include. The use of a rhetorical table of contents, in which Littlebird's story is placed under the category of "Definition," would support this interpretation. Nevertheless, the editors' language seems to reinforce the fiction-nonfiction dualism that has been a mainstay of nature-writing criticism and a hindrance to a more diverse appreciation of the varieties of nature-oriented literature.

Finally, let me also note that reinforcement of nonfictional prejudice is not limited to anthologies of primary materials but is also a problem in the first anthology of ecological criticism, *The Ecocriticism Reader: Landmarks in Literary Ecology*. Editors Cheryll Glotfelty and Harold Fromm state that "the essays in this anthology provide an answer to the question, 'What is ecocriticism?' These essays will help people new to this field to gain a sense of its history and scope, and to become acquainted with its leading scholars."[27] A review of the volume's contents indicates that the essays selected here define that "scope" primarily in terms of nonfiction. Works of fiction turn up on only twenty-one of the nearly four-hundred pages devoted to critical essays and only one essay out of twenty-five treats poetry. Given that some of the nonfiction nature writers cited in these essays have also written novels, short stories, or poems—including Abbey, Austin, Dillard, Barry Lopez, and John Van Dyke—it seems curious that the selection process all but ignored literary works that do not meet the criterion of being "nonfiction."

The Multiple Modes of Nature-Oriented Fiction

The nonfictional prejudice arising from the treatment of nature writing as factual, nonfictional, experiential works of observation and description directs readers and critics toward expecting environmental fiction to be thinly disguised autobiography or biography or realist fiction in the traditional sense of the term. The significance of the correlation of nature-oriented literature with autobiography is suggested by Michael P. Cohen's decision in "Literary Theory and Nature Writing" to answer the subheading question he poses, "Is Nature Writing Nonfiction," in terms of theoretical conceptions of author and autobiography.[28] But such a direction defines the terrain too exclusively by establishing a set of universal criteria for a vast array of literary regions. Dan Flores's argument about the writing of environmental history is pertinent to the writing of the critical history of environmental literature: "The particularism of distinctive *places* fashioned by human culture's peculiar and fascinating interpenetration with all the vagaries of topography, climate, and evolving ecology that define landscapes—and the continuing existence of such *places* despite the homogenizing forces of the modern world—ought to cause environmental historians to realize that one of their most crucial tasks is to write well what might be called *bioregional* histories."[29]

Nature-oriented fiction partakes of the kind of diversity that Flores calls for in writing environmental history, in terms of both its subject matter and its representational modes. What the works of nature-oriented fiction I have read have in common is a continued reliance on narrative, but not necessarily a common emphasis on plot, character, or setting. They do not share a common mode of depicting reality nor for addressing depictions of nature or environmental themes. Rather, writers of nature-oriented fiction utilize multiple modes of representation in the service of drawing attention to environmental issues, environmental conditions, and human-nonhuman interaction.

Enlightenment Realism

Traditional realism has its place in this writing, but it is not nearly as prevalent as one might expect, and it is highly diverse in its narrative strategies and settings. I have chosen to illustrate the mode of traditional realism, what I will call *enlightenment realism*, by means of a group of novels that are significantly different in setting, environmental attitudes, narrative emphases, and tone. By enlightenment realism, I mean a strategy of representation that treats the Western, secular, observable conception of everyday reality as a universal truth. The critic Ian Watt has referred to this type of fiction as "formal realism," and Don D. Elgin comments that in Watt's view, "the idea of a more formal, scientific approach to the presentation of *external* reality, then, was what the novel was all about."[30]

A novel that would fit most readers' stereotypical image of nature-oriented fiction is Wendell Berry's novel *A Place on Earth, A Revision,* which portrays the daily lives of a Kentucky farming community and includes extensive descriptions of the people, the land, and how they interact. Although written in the 1960s and revised in the early 1980s, the novel is set during World War II, creating sufficient distance between the time of the narrative and the time of the reader that it cannot be read as an ecological polemic or criticism of particular public policies or social practices, the way that many of Abbey's novels are read, for instance. Yet it is still relevant to contemporary politics and social change, in part because Berry creates no distance between the perspectives of the characters and that of the narrator.

Barbara Kingsolver's *Animal Dreams* is very much a novel of the present and has a somewhat more complicated narrative structure than the other novels mentioned under this category. It is much more overtly political and environmentalist than *A Place* and much more plot driven. Whereas *A Place* is very much about ways of living in the world, *Animal Dreams* is largely about human destruction of the world and ways of addressing or halting that destruction. As if to heighten its themes of individual responsibility and political engagement, Kingsolver utilizes first-person narration with a high level of self-reflexivity.

The other two works that I want to mention in this category are Jane Smiley's *A Thousand Acres*, set in Iowa, and Chris Bohjalian's *Water Witches*, set in Vermont. Both treat a community undergoing change, the former in the third person and the latter in the first. Smiley focuses on a woman in the midst of a family crisis who must break with the family and community to survive. It is a recommended compliment to *A Place*, because while Berry portrays a group of people struggling to develop a healthy relationship to the land, Smiley depicts the disastrous physical and psychological effects of the dominant mode of modern farming. Berry might define his work's mode of farming as agrarianism and the type Smiley depicts as agribusiness. Berry's women and men live and work relatively harmoniously, while Smiley emphasizes the oppression of women at the hands of the family patriarch and patriarchal values.

Bohjalian's novel, like Smiley's, addresses land-based industry, commercial ski resorts in this case, focusing on a man who experiences a crisis of consciousness that changes his relationships with community and family. Through the course of *Water Witches*, an environmental tale of compromise and coexistence unfolds, with the male protagonist—a lawyer—initially representing logic and admissible scientific evidence, while the members of his wife's family represent empathic understanding and intuition. His daughter's experiences and his own open-mindedness, however, turn the apparent dichotomy between scientific logic and intuition into a cultural synthesis. The use of water witchery to realign underground streams and increase the water flow of a river may cause some readers to dismiss this novel from the category of realism, even though Bohjalian goes to some lengths to establish its plausibility.

The land, the place, is integral to all of these novels. And regardless of the time frame of their setting, these are novels of the present and of the present-day difficulties in clarifying one's role in the larger scheme of a culture undergoing environmental self-criticism. While Berry emphasizes an agrarian way of life that is rapidly disappearing but that needs to be preserved and revived, Smiley suggests that the ideology of agribusiness has already permeated most American farming with capitalist patriarchy obliterating the positive, nurturing characteristics of husbandry that Berry holds up for emulation. Kingsolver, in contrast to Berry and Smiley, tells a story that emphasizes agency and resistance to further ecological damage in a conflict between business and community. She identifies southwestern Native American cultures as an alternative environmental ethic active in the present. Her emphasis on their contemporary viability counters any potential charges of nostalgia like those that are often raised against Berry's novels, of which all but one are set in the past. While Berry implies loss and Smiley depicts it explicitly, Kingsolver emphasizes gain and the possibility of restoration. Bohjalian also plots a trajectory of agency, but one that works much more in the framework of compromise than that of Kingsolver's confrontation. Although Bohjalian does not project a net gain, he suggests that there are compromises on behalf of environmental integrity that can prevent further loss to industrial and commercial development.

Each of these novels goes beyond nature literature to become environmental in orientation, emphasizing human-nonhuman interaction and its systemic transformative potential. All of the major characters are participants in the world rather than observers of it. Each novel addresses allegiance to land and place, or else its loss and cost, through historically based narratives that depict typical events and circumstances for the respective time periods. While none provides extensive historical information, each relies on readers' knowing or gaining knowledge of such factual matters as the expansion of tourism in the 1980s and 1990s, mining practices and pollution, the mechanization of agriculture after World War II, federal agricultural policy and bank interest rates in the 1970s, and erosion and flooding problems due to Great Depression–era government dam building.

Alchemical and Situated Realisms

I want to contrast the type of realism found in the preceding novels with alchemical realism and situated realism. An alchemical realism is one that posits "a seemingly magical power or process of transmuting," which is the second definition of *alchemy* provided by the third edition of *The American Heritage College Dictionary*. A situated realism is one that relies on the consensual reality of a given people in a given locale, but that is not represented as a universal truth. There are many indigenous peoples, such as Native American tribes in the Southwest, that have a particular emergence story that is part of their consensual reality. They do not, however, attempt to impose this origin myth on all human beings and do not treat other peoples' origin myths as mutually contradictory or competitive. The following novels can be defined as either alchemical or situated, and sometimes as both: Margaret Atwood's *Surfacing*, Ana Castillo's *So Far from God*, Linda Hogan's *Mean Spirit*, Edna Escamill's *Daughter of the Mountain*, Kiana Davenport's *Shark Dialogues*, and Louis Owens's *Wolfsong*. The novels by Castillo, Escamill, and Hogan will be discussed in later chapters, so here I will elaborate only on those by Atwood, Davenport, and Owens. All of these novels extend considerable space to narration devoted to natural setting and environmental depiction even as they depart from enlightenment realism.

Most of Atwood's *Surfacing* appears to conform to standard expectations of realism, but the later part focuses on a process of character transformation that is clearly magical and environmental. The female character undergoes an alchemical rebirth into someone better and more unified than she was at the beginning of the novel. This transformation begins with the gradual shift in her actions and her ideas from searching for her missing father to searching for her missed mother, which may also be interpreted as a shift from seeking death to seeking life. It is accompanied by a shift from a nationalist concern for U.S. exploitation of Canada to an environmental concern for U.S. and Canadian patriarchal capitalist exploitation and destruction of the land she inhabited as a child.

To establish a new identity as an empowered woman in contemporary Canadian culture, the narrator metamorphoses from a civilized human into a natural animal under a quarantine from all types of cultural trappings, including shelter and clothing, until her psychic rebirth is accomplished. In the end, she does not light out for the territories to be free from culture in some idealized untrammeled nature but returns to civilization with a new environmental awareness that links her oppression as a woman with the exploitation of nonhuman nature. That awareness provides the basis for a commitment to nurture the birth of a new kind of human being, one who is ennatured rather than alienated. Implicit is the belief that such an ennatured person would also be nonsexist, since human alienation from nonhuman nature and male alienation from female nature are intertwined and must be mutually transformed.

Kiana Davenport's *Shark Dialogues* fundamentally emphasizes the supernatural or *ultranatural*, to use Charlene Spretnak's term (see chap. 12), as part of being situated in the Hawai'ian historical milieu. A historically wide-ranging family saga, *Shark Dialogues* emphasizes the multiracial, multiethnic melding of a contemporary Hawai'ian cultural identity. Due to Hawai'i's racial mix as a result of European domination and related immigration from other, predominantly Asian, countries, and also to their being rapidly outnumbered and displaced from much of the land by that domination, Hawai'ian people, according to Davenport, must retain and recover their deeply rooted relationship to the land. Such rootedness must survive through certain kinds of working relationships not only to the soil but also to the geological formations upon which it rests and the ocean and its inhabitants that surround the islands.

While displaying some elements of postmodern style, *Shark Dialogues* is fundamentally structured as a saga that provides space for the provision of all kinds of historical detail. A fact-filled book, Davenport's fiction provides more information on the historical and political realities of Hawai'i than most readers are likely to have encountered elsewhere. Like nonfiction nature writing, *Shark Dialogues* educates the reader in detail on the fauna and flora and the history of human inhabitation of the islands. But like historical fiction, it also weaves into such detail a political interpretation of historical events that leads to a politically sophisticated analysis of Hawai'i's current ecological threats and crises brought about by U.S. domination in general and worldwide tourism and retirement living in particular. Davenport also takes her narrative beyond the confines of much of the historical-novel genre by breaking with the mode of enlightenment realism to present an alchemical relationship with the land in terms of the ultranatural powers of the kahuna and the legendary, mythic relationships of Hawai'ians with shark deities and the possibility of human-deity metamorphosis.

Louis Owens's *Wolfsong* is a Native American novel that displays an ultranaturalism that is situated and alchemical and fully integrated with the environmental orientation of the story. Owens's emphasis, however, is much less on the alchemical and the transformative potential of metamorphosis than either Atwood's or Davenport's novels. Like *Shark Dialogues*, in contradistinction to *Surfacing*, *Wolfsong* focuses strongly on environmental activism and environmental crisis. This latter attention by both Davenport and Owens may reflect the heightening of ecological awareness between Atwood's writing of *Surfacing* and the time of their work. It may also reflect the distinction between Atwood's emphasis on gender and the individual, Davenport's on gender and an oppressed people, and Owens's on an oppressed people and an individual member of such a group.

Wolfsong begins with ecosabotage being practiced by a very old Native American named Jim Joseph, who is on the verge of entering the spirit world through death. Working in the shadows of the forest he has become almost more a spirit warrior than a human one. His funeral brings the novel's protagonist, Tom Joseph, home, and his metamorphosis toward assuming the mantle of ecowarrior slowly begins. The bulk of the novel, however, focuses in realist fashion on the difficulties of homecoming when one's knowledge of the land, the animals, and the environment is based on a world being destroyed by the plunder of natural resources. At the novel's end, Tom has accepted the spirit calling of the wolf song, following in the footsteps of his uncle. Like Atwood's, Owens's narrative provides extensive detailed description of place and environment, but appropriately, given the narrative perspective, relatively little factual information akin to that found in *Shark Dialogues* is provided. Rather, Owens focuses on the same issue of activism that Davenport addresses. In both cases, that activism cannot be separated from the alchemical or the situated dimensions of the novels.

Postmodernism

Postmodernist novels are specifically structured to disrupt reader complacencies regarding consensual reality, rules of causality, and assumptions about order, coherence, and progress in human culture. Such texts are some of the least likely to be addressed in ecocriticism because they are often the farthest from any representation of observed facts or actual individual experience. They refuse to comply with the protocols of that verisimilitude, while not being amenable to an allegorical reading that treats them as "thought experiments," in the way that animal fable stories, such as Ursula

K. Le Guin's "Buffalo Gals Won't You Come out Tonight" and Robert Franklin Gish's *When Coyote Howls,* can be treated. These are also the types of novels to which I have devoted the least attention in my own reading. One postmodern novel that will be discussed in a later chapter (chap. 10) is Karen Tei Yamashita's *Through the Arc of the Rain Forest.* Rather than outline that analysis, I will use it and some other illustrations here just to clarify the distinction I make between the modes of alchemical and situated realisms and the postmodernist mode. (In chap. 4 I discuss postmodernism in greater detail in relationship to ecofeminism and conceptions of agency.)

As Kristin Cashman notes, building particularly on the work of Dale Spender, "what we see in the world around us depends largely on the principles encoded by language in our knowledge system."[31] This claim applies to the critical world as much as it does to the phenomenal world, a term for which there are multiple and contradictory interpretations. Two terms that have been flung about rather indiscriminately in literary criticism are *magic realism* and *postmodernism,* with the former generally seen as a subset of the latter. Magic realism originated as a label to describe certain literary techniques practiced specifically by Latin American writers under conditions of government censorship of overtly political works of literature. While they employ events, characters, and devices that can be compared with similar features in works of alchemical realism, magic realist and alchemical realist novels need to be distinguished in terms of their ontological claims.

Alchemical realist novels do not treat their supernatural depictions as fabulous contrarealistic devices but as part of a referential orientation toward a different conception of reality than the culturally dominant one. In contrast, magic realism, as part of the postmodernist literary movement, foregrounds the unreality, the absurdity of their magical devices in order to emphasize their figurative and allusive signification. Depicting a man with enormous wings in a work of magic realism is not meant to be an ontological claim about the existence of angels in the contemporary world, whereas for Ana Castillo the kinds of miracles she depicts in *So Far from God* are meant to refer to aspects of an actual cultural reality. As a result of this distinction, critics who are cultural outsiders ought to be very cautious in labeling works arising from different cultural perspectives as magic realism, since such a label may be seen as dismissing others' spiritual beliefs, particularly of indigenous and inhabitory peoples, as merely myths or literary devices.

In like manner, care needs to be taken in deciding to label a particular work as postmodernist. First of all, although many first-world-dominant cultures could be defined as being part of postmodernity—a particular cultural condition in the second half of the twentieth century—it is erroneous to suggest that everyone in the world lives within the confines of such a worldview, even if they are culturally, economically, or politically affected by it. Similarly, it seems to me erroneous to suggest that any literary work of value in a given period must reflect the features of the most critically regarded or most avant-garde aesthetic movement.

But then what should and should not be labeled postmodernist literature? If it is written today without being postmodern, what is it? For the purposes of this particular project, let me define literary postmodernism as a particular type of writing that shares the philosophical orientation arising from the condition of postmodernity and that tends to display certain stylistic aspects that would proceed from or reinforce such an orientation. A break with traditional realist conventions is one blatant feature; another is a break with the kind of focus on epistemology as the key to meaning and understanding found in much modernist literature of the first half of the twentieth century; a third is a disbelief in a master narrative or universal structuring principle for the world—much less the literary text; another is a tendency toward stylistic experimentation favoring the arational, the non-linear, and the indeterminate, with high favor for parody, satire, and excess; and, perhaps most important, is a tendency to cast doubt on the possibility of intentional human agency. Many of the stylistic features found in works that are labeled postmodern either by their authors or by authorial acceptance of that label by critics can also be found in literary works by Chicano/a, Native American, African American, and Asian American writers—just to limit the review to U.S. literature.

But are such works necessarily postmodernist? I think not, primarily because such works tend to affirm the possibilities for intentional human agency rather than cast doubt on it. *Through the Arc of the Rain Forest* does cast doubt on the intentional possibilities of human agency, and it is on that basis more than on the basis of its stylistic experimentation that I label it postmodernist. Many other visibly ethnic writers refuse the label of postmodernism, arguing that the devices that are similar arise out of a different aesthetic tradition and a fundamentally different worldview. Alice Walker's *The Temple of My Familiar* uses some devices that could be labeled postmodern and her spiritual beliefs could be aligned with New Age mysticism, which might be seen as part of postmodernity, but reincarnation in the novel functions as more than a literary trope or a figurative device. It is a profession of spiritual belief reiterated in Walker's essays in *Living by the Word*. And it is therefore fundamentally no different from the professions of Linda Hogan, which proceed from an indigenous spiritual philosophy and practice and not from a postmodernist perspective, as indicated in both of her novels, *Mean Spirit* and *Solar Storms*, and her essay collection, *Dwellings*. Similarly, Leslie Marmon Silko sees the features of *Almanac of the Dead* as arising from a native oral storytelling tradition.

In contrast, Gerald Vizenor, another Native American author, does label himself a postmodernist writer, and I think we should accept that decision regarding his own identity politics. His environmental fiction, *Bearheart*, then, could be studied profitably as a postmodern work. I do not think, however, that critics should generalize from Vizenor's claim to label as postmodern all Native Americans who use similar literary techniques.

Kiana Davenport's decision to open *Shark Dialogues* with reference to the term *talkstory*, which places her work in an aesthetic tradition related to Maxine Hong Kingston's own *talkstory* novels, suggests an authorial distinction between postmodernist strategies and the ground for her own strategies. Many visibly ethnic authors have clearly been influenced by literary postmodernism, but unless the ontological orientation of their texts appears to bear strong resemblance to the work of someone like John Barth, I will refrain from labeling them postmodernist writers, preferring instead to see them as more likely working as alchemical and situated realists. And while these are my own terms for their work, they proceed from my perception of the authors' ontological and cultural orientations as revealed in their writing rather than from my trying to make them fit into some dominant, universal paradigm.

Science Fiction and Fantasy
In contrast to postmodernist novels, fantasy and science fiction,

although frequently dismissed from consideration as nature writing for obvious reasons, have been the subject of ecological criticism. Don D. Elgin's *The Comedy of the Fantastic: Ecological Perspectives on the Fantasy Novel* is the prime example of such treatment. Unlike postmodernist novels that challenge ontological assumptions, fantasy novels reinforce a comedic ontology about the way the world works. Elgin claims that the fantasy novel "has adopted a comic conception of humanity, placing its emphasis upon humanity as part of a total environment or system and acknowledging the absolute dependence of humanity upon that system."[32] As Elgin observes, the plots of many fantasy novels revolve around the discovery of the laws that govern the imaginary world rather than the character's heroic behavior or transcendent morality. Certainly, only some of those imaginary worlds provide readers with insights regarding the ecological dimensions of their own world.

Science fiction novels may be less disruptive than postmodernist ones in terms of the reader's assumptions about consensual reality because they tend to contain so much narration devoted to establishing the textual world and its internal consistency. At the same time, they are much like a thought experiment in that they place human beings in settings that foreground certain problems and dilemmas regarding human behavior and awareness. Eco–science fiction, then, would be those novels that focus on conflicts whose resolution is dependent upon working out an appropriate systemic relationship between the human and the nonhuman, or those that reveal the formation or adaptation of human character in relation to environmental influences.

What I am proposing here, then, is a study of the foregrounding, or significant depiction of, environmental issues and ecosystemic relationships in a set of novels chosen because they provide a range of modes of representation from traditional realism to postmodernism, from the observable world of immediate reality to the imagined worlds of unreality. I am going to consider all of these novelistic variations nature-oriented literature because they are aesthetic texts that tell stories about humanity's relationship to the rest of nature. Rather than going into detail on two or three selected examples, in the next few paragraphs I want to emphasize through half a dozen or so examples the variety of the field awaiting critical attention.

John Bruner's *The Sheep Look Up* is a typical, although structurally complex, science fiction novel utilizing extensive postmodernist techniques. Its typicality comes from Bruner's extrapolating certain tendencies in the contemporary environmental crisis to project an American culture on the verge of ecological chaos and self-destruction. While set in the near future rather than the present, it provides more information about ecological problems than perhaps any of the other novels mentioned in this chapter, with the exception of Davenport's *Shark Dialogues*. Bruner's highly activist-oriented conclusion has virtually all of the United States engulfed in a system-purging conflagration, the apocalyptic overtones of which may explain the title's source in the Puritan poetry of Milton.

In contrast to *The Sheep Look Up*, William Gibson's cyberpunk novel *Neuromancer* treats nontechnological nonhuman nature as an almost vanished background for the playing out of its posthuman cyborg plot. But in the future culture's neglect and dismissal of wild nature, it delivers a shrill warning about the future of a virtual-reality United States. It also strongly reminds readers that it is only human hubris rather than human knowledge that tends to cause us to treat all other entities in the world, organic and inorganic, as beings-for-us rather than as beings-in-themselves and, perhaps more significantly, beings-for-themselves.

In Ursula K. Le Guin's *The Dispossessed*, nature is not at the center of the plot, but it is at the origin of the culture from which the protagonist arises. The impact of the environment on cultural evolution is explored extensively throughout the novel, including the ways in which the environments of the various planets affect gender and class relationships. And through the lessons of an ecologically destroyed earth near novel's end, Le Guin emphasizes the necessity of gaining an understanding of human-ecosystem interrelationships before human destructiveness becomes self-destructiveness.

Sherri Tepper's *Grass* functions along similar lines regarding human destructiveness becoming self-destructiveness but focuses on human beings faced with the need to recognize a world ecosystem in which they are an exotic and subordinate animal in the planet's predator-prey hierarchy. One of the planet's highly sentient creatures—far more sentient than the humans are allowed to know—uses the alien human beings as the equivalent of hunting dogs to exterminate a rival sentient species. Here, through the use of native creatures rather than the artificial intelligence entities of *Neuromancer*, Tepper emphasizes the degree to which human beings can be the alien in relationship to other animals. She reminds the reader that other creatures can function as beings-for-themselves and that they can also make humans function as beings-for-others, using the human propensity for species extinction against both their native rivals and against the human settlers themselves.

Joanna Russ's *We Who Are about To. . . .* takes these ideas of cultural evolution, ecosystem interdependence, and human destructiveness leading to self-destructiveness a step further than Le Guin and Tepper. In Russ's novel a group of space travelers crash-land on a plant never before violated by human presence. The female narrator-protagonist is a nonconformist who seeks to secede from the replication of patriarchal hierarchy that the other shipwrecked people start to establish. Early in the novel she realizes that the food rations and other emergency gear upon which the survivors are relying are designed not so much to protect humans from possible toxins in native plants and atmospheric gases but to protect the native environment from the potentially toxic humans! In her quest to remain outside patriarchal oppression, she chooses death with dignity over survival at any cost and, through her resistance, is unwillingly involved in the extinction of the small survivor population. Russ embodies through this work of feminist science fiction the idea that some wilderness areas would ecologically benefit from being human-free.

It is also useful to look at fantasy novels. Patricia McKillip's three-volume *The Riddle-Master of Hed* and Buchi Emecheta's *The Rape of Shavi* work as a study in contrasts. The former is an epic fantasy in which the world does not change in the sense of altering its own dynamic processes in the face of sentient manipulations. Rather, its complexity and the interrelationships of its various humanoid creatures with the rest of the imagined world's nature is revealed to the protagonist, Morgon of Hed, and the reader simultaneously through a long journey of homecoming. This quest to achieve grounding transforms Morgon and helps him realize his destiny along with that of the world of which he is an integral part.

The Rape of Shavi is a postcolonial dystopia in which a small group of British subjects flee an anticipated nuclear apocalypse and crash near an idyllic African village. The destruction and reconstruction of the villager's environmentally sustainable way of life forms the plot of the remainder of the novel. Emecheta's dystopia is actually more allegorical than many animal fables. As a result, in terms of its environmentalist argument it is more similar to *Animal Dreams* than to *The Riddle-Master of Hed*, which could be said to have more thematically in common with *A Place on Earth*. On such a basis, the first two works could be classified as environmental fictions while the latter two could be classified as nature fictions. In the case of *A Place on Earth*, however, I think its categorization and interpretation would depend heavily on whether the reader was familiar with the author's non-fiction prose and poetry.

In looking at these seven works of science fiction and fantasy, one can see several varieties of nature and environmental engagement. First, there are science fiction novels, such as *The Sheep Look Up*—which is part of the category of near-future science fiction set on this planet—that can both provide factual information about nature and human-nature interactions as well as provide thematically environmentalist extrapolations of conflict and crisis based on such information. Second, works of both science fiction and fantasy, such as Le Guin's, Tepper's, and McKillip's, can provide analogous depictions of ecosystems and human interaction with such systems. Third, science fiction and fantasy works, such as those by Tepper, Russ, and Emecheta, can demonstrate the disastrous consequences of exploitative relationships between humans and other humans, humans and other sentient beings, and humans and ecosystems in which they are an exotic.

An Inclusivist Approach to Fiction

The examples briefly discussed in the previous sections range across works by men and women of various ethnicities and nationalities, including African American, Euro-American, Asian American, Chicana, and Native American, as well as African, British, and Canadian.[33] Such a selection attends to multiple modes of representation of the environment in literary fictions. While it relies on categorical labels for organizing the texts into separate groups, these are heuristic rather than foundational. I would strongly urge that the degree to which nature is addressed as theme, as character, as philosophical worldview in these works and others be treated in accordance with its depiction in each text, rather than from a one-analytical-method-fits-all approach. That is to say, I have provided multiple sets of texts in order to encourage an architectonic rather than a generic approach to their analysis. By architectonic I mean an analysis of the specific structural system of each work and how that work's parts function in regard to the whole, and how form and content are mutually complementary, a point I will address in more detail in chapter 3.

By considering the diversity of depictions and representations of the environment found in the novel form, and by considering the depiction of the land in these novels as more than a scape, as more than mere setting or refuge, I intend to advance an argument about the need for a more inclusive definition of nature-oriented literature than the nature-writing paradigm can provide, or that terms such as nature literature or environmental literature or ecofiction can encompass.[34] I also intend to bring greater attention, by my explicit selection of examples, to novels that either have not received much critical response or have been subjected to critical analyses that ignore or downplay their nature-oriented dimensions. And, finally, by stimulating interest in these examples I hope to enhance my reader's appreciation for such fiction and suggest a way of reading it that also has serious implications for the way we live in and sustain or denigrate the world of which we are a unique part. The reading of such novels and of such critical arguments as this one takes readers away from the rest of nature in order to think about it through imaginative literature and its criticism. But I intend for such reading and critical reflection to propel people back into the rest of nature with new perspectives and frames of reference.

2

Environmental Literature

Beyond Nature Writing and the Fiction of Nonfictionality

OR SEVERAL YEARS I have been inveighing against the limitations of the narrow concept of nature writing as defining the field of criticism that endeavors to study the relationship of literature and environment. In the introduction I argued for the need to have a more discriminating taxonomy of the literature that could be defined as nature-oriented and established my distinction between nature literature and environmental literature. With such a taxonomy in mind, I made a case in chapter 1 for why the novel has been slighted in ecocriticism with an emphasis on what I have labeled the nonfiction prejudice. In this chapter I would like to bring together that initial distinction between nature and environmental literature with that concern for a nonfiction prejudice through answering three multipart questions: What is nature writing and what is environmental literature? My answer to this question will recap some of my previous remarks and address these concepts from additional angles. What is the fiction of nonfictionality, and why do we need to move beyond it? Here I will return to the nonfiction prejudice, emphasizing the problems it creates in ecocriticism. And what are the implications of defining the subject of ecological literary criticism as primarily environmental literature rather than nature writing? In answering this question I will present an argument for why I think that such a shift in focus is not only a matter of descriptive emphasis but also a matter of thematic and ethical responsibility.

Nature Writing versus Environmental Literature

For a professor of American literature to teach nonfictional essays in a course, he or she must be able to demonstrate that the works contain some aesthetic dimension and have sufficient literary qualities to fit the purview of the discipline and the English department. With the advent of cultural studies as a field, the inclusion of nonfiction has become somewhat easier in many cases, but the problem remains in courses defined as studying literature. While a New Critic might take delight in studying a verse essay by Alexander Pope, it would be the verse component that justified the study because New Criticism is a type of analysis that militates against any significant inclusion of nonfiction in literary study.

And yet, the triumph of New Criticism within American universities came during the decade after its fundamental premises were already being challenged. In the 1940s, a host of literary scholars were developing a historical, cultural, and political orientation toward the study of American literature, because they were concerned with demonstrating its American specificity, which New Criticism could not do. I think here of such theorists and critics as Alfred Kazin, F. O. Matthiessen, Robert Spiller and his coeditors who compiled the *Literary History of the United States* (1946–48), and the critics who defined themselves as literary historians. Soon after there developed the rising interest in the Puritan period of American culture. Given that the *Literary History* made no mention of the nature essay, as Tom Lyon points out, and had little to say about other types of nonfiction, the Puritan scholars had to justify the study of apparently nonliterary materials as part of the literary heritage by means of historical and cultural criteria.

In opposition to the triumph of the New Critics in the 1950s, then, there developed a nascent American studies that, while focused on literature, was historical, cultural, political, and economic in orientation. By the

1960s a new consciousness was developing at American universities, one quite different from the Cold War ethos of the previous decade, which had been very intent on defining American cultural and political uniqueness in opposition to the communist countries in Europe and Asia. Part of the critical review of culture that was questioning the American economic system and its image as the bastion of democracy and representative of the world's future was a rising feeling of environmental crisis. That, perhaps more than anything else, provided the opening for a range of new courses in English departments titled "The Literature of Nature," "Man and the Natural World," and "Nature Writing."

The word *writing* in some of these course titles revealed the intention to include alongside *Walden, Moby-Dick,* "The Bear," and other such canonical texts materials for literary study that were clearly nonfiction and often rhetorically or thematically (rather than aesthetically) structured. *Nature writing* was being defined by its teachers as a type of nonfictional prose focused, as Lyon contends, on "natural history and experiences in nature." The teachers were concerned as much with imparting information about the natural and wild world to an increasingly urban student body as with introducing them to another form of literary expression. At the same time, they felt compelled to balance that sense of the need for timeliness with the canonical conception of timelessness in order to claim worthiness for academic analysis.

But, even as professors and critics were achieving success in teaching such material and publishing on the subject, they were finding themselves unable to limit their selection of texts to nonfiction and experiences, and they were unable to address sufficiently the aesthetic characteristics of much of the writing they most admired. Their definitions of the subject have shifted and changed, which necessitates making the distinction between nature writing and natural history writing that many critics ignore or blur— Don Scheese in 1996, for instance, defines nature writing as a "descendant" of "natural history, for its scientific bent."[1]

When natural history as a field developed such a "scientific bent" in terms of science in the modern sense remains open to debate. While there are certainly forerunners of Carl von Linné, his *Systema naturae* published in 1735 is generally treated as the foundational text for the contemporary methods of scientific classification used by natural historians since his time. And it is this type of science that I believe ecocritics such as Lawrence Buell, John Elder and Robert Finch, Lyon, and Scheese have in mind. Michael Branch in his essay "Early Romantic Natural History Literature (1782–1836)" names an eighteenth-century change in religious perception as also crucial to the rise of modern natural history writing and nature writing in North America: "During the eighteenth century the confluence of several currents of European thought helped mitigate the American aversion to wild nature. Of primary importance was the influence of deism. . . . Behind the deist association of God and nature were the century's vast accomplishments in natural science."[2] From the mid-eighteenth century into the twentieth century, natural history as a form of scientific writing, rather than as a type of natural theology with which such figures as John Ray and William Paley were associated, continued to winnow out individual subjectivity, myth, anecdote, and religious belief.

But nature writing as ecocritics such as Branch, Lyon, and Scheese define it is different from natural history. These critics tend to converge on the early nineteenth century in the United States as the period in which nature writing as a distinct mode of representation of experience becomes established. Such a type of writing makes use of natural history and scientific observation techniques, relies on direct field experience, and refuses to give up the inclusion of the personal, the subjective, and the literary. The only element that might separate it from being labeled nature literature is the continued emphasis on nonfiction. Coterminous in American literature, then, is the rise of a nonfictional aesthetic nature writing, increasingly distinct from natural history, and a fictional aesthetic nature literature, distinct in subject, depiction, imagery, and theme from the rest of American fiction and poetry.

Such nonfictional nature writing and fictional nature literature continue to be written today, as I suggested with my introductory taxonomy. Nature writing is a genre, but one within a mode, and it is the mode that mainly concerns me in this chapter. Nature literature as a large category would mean an orientation toward writing, regardless of genre, as exhibiting an attention to the details of the natural world and a concern for human-nonhuman relationships, and a representation through imagery and narration of a philosophy toward the place of humanity within the whole of nature. We often find in nonfiction prose the implicit authorial belief that a reader will be moved to deepen or change his or her views about nature and human nature through learning more information and through being presented with the author's own epiphanies. There is a faith in the contagiousness of nature appreciation and a belief in the timelessness of epiphanic experience throughout much nature literature.

Environmental literature, in contrast, does not presume contagion by shared appreciation and tends to be more concerned with timeliness rather than timelessness. It does presume a high degree of self-consciousness about ecological relationships and environmental crises, while sharing the other attributes of nature literature. Quotes from two recently published works labeled as nonfiction prose help to demonstrate my distinction as it is manifest in contemporary writing. The first, by Jack Wennerstrom from *Soldiers Delight Journal*, is an example of recent nature writing clearly based on the natural history tradition. In the introduction Wennerstrom explains his purpose: "Both natural and human history were the objects of my scrutiny, though with clear emphasis on the former. I have tried to describe a representative number of intriguing flora and fauna, and have by no means attempted to list all of the area's species. . . . I hoped to get a handle on those imponderables that attend all closeness with the outdoors to, now and again, hold up nature's glory for inspection and turn it in the light."[3] Following is a representative example of this text:

> This morning Donna and I walked the northwest sector. As we left the parking area west of Ward's Chapel Road, I looked up to see an adult bald eagle soaring against the blue. It was probably in migration north. I have now seen both North American eagle species at Soldiers Delight, for I found an immature golden eagle, by far the rarer of the two, in the eastern sector the autumn before last. It had been perched high in a dead tree not a hundred feet away, and I inadvertently spooked it as I passed. Unlike the adult, which is uniformly dark with tawny highlights, the immature golden eagle has a white-banded tail and white wing patches, and these were apparent as it pushed aloft and circled in the autumn air.[4]

The second text, Pete Dunne's *Before the Echo: Essays on Nature*, is an example of environmental nonfiction writing:

> Like a piebald shadow, the animal ambled across a landscape that looked as if it had been tortured. . . .
> . . . [T]he skunk ambled up the blacktop driveway heading for the location of its old den under the wind-blown tree—the one that used to be right where Bob's garage was now. . . .
> Puzzled, the skunk coursed beneath the somewhat overprized symbol of Bob's promotion, sniffed the wheels, and, frustrated, began a reconnaissance in search of the opening to its misplaced den.[5]

In the latter passage, indictment of human behavior is almost continuous within the narrative description, as we see from the use of "tortured," "overprized," and "misplaced." In the introductory remarks from *Soldiers Delight*, in contrast, the author makes certain assumptions about the affective power of accurate description, focusing on the apparent benefit of a sense of wonder, without any clear indication of what kind of positions a reader might take as a result of feeling a sense of wonder. In the passage from *Before the Echo*, the author relies largely on rhetorical devices and highly connotative language to make an implicit political point about how suburban expansion is destroying wildlife habitat while defending the behavior of wild animals in the face of human incursions into their domain.

It seems to me that as awareness of environmental crises becomes more widespread it will become increasingly difficult for contemporary writers to produce a nature literature that depicts a deep appreciation for wild nature and relishes the kinds of observations that Wennerstrom makes without including environmental statements in their work. They will be hard-pressed to avoid turning their observations into implicit environmentalist manifestos in terms of condemning certain kinds of human behavior and in promoting other kinds. And certainly the likelihood of readers interpreting nature literature as environmentalist will outstrip any means of authorial thematic control.

A case in point is Marcia Bonta's *Appalachian Autumn*. Bonta had established her reputation as a nature writer prior to publishing this book, particularly through the success of *Appalachian Spring*. She notes on the first page of her introduction to *Appalachian Autumn* that "this book was to be a praise-song for an Appalachian autumn, full of the happenings and special beauties of this loveliest of Pennsylvania's seasons, and so it is."[6] In other words, it was intended to be a classic work of American nature writing. But then, as Bonta continues, this book became something more than the nature writing she originally intended:

> Those resources belong to everyone, and if they are destroyed, we will be destroyed too.
>
> Unfortunately, though, many landowners consider what they do to their property to be their own business, even if it impacts their neighbors. That has been the situation here for most of the years we have lived on our wooded mountaintop, particularly in autumn when, several times, adjacent landowners decided not to harvest their woodlots sustainably, but to either take off all the big trees or, in the worst-case scenario, to clear-cut the steep mountain slopes with no thought of those living below. . . . Must we again try to stop their irresponsible rape of the forest?[7]

Although Bonta began with the intention of writing in the same way that she had written in the past, she found herself including more and more passages that were much more akin to Dunne's *Before the Echo* than Wennerstrom's *Soldiers Delight Journal*. Although she would wish to describe the beauties of nature writing as an amateur naturalist, by page 222 Bonta defines herself as an "environmentalist." Her experience exemplifies my point about the shift away from a detached nature writing to an increasingly engaged environmental writing in regard to nonfiction.

To summarize, nature literature and environmental literature are labels I am applying to two different modes of writing about nature and human-nonhuman relationships. These modes can be practiced in any genre. Nature writing is a genre within a mode, while environmental literature is a mode with several genres, one of which is environmental nonfiction writing. The modes rather than the genres ought to be defining our field of study. We also need to recognize that, if we privilege nature literature as the more general category including environmental literature, or if we privilege environmental literature as including nature literature, there are certain ramifications in terms of course organization, pedagogy, and political and ethical stances, which I will address in my conclusion to this chapter.

Moving beyond the Fiction of Nonfictionality

The fiction of nonfictionality consists not so much of the belief that information can be presented in some unmediated way, but rather of the treatment of works that are labeled nonfiction as if they contain no fabrications and the pretense that objective facts when personally experienced have greater validity than speculations or fictive events in representing natural processes or generating truth. Two related debates that took place on the Association for the Study of Literature and Environment Internet discussion list provide evidence of such a situation. In the one case, Edward Abbey was resolutely defended for the nonfictionality of his work *Desert Solitaire* because he allegedly engaged only in the omission of facts, not in fabricating parts that would be treated as facts—although other contributors cast doubt. In the other case, Annie Dillard was vehemently attacked by some participants because she invented the story of the giant water bug in *A Pilgrim at Tinker Creek*.[8] In fact, the only part that was fabricated was the claim that her knowledge of the water bug came about through direct personal experience rather than through reading the works of other naturalists. But, as Scheese notes, "Dillard immerses herself in the 'book of nature,' in both the primary and the secondary senses of that term. She stalks authors of natural history as well as the phenomena of nature, reading and quoting naturalists from Pliny to Edwin Way Teale."[9]

The furor, then, seems to derive not from the scientific accuracy, the nonfictionality, of the description of nature, but from the narrative means by which the author frames that information. Some readers apparently felt deceived because they could no longer be sure that everything described actually happened to Dillard, or, perhaps, even happened at all. In other words, the claim of nonfictionality seems to be wrapped up in an idea of writing with a "scientific bent" and also in writing based on direct personal experience. Yet this very emphasis is based on the importance of subjective experience and perception, and the communication of such is further dependent upon the ways in which authors artistically conceptualize the best way to represent such experience and perception. Dillard apparently concluded that drawing on a scientific description of an event observed by someone else would better further her representation of her subjective, personally experienced perceptions of power, reality, and justice in the natural world than relying on some event recorded in her Tinker Creek journal.

Does that make Dillard's philosophical claims or her own religious epiphany less true, or the depiction of the water bug less factual? Even readers who answer no to this double question might reply that it does eliminate her book from the ranks of nonfiction, but whose label is that in the first place, and what cause does such a label serve? *A Pilgrim at Tinker Creek* certainly meets Buell's criteria for an emphasis on "outer mimesis," but such mimesis doesn't finally determine whether a work of literature is fiction or nonfiction, unless the narrative framing of the features of "outer mimesis" are also required to be nonfictional in the sense of directly, personally experienced.[10] But should they be, or should the generic classification of the work be determined precisely by that narrative framing of the facts?

To my mind, the fiction of nonfictionality is a more serious problem than just the difficulties raised by the preceding questions because it reinforces the canonical illusions of timelessness and universality. If facts can be presented in unmediated language—as indicated by that idealistic axiom of "let the facts speak for themselves"—then there must be a single mode of representation that can present the truth more accurately than other representations, which is something Lawrence Buell seems to be headed toward in *The Environmental Imagination*. One of the problems with privileging nonfiction as a foundational criterion of nature writing—and then extending that term to cover all forms of nature-oriented literature as some critics are wont to do—is that it ignores the realities and traditions of literary production and the political climates in which authors must operate from country to country and decade to decade.

The problems of translating pronouns between languages and representing an individual's relationship to others should remind us of the dangers of universalizing ideas about discourses and writing. Where an Anglo-American might say, "the four of us crested the hill and I saw my very first mountain lion," rendering the experience as individually personal and possessive, an indigenous person might say, "hill-cresting our party and the inhabiting mountain lion met; we looked at each other with caution," emphasizing the group experience and identifying both human and lion as subjects participating in the mutual moment of recognition. How also, for example, might Japanese cultural and linguistic norms affect the representation of this event, given that Japanese sentences often avoid directly naming the agent of an action and place the verb at the end?

Some might object that all of these microstories are nonfictional, since in each the fact of the mountain lion is taken for granted. But I would contend that the significant aspect of these stories is precisely the accuracy of the culturally located point of view. Each is an interpretation of reality and also a construction of it with practical ramifications. For readers and their relationships with the rest of the world and their behavior toward their immediate environments, the representation of a more accurate point of view about how nature works maybe be far more important than whether the people saw a mountain lion or a cougar and whether the event was experienced by the narrator or imagined on the basis of the experiences of others.

In other words, the really salient feature of an environmental literary work may be its impact on the reader's point of view, which can be accomplished through fictional stories as well as nonfictional ones. But the typical definition of nature writing, with its emphasis on nonfiction and natural history, tends to work against such a recognition, and in literary studies it has inhibited American attention to fiction and inhibited international attention to certain literary histories of various countries, making nature writing not necessarily a particularly useful genre for environmentally conscious writers.

We must move beyond the fiction of nonfictionality for several reasons. The uncritical reliance on the nonfiction natural history essay as the paradigm for studying literature that engages nature inadvertently validates universalizing claims of the Eurocentric Enlightenment that have been extensively critiqued from a number of poststructuralist and feminist angles. The Anglo-European natural history orientation is also fundamentally Judeo-Christian in its postlapsarian vision of the fallen state of humanity, a vision that constitutes alienation as the necessary condition of all human cultures and that is reinforced through efforts to define nature writing as invariably pastoral. Critics, I think, need to ask to what degree alienation becomes an ontotheological foundation for the privileging of this mode of writing over other forms of literary representations of nature.

The privileging of alienation, individual experience and personal epiphanies, and factual discourse has limited the ranks of those who have been studied as writers of nature-oriented literature. It is not atypical to find a book-length study of nature writing focusing on five or six authors, all of whom are white and only one or at most two of them female.[11] Rather than asking what are the traditions and discourses in which people around the world write about nature, those who rely on the nature-writing tradition, in effect, ask whether anyone else can write like the white male natural historians who are the foundational figures of the field. Donna Haraway has documented the ways in which gender bias has affected the history of anthropological research on primates, and Evelyn Fox Keller, Sandra Harding, and others have addressed the same problem in other scientific disciplines. No one should imagine that the nature-writing tradition has avoided such problems when it works so closely with the same discourses and worldviews. Even as women begin to infiltrate the lists of authors under study, we still have to ask whether the nature-oriented literature of minority writers can be accommodated by definitions of genre and mode that proceed from the typical definitions of nature writing now circulating.

The fiction of nonfictionality also creates an environment in which authors are not only expected to feel philosophically alienated, but also to conceptualize themselves as observers more than as participants, as if one could observe without participating. This position encourages the phenomenon that occurs too frequently in anthologies, where there are no works by Native Americans but there are several essays by white anthropologists about Native Americans. Indigenous peoples are limited to being informants rather than authors, their voices silenced in an allegedly unmediated representation that objectifies them as another natural object.

This observational emphasis also militates against the inclusion of overtly political themes and discourses within narratives about nature, thereby working against the environmental-literature orientation. Authors who perceive their writing about nature as part of other struggles, such as anticolonial, antiwar, and antiracist, may feel discouraged from participating in nature writing. This discouragement does not come directly from feelings about whether they can write nonfiction, but from a recognition that their nonfiction is partisan and participatory and not in the pastoral tradition often associated with nature writing.

The prescriptiveness that goes along with embracing the fiction of nonfictionality and the narrow nature-writing tradition risks stifling new, fresh, developing writing. It runs the risk that prescriptive criticism and canon formation always do, the risk of killing the genre through baking it into a rigid mold. The emphases on nonfiction, on the essay, and on prose all point in this direction of deadening.

These problems result not from some intrinsic evil of nonfictional nature writing, but from the ways in which critics and anthology editors have elevated it to the preeminent and most authentic form of nature representation, and from their failures to critique their own cultural assumptions, gender biases, or stylistic prejudices. Until we can admit the aesthetic manipulation and fictionalizing maneuvers taking place in any text of literary nonfiction, we cannot recognize the degree of truth and the range of information found in other genres of literary representation of nature and human-nonhuman relationships.

Defining the Subject as Environmental Literature

A shift from nature writing to environmental literature as a starting point has several implications. It significantly broadens the range of literary texts appropriate for ecocritical analysis, and it opens the entire range of the history of literary production for consideration. Using the terms *nature literature* and *environmental literature* can increase the inclusiveness of the field of critical study, as long as these terms are recognized as modes of describing representation, rather than subgenres. While genres may be fairly stable, subgenres come and go (such as the Western epic poem) or undergo significant transformation (such as pastoral poetry).

Postmodernist forms and media technology have also increased the frequency of the appearance of hybrid forms, such as mixed-genre books and combination art and text works, as well as video, film, and mixed-media presentations. We ought to have a conception of aesthetic representations inclusive enough to be able to comment intelligently and critically on such works. Environmental literature allows us to consider works of any time period that demonstrate an environmental consciousness within the cultural, historical, religious, and philosophical particularities of the time. There are, for example, ancient treatises, poems, plays, and other literary forms that comment on human-nonhuman relationships and environmental changes prior to the rise of the scientific method that undergirds the contemporary concept of nonfiction in the dominant definitions of nature writing. While such environmental consciousness may not be ecological in any scientific sense of the term, it may represent a more interdependent and systemic view of natural relationships than was prevalent in its day.

Shifting away from nature writing also encourages a greater inclusion of historically marginalized and suppressed voices—peoples who are on the front lines of global environmental destruction. Once we break with the notion of a particular genre defining the field, we are open to studying the diversity of literary representations from cultures around the world with their own nature traditions, their own environmental philosophies, and their own contemporary responses to global environmental issues.[12] The concept of environmental literature, for example, enables us to analyze the very different way the contemporary revival of an ancient work, such as the Aboriginal epic songs of Australia, might affect contemporary readers' or listeners' understanding of environment, politics, and local sustainability. Instead of being informants for Anglo-European essay writers, indigenous peoples can be recognized as authors and speaking subjects in their own right, without necessarily working in the literary forms popular in the United States or England.

Working with the environmental-literature mode facilitates the development of a criticism supportive of continued innovation in nature-oriented literary production. In particular, it will be able to accept, appreciate, and interpret the subjectivity, partial perspective, and positionality in much contemporary writing, particularly in regard to English-language literature by women of color, who are largely absent from critical studies and anthologies of nature writing.

Environmental literature challenges the configuration of traditional course offerings and academic departments, conceptions of canon formation and reader competence, and the parameters for historicist and contextualist criticism. Environmental literature by definition encourages the structuring of courses that include works from several genres, and it includes consideration of science fiction and fantasy, since these forms can represent human-nonhuman relationships and address environmental issues as well as realism. Environmental literature also calls for courses that include literary and rhetorical texts, because it recognizes that information and representation are part of a web of conceptualizations and human experiences, and because such courses can contribute to the development of ecological literacy among students. Ecological literacy can then become a criterion by which students are determined to be competent readers of literature, and environmental literature can be used to alter their awareness of what they need to know to function in the world.

Certainly it calls for a reconsideration of the mainstream literary canons, because it can both analyze nature and environmental literatures and because it facilitates an ecocritical review of canonical works in terms of their relative merit to contemporary readers. Working with the mode of environmental literature also places demands on contemporary cultural studies and critical theory, by demonstrating that literature has already brought nature onto the stage of culture as a speaking subject, as a participant in history, and any critical school that fails to acknowledge this fails to be comprehensive or even competent in its literary analysis.

Finally, environmental literature provides a noncentric basis for genuinely cross-cultural analysis of literary representations of nature and human-nonhuman relationships. Because it does not privilege any particular genre or style of expression, it does not establish a foundation, such as the nonfiction prose essay, against which other literatures and literary traditions are measured. Romantic poetry is not automatically privileged over haiku, or nonfiction essays over speculative meditations. It would be able to recognize that the use of a particular style or language in one context might be entirely appropriate and thematically effective, while reactionary in another.

Conclusion

Let me conclude this chapter by clarifying one final point. While I believe that it is a mistake to use nature writing as the paradigm for critical analysis of all forms of nature-oriented literature, I do not advocate that everyone proceed from the environmental-literature-mode orientation that I recommend here. One can also proceed from the nature-literature mode, but readers and critics need to understand the implications of deciding to privilege nature literature over environmental literature as the major category. The fundamental distinctions in this choice are the difference in the concept of advocacy in the literature to be emphasized, the author-reader relationship in terms of the potentially transformative function of literature, and the implicit attitude toward the severity of the global environmental crisis and the responsibility of the critic not only as literary interpreter but also as participative inhabitant in the world. We will not all see eye to eye on any of these points, but perhaps more self-conscious reflection on these issues may help us to understand our differences.

In my approach, I view nature literature as being implicit in areas where environmental literature is explicit, in stopping at the point of description or analysis just where environmental literature would begin, and as being less crisis oriented. In regard to this last point, it is my belief that through emphasizing environmental literature as part of an ethically engaged literary criticism, I may contribute to the kind of gradual cultural change that will allow nature literature to become again the more appropriate form of writing because the global ecological crisis will have been lessened.

3

Refining through Redefining
Our Sensibilities

Nature-Oriented Literature as an International
and Multicultural Movement

Refining and Redefining

I ECOCRITICISM HAS been hindered by too narrow an attention to non-fiction prose and the fiction of nonfictionality, it also has been limited by a focus on American and British literatures. In order to widen the understanding of readers and critics, it is necessary to reconsider the privileging of certain genres and also the privileging of certain national literatures and certain ethnicities within those national literatures. Such reconsideration will enable a greater inclusiveness of literatures from around the world within the conception of nature-oriented literature. It will also enable critics and readers such as myself, who focus primarily on American literature, to place that literature in an internationally relative and comparative framework. I see such reconsideration as one of the ways by which we can refine our awareness and expand the field of ecocriticism.

Therefore, I begin this chapter by posing two questions: What should be the character of our spirit of inquiry when investigating nature-oriented literature and thinking about ecocriticism as an international and multicultural movement? And what should our expectations be regarding the degree to which other cultures and literatures can facilitate the analytical processes that flow from such a spirit of inquiry?

Let me answer the first question with an untitled poem by Lew Welch:

Step out onto the Planet.
Draw a circle a hundred feet round.

Inside the circle are
300 things nobody understands, and, maybe
nobody's ever really seen.

How many can you find?[1]

And let me answer the question about expectations with another poem,
this one by Yu Kwang-chung, "Noonday Slumber of a Faun":

"Is the faun at home?" lightly I ask.
A long pause without an answer.
Nothing but cool breeze and chirping birds,
And impenetrable remains the wood.
"Is the faun at home?" again I ask.
And again silence is the response.
So the bulldozer's impending arm
Will not knock on your door today,
Where dense and dark foliage droops.
Nor will loudspeakers and traffic
Break in upon your profound sleep.
Listen, nothing but silence.[2]

Readers and critics could benefit from refining their sensibilities
through some redefining of the concepts that are meant to articulate those
sensibilities. What do I mean by *sensibilities*? The first definition of "sensibility" is the basic concept of physical interconnection—the capacity for
physical sensation, the power of responding to stimuli, the ability to feel.
This ability to feel by means of one's senses tends to be culturally downplayed, however, in relation to the ability to feel mentally and symbolically.
The word *sensibilities* indicates a capacity to be affected emotionally or intel-
lectually and a receptiveness to impression. Further, sensibilities are the
capacity to respond perceptively to intellectual, moral, or aesthetic values.

Through the popularity of mind-body dualism, we can see how the dictionary definitions here slide from sensory interaction to impression to perception, with the stimuli changing from the material world itself to mental interpretations of that material world to cognitive concepts. Yet, all of this sliding along the chain of signification reveals the possibility, which I claim as a necessity, to link indissolubly the ability to sense physically and the capacity to respond perceptively.

Intellectual sensibility about literature is inextricably interwoven with our physical sensibility about the world, as the two opening poems suggest. The epithet that someone is "out of touch" should not be understood as only a metaphor. Refining our sensibilities, then, toward literature and through literature to the world from which it arises requires, among many other things, redefining concepts, terms, territories, and, possibly, our self-conceptions of sensory awareness. As Joy Harjo has remarked, "In European culture the world is supposed to have only three dimensions. It's constructed in a way that only the five senses can maneuver. There are probably more than five senses; there are probably ten, twelve, fourteen, a hundred senses—and we haven't developed them."[3]

In relation to such refining through redefining, I want to emphasize the international extent and the multicultural character of literature that depicts nature beyond human culture and also human interaction with the rest of nature. Implicit in that previous sentence is my definition of human culture as a manifestation and a part of nature, not something separate from, independent of, or foundationally in contradiction to nature. I define nature as the systemic processes of interacting physical entities that manifest the energy pathways and metamorphoses of the universe.

Those of us operating within the paradigms of dominant U.S. culture, or attempting to operate through other paradigms but indoctrinated into that culture in family life, school, and elite and mass cultural productions, too often confuse particularities with universals because that is the way we have been educated, that is the way mass American culture functions. Too often we confuse historically and culturally specific forms, attitudes, approaches, and concepts with global ones. The practice of universalization and generalization foregrounds some information and suppresses other information, as I have just done in my claims about "those of us."

Let me use a generic example about this problem of universalization, generalization, and foreground-background suppression. What is a novel? A novel is a long, written, prose narrative, with characters, events, and one or more points of conflict and climax—invented by the Chinese a very, very long time ago, enhanced by the Japanese at least ten centuries ago, and discovered as a significant literary form by the English in the past three hundred years. If we eliminate the word "written" from the definition, the origin of the form is lost to antiquity. Given these facts, one wonders how anyone could write a book about "the rise of the novel" and begin the discussion with British literature and treat only the Western dimensions of the novel tradition, yet people have done just that. Fortunately, fewer people would feel comfortable doing so these days. Indeed, fewer and fewer eco-critics feel complacent about their knowledge of the parameters of nature-oriented literature as we begin to think more in terms of the gestalt, more in terms of attending to the background that the foreground requires in order to function, but which has been suppressed. Paula Gunn Allen trenchantly observes that "Westerners have for a long time discounted the importance of background. The earth herself, which is our most inclusive background, is dealt with summarily as a source of food, metals, water, and profit while the fact that she is the fundamental agent of all planetary life is blithely ignored."[4]

One way of defining parameters for a field is to use a few generally acknowledged preeminent texts to establish criteria for evaluating other works. In other words, carve a foreground out of a differentiated but not hierarchically constructed tableau of literary production. In this way, the characteristics of a set of texts that were conceptualized as scientific natural history writing have been used to define certain key features of the nature writing that comes after them. That writing, however, does not quite conform to the earlier criteria, but since critics don't want to dismiss the later writing they adjust the definition. As with the definition of *epic* in the Western tradition, the definition of *nature writing* has to be adjusted with each new work that people find significant. As the Russian formalists argued, significance often results from innovation, from *oestrayenie*—estrangement and defamiliarization—from breaking with the past descriptions that have become prescriptions. As a result, any genre definition is effective only as a retrospective and ineffective as a predictive mechanism of analysis. Any approach that uses description for prescription and prediction also uses it for proscription, which guarantees what Ursula K. Le Guin has referred to as the colonization of the future by the present.[5]

I do not know whether a literary study that attends to form, style, and structure in any less of a reductive way is possible, although an emphasis on architectonics over genre might help some. Architectonics consists of the study of the unduplicated, particular structure of an individual work, which could be defined as the structural-interpretive method antithetical to genre analysis. If we do not know how to proceed other than by formulating reductive definitions based on past works, which can never fully account for the characteristics of new works, and we want to be careful not to exclude the innovative, the departive, the paradigmatically distinct from the study of aesthetic works that treat human–rest-of-nature interactions, then we need as diversified a sense as possible of the kinds of nature-oriented literature that exist today and that have existed in the past—those three hundred things that Lew Welch calls on us to find.

While the readers I know don't go to John Muir for sheep raising, or to Pat Mora for the *remedios* of a *curandera*, or to Paula Gunn Allen for channeling, they do go to them for information, of sorts, which often consists most significantly of a representation of sensibilities about human relationships with the environments in which humans find themselves. It is the thematic horizon more than the aesthetic one that predominates in the ecocritical vision of reading, although it is the aesthetic quality of certain works that keeps readers coming back (although not all readers appreciate the same aesthetics equally, and hence they have different literary favorites among their thematically important top choices, whether those works are nature writing, environmental fiction, or nature poetry). To some degree that primacy of communication and theme has hindered the parametric expansion of the ecocritical purview, because there has been an unstated and often unrecognized conflation of form and content in the analysis of literature.

The nonfiction prejudice within the nature-writing critical tradition has impeded appreciation of representations of nonhuman nature and human-nonhuman ecosystemic interaction in literary works that do not stylistically conform to canonical expectations. A case in point is the work of many Native American, Chicano, and Latin American authors, who write outside the traditional realism that Lawrence Buell champions as the defining feature of an "environmental text."[6] While the founders of Enlightenment science had no difficulty in writing about witches and supernatural manifestations in the material world, many people today rely on the Enlightenment's legacy of a secular, mechanical materialism for a definition of realism and a conception of reality.

In contradistinction to such a perceptual orientation, Harjo has commented that "the physical world is just another vibration, another aspect of the real world."[7] Think about the weakness and simplicity of a conception of reality based exclusively on observable phenomena for considering the vast range of the light spectrum, part of which is visible to other animals but beyond what our visual sense can process. There are all kinds of things, processes, and actions that nobody has ever really seen. Since there is far more visible to other entities than the naked human eye can see, why should people imagine that current conceptions of genre, current lists of exemplary texts, current course titles, or current ways of organizing academic fields of study are accurate or even adequate to the range of literary phenomena being produced around the world that might be treated as nature-oriented literature?

Louis Owens, in "'The Song Is Very Short': Native American Literature and Literary Theory," observes that, "With the recent emergence of what Arnold Krupat calls the 'voice in the margin,' there seems to be a widespread sense that a new kind of critical-theoretical approach is needed if multiculturalism is to be more than another aspect of the familiar discourse of dominance, what has been called critical imperialism." Owens goes on to highlight a "twofold kind of resistance" that impedes the development of such a new approach: "(1) The resistance of the so-called 'other' who very rightly suspects and frequently rejects the critical discourse of the metropolitan center as little more than further colonialism or cultural imperialism. And (2) the resistance of the privileged center itself which continues, in the face of what strikes me as often hypocritical posturing, to ignore the voices of Native Americans who would seek to construct and represent themselves."[8] When American academics ask if the nature-oriented literature faun is at home in the literatures of the world, attentive to its multi-cultural and international dimensions, they should not be surprised if no answer is immediately forthcoming, or if the answers given seem laboriously circuitous or highly opaque. Nor should they use the lack of an easily translatable invitation to sit at the table as an excuse to remain Eurocentric and Anglophilic.

For example, Gregory Cajete, when writing about a theory of indigenous education, and Rush W. Dozier Jr., when writing about new research pertinent to evolution theory, and many others, have noted that "recent studies indicate that the act of seeing and repeating a word has different neural pathways than hearing and repeating a word."[9] People who participate extensively in oral performances and audiences brought up in oral-transmission cultures develop different synaptic connections from those predominantly educated through print. As a result, in studies of the degree of natural depiction or environmental implications in literary works deriving from predominantly oral cultures, critics ought to be taking into account the differential structures of cognitive associations within the minds of the works' audiences. They also need to consider the degree to which the authors utilize this physiological phenomenon in their imagery and narrative and rhetorical strategies. In other words, according to Maria Chona, whom Owens quotes, "the song is very short because we understand so much."[10] Anyone who has read Larry Evers and Felipe S. Molina's *Yaqui Deer Songs* will recognize the accuracy of this terse statement.

Along a somewhat different path, Owens's warning can also help with consideration of works that appear to be clearly written, at least initially, in recognizable western literary genres. Joni Adamson, in her book *The Middle Place* (in press), extensively demonstrates the degree to which the word *almanac* in Leslie Marmon Silko's title *Almanac of the Dead* is heavily indebted both to the Mayan almanac tradition and the early European colonists of North America's printing of various almanacs. *Almanac* provides the opportunity, then, for one to consider judiciously the relationship of Silko's writing to literary postmodernism in terms of parallelism rather than influence, adaptation rather than adoption, and as a supplement to the main influences on Silko's writing rather than as source.

While it may be impossible to avoid reductionism as a constitutive category of literary analysis, it may be possible to offset its tendencies by remaining always restless in the face of previous categories, labels, and definitions, seeking always not to make the newly discovered Maori *novel* or Bedouin *pastoral* poem fit familiar genre expectations, but to make up new categories to conform to the diversity of literary production. For instance, although in a previous chapter I distinguished nature literature from environmental literature, perhaps those terms do not suffice, even if momentarily productive. In addition to talking about the literature of place or the new regionalism, two current terms, it might be as accurate and productive to distinguish between *indigenismo* literature, inhabitory literature, and reinhabitory literature, emphasizing the historicity of various human-place relationships rather than lumping them all together. Such relabeling will, I believe, contribute to the ongoing transformation of ecocriticism to the level of sophistication that literary representations of nature and human-environment interaction require. As Joy Harjo notes in a valuable act of refining through redefining, "transformation is really about understanding the shape and condition of another with compassion, not about overtaking."[11]

Location, Location, Location

Many people involved with ecological criticism, with the study of nature in literature, and with finding ways of being in the wild are skeptical of postmodernism and poststructuralist theorizing, and rightly so. But periodizing the contemporary age as postmodern and the intellectual discussions about this condition as poststructuralist have enabled us to envision the dethronement of the idea that there is a single universal story to which all great literature aspires. As ecological criticism gains momentum as an international movement and establishes itself as an academic discipline, its practitioners need to be vigilant about avoiding the impetus toward canon formation. They ought to be wary of prescriptive critical formulations.

One way to maintain such vigilance is to pay careful attention to location, location, location. The first of these locations is geographical, the second historical, and the third location is the awareness of where actual readers and critics stand, of their own geopsyches, of their own subject constructions, of their own narratives and storied residence. Let's take a little walking tour through these three locations in the style of what John Burroughs and other American naturalists might call a ramble.

Geographic Location

Anyone engaging with any kind of literature attentive to the natural environment as setting, character, or subject will invariably be aware of the specificities of location. In order to sharpen this focus on geographic location, I will allude to the literature of only the past two hundred years. With this literature readers want to know where the action takes place and how the main character views it. Do they have another London urbanite coming upon the Scottish moors for the first time and seeing them through a rosy filter well deployed by Sir Walter Scott or Robert Louis Stevenson? Or do they have instead the images of a daily life in intimate, and therefore rarely romantic, contact with the soil and the land through labor, as in Patrick Kavanagh or Emily Lawless? Do they have the vision of the coast range, the ocean, the cypresses, and the rocks and crags that almost guarantee a story of human tragedy etched across the face of an inhuman world, as in the long narrative poems of Robinson Jeffers? Or do they see a desert landscape deadly to many but enriching to those who fit their lives to its rhythms and patterns, as lovingly depicted by Mary Austin? Or, as final examples, do they have a meditative speaker, such as William Wordsworth, wandering through the Lake District with the help of his sister, Dorothy, finding philosophical lessons for humanity in wildflowers and running streams, while his friend Samuel Taylor Coleridge conjures lurid allegorical images of the sea and the albatross?[12]

Such descriptions ought to be familiar enough to anyone who has spent time with the major anthologies of the literature of nature or nature writing. Yet they are exclusively Anglo-Irish-American, just as the current anthologies tend to be. That is all right as long as readers continuously remind themselves that such books contribute to the defining of traditions within just a few national literatures, omitting a great deal even from these literatures along the way, particularly in terms of indigenous and other visibly ethnic writers. Still, these anthologies and my previous examples do not adequately represent the diversity of depictions of nature and human inter-action with the rest of nature in English-language literature.

When readers turn to the English-language literatures of the Caribbean, Australia, India, and Africa, they will see again signal differences in emphasis. In Jean Rhys's *Wide Sargasso Sea*, the vitality and chaotic com-plexity of the jungle and the fecundity of the young female protagonist are set against the pallid Rochester and his visions of well-manicured lawns and stately gardens. The desired domesticated nature of England set against the repelling wild vegetation of the Caribbean tells a story of not just sexist domination but also of colonial oppression and cultural destruction. Not surprisingly, much recent Caribbean literature focuses on the return from the metropolis as a process of recovering identity, and such recovery is dependent upon a return to a relationship with the land, its rhythms, cycles, and bounty (see the related discussion of Michael Anthony's *Green Days by the River* in chap. 6).[13]

While *Wide Sargasso Sea* focuses on the colonizer versus the colonized, the literature of some other English-speaking areas is even more compli-cated. Just as the United States began as a settler colony, so too did Australia and New Zealand, and in every case one finds a complexity in defining the national literature, since there is the literature of the migrant populations who have become the dominant cultural, political, and economic force but have not clearly or successfully established themselves as inhabitants of those places. Originally suppressed but now avidly studied, readers also have the literatures of the indigenous peoples, who have taken up the colonizer's language as unavoidable or necessary for disseminating much of their own literatures and their own writing about nature to a wider audience. When readers look at Australia, the outback and the bush loom large, but there are vast differences of representation between contemporary Aboriginal epic songs and novels and much of the natural history writing, nonfiction, poetry, and fiction of the white settlers.[14] What one group called home was perceived as a perilous wasteland and a deadly jungle, with weather another of its weapons against the encroachments of European civilization. The impact of colonization and settlement upon this region can perhaps best be understood in the title of the novel by Mudrooroo, *Dr. Wooreddy's Prescrip-tion for Enduring the End of the World.*

Could there possibly be any other nation-state as complex as India? It is important for readers confronted with this particular location to admit the degree to which a colonizer's literature, much of which is not even written by settlers but by tourists, visitors, and military men and their family members, dominates our impressions of the land, its people, and its natural diversity. When readers come across the literature arising out of the Chipko movement—the women's movement to protect the northern forests from clear-cutting and destruction for the introduction of exportable cash crops and urbanization—they must step back for a moment.[15] Nothing in the works of Rudyard Kipling or E. M. Forster prepares readers for a literature critical not only of the multinational corporations and their continuing postcolonial exploitation, but also of the comprador bourgeoisie who have no understanding of the forest communities who resist the ecological destruction of their habitats. And when readers come to the writings of someone like the Bengali author Mahasweta Devi, they must be cognizant of the degree to which colonial and transnational exploitation are bound with perceptions and representations of nature in contemporary postcolonial writing.[16] This type of binding is not limited to India and the Caribbean.

For example, just in those areas of Africa in which the dominant language for literature is English, many contemporary African writers find that the environment cannot be treated without attention to violence, warfare, government corruption, and transnational corporate greed. From Chinua Achebe to Ayi Kwei Armah, Wole Soyinka to Alex Laguma, ecological destruction is depicted as part and parcel of postcolonial governmental corruption and the insanity of civil wars. It is impossible to treat even the study of animal behavior in Africa without recognizing the impact that war has on every aspect of human and nonhuman nature.[17]

War and environment are, however, a far cry from the literature that emphasizes solitary individuals spending a long, slow, meditative day at the ocean watching the comings and goings of creatures all smaller than one's hand. Yet, in understanding the significance of geographic location in the practice of ecological criticism, in the practice of the study of literature and the natural environment, readers must figure out how to develop paradigms and critical orientations that enable them to encompass such a range of material, from Rachel Carson's *Silent Spring* to Ngugi wa Thiong'o's *Petals of Blood*. These paradigms must help one to realize the extent to which, when thinking of geographic location, such geography includes the human, the cultural, and the economic as much as it does geological formations, animal migratory behavior, and weather patterns. If indeed the International Panel on Climate Change's estimations of global sea-level rise due to the greenhouse effect are borne out, the understanding of the impact of climate change on the high-water marks along the Thames River in London will be due to a nature made more wild by the material effects of human cultural practices in specific geographic locations.

Historical Location

Unless a critic has given at least some thought to the environmental implications of *The Epic of Gilgamesh* or *Shan-hai ching chiao-chu* (Guideways through mountains and seas), for example, then he or she is probably not looking far enough back in time to understand the traditions, cultural influences, sociopolitical factors, and environmentally shaping effects on the formation and development of nature literature through the centuries.[18] The American transcendentalists and their peers were heavily immersed in the texts of classical Greek as well as Roman pastoralism. They often came to natural history writing out of their own interests rather than through formal training; Laura Dassow Walls, for example, notes of George Perkins Marsh that he "offered a vision of participatory and democratic natural science quite similar to Thoreau's in his popular book *Man and Nature.* Yet Marsh did so not as a practicing scientist but as an avowed amateur."[19] The Humboldt brothers and their German philosopher peers heavily influenced their idealist thinking, while Edgar Allan Poe's nature fantasy, *The Narrative of Arthur Gordon Pym*, reflected the infatuation American authors had for the rapidly developing field of Egyptology. Egyptian hieroglyphics and their decipherment became part of the intertextuality of amateur efforts to read Nature's book in the United States of the nineteenth century.

Where do the Druids fit in the tradition of English nature writing? To what degree do readers need to take a look at the influence of various modern popularizations and fantasy inventions of medieval nature worship to understand some of the late twentieth-century American and British authors? Gary Snyder, for instance, was heavily influenced by Carl G. Jung and by Robert Graves's *White Goddess* while he was in college, reading them alongside the anthropological recovery of ancient Native American myths through the work of Franz Boas and others.[20]

My point here is that many oral traditions have infiltrated, been revitalized by, and formatively influenced the perceptions of nature by many of our contemporary writers, even though those oral traditions have been rendered through anthropological transcriptions, folklore, and fictive revisions by their contemporaries and immediate precursors. In rethinking the historical location of much of our modern writing we need to ask in what ways the landscape of Broceliande in the Breton Lays or, closer to home and more proximate in time, the pastoral characteristics of J. R. R. Tolkien's Middle Earth have shaped the imaginations of our current ecological writers.

The writing of the present day is my focus, and I tend to read the literature of earlier times through that particular lens. Such a focus works for me as well as the trifocals I wear, but I recognize that it is a limited perspective. As Carolyn Merchant in *The Death of Nature* has observed, Europe went through a series of human-induced ecological crises throughout the Middle Ages, into the Enlightenment, and continuing to the present. The Greeks and Romans faced such ecological crises even earlier than northern Europe, which may have been coping more with weather-induced ecological change, and archaeologists can no doubt tell us much about agriculture-induced erosion and ecosystem damage in ancient Mesopotamia, India, and China. Surely, then, the tendencies in literary history toward universalization and canon formation based on the alleged universality and timelessness of great works have suppressed literature that focused not on the more allegorical characteristics of the pastoral but on the warning signs of the nature-culture conflict. What kind of work is needed to recover a counterculture of literature that may have been earth oriented, like the ecological writings of that medieval abbess Hildegard of Bingen, for instance?[21] Why was the work of seventeenth-century English poet Thomas Traherne buried for so long and even now relegated such a minor place in the anthologies? Perhaps he has appeared to be too much of a tree-, sun-, and flower-hugger in his *Centuries of Meditations* to fit into the parameters of the metaphysical tradition.

Ecocritics have been busily engaged in recovering and promoting neglected works through writing about them, getting them brought back into print, and teaching them to keep them in print. But there is a need to move beyond the enclosure and initiate or intensify efforts to rewrite the general canon, not only of various national literatures, but also the general canons of Western and world literatures. As work with travel writing has shown, the recovery of neglected texts must go hand in hand with rethinking the historical location of literature, its situatedness within ideologies of domination, oppression, and liberation. Colonial literature, for example, particularly needs to be rethought in terms of the environmental and natural philosophy of travel writing, science writing, anthropology, race relations, and missionary records.

Self-Situated Location

Just like a character in a novel can be a Londoner suddenly transported to the Scottish moors, or an English gentleman lost in a Caribbean jungle, or an African student transported to a college located in an inhospitable climate beneath constellations he has never before seen, so can readers and critics come upon literature that they have not previously encountered. And like those characters, readers scan these new horizons, looking upon these strange locales from a perspective already well established, one that may have stood them in good stead on the safe and familiar terrain of the canon—the officially good literature—but that often does not suffice for determining their bearings.

In addition to geographical and historical location, there is also one's own personal location, or situatedness. Where was a person born? What was his or her relationship to the surrounding natural environment, and how much contact was there with that environment? Was a person a sickly child shut up with books as friends rather than out on the playing fields getting muddy? I grew up in a small town in the American Midwest and spent time playing in barns, wading in creeks in summer and skating along them in winter. I played army in the woods, built tree houses, underground forts, snow castles, and tunnels through ripe wheat fields. In high school I cut the corn out of the beans in the field behind my house and later strung barbed wire and buried dead cattle. Today I take care of about three acres on the edge of town and have observed up to ten white-tailed deer at a time in our yard. Genetics also affects my relationship to the rest of nature. I am color-blind and therefore discern far fewer colors in the world than many of my peers.

Personal situatedness, built through individual contact with the natural environment often against the grain of the culture, affects a reader's location in relation to the literature he or she studies and helps to explain why an individual enjoys certain kinds of literature more than others, and different types at various times. There are also the myriad currents of cultural formations that have influenced, and at times determined, a person's initial reactions to insects, large mammals, the oceans, and the mountains. There are the religious and scientific values through which readers have been brought up to believe that they inhabit a fallen world or else a world perfectible through technology. Without reflecting about individual self-location—a person's particular situatedness through nature, culture, and individual physiology—people are more likely to be determined by belief systems, philosophies, and prejudices, ones they might very well reject as a result of careful consideration, than if they take the time for such understanding of the I-as-particular-reader, rather than as a general reader.

When Cajete defines the *geopsyche* as the way that all the aspects of one's individual mind are shaped and influenced by a person's place of birth and upbringing, he is referring both to that phenomenon so many displaced people experience of arriving somewhere they have never been and feeling suddenly as if they had come home, and to the way that one's culture interacts with place and shapes the mind of each member of the culture. Formative factors include the direct contact with the natural world in which one is raised and the ways that one's culture, community, and family—at times in contradiction to each other—shape the preconditions and the interpretations of that direct contact, reinforcing certain impressions and reactions and rejecting or resisting others. The unconscious is affected by such overt cultural pressures and also by the rituals and rhythms of the community.

As discerning individuals, critical readers need to recognize the manifestations and representations of such psychic patterning in the literature that they choose to read. For instance, in the United States there were two contemporary famous Johns, Muir and Burroughs. Muir often portrays himself as a heroic individualist who relishes the isolation and danger of the solo mountain-climbing expedition and lavishes poetic language in his essays in appreciation of the sublime, which also contributed to the cultural popularity of that concept. Burroughs largely repudiates the sublime, warning in one of his essays against building one's house in a location with the most scenic overlook because one risks becoming overstimulated (I give additional attention to this point in chap. 11).[22] People appear regularly in his essays, often as companions on a fishing or hiking expedition or as inhabitants of the land through which he travels. How does one account for this dichotomy between Burroughs and Muir? Their diverse reactions to Alaska on the Harriman expedition indicate quite clearly that their differing viewpoints were not the result of the locale each traversed, but rather some orientation toward nature deeply ingrained in them much earlier in their lives.[23]

Likewise, how can readers come to terms with the immense variety of cultural and geographical backgrounds of today's international community of environmental writers? Readers must remind themselves repeatedly of where they are standing and of what they look like—both how they imagine themselves and how they are likely to look to these writers—as they seek to understand and to evaluate their work.

Conclusion

Across Great Britain as across the United States the definitions of such terms as English literature and American literature are becoming ever more complicated. Further, the literary and cultural traditions that inform that literature are becoming more diverse as the ethnic and religious minorities—whether recent immigrants or ancient inhabitants—remain unassimilated, if not in language then in terms of culture, religion, and family structure. In some ways, this diversity may prove to be even more pronounced when looking at contemporary literature treating nature and engaging environmental issues. While many contemporary ethnic writers may draw on the dominant written literary tradition for their style and aesthetic inspiration, they often draw on their ethnic cultural heritage (particularly the oral traditions) and their ancestral lands, religious beliefs, and healing practices for their intellectual, empathetic, and sensory engagement with the uncultured dimensions of the world. While it is the case that the term *nature* and its various meanings are cultural constructs, human perception is sensory as well as cognitive.

More to the point, much in the world remains fundamentally and utterly uncultured, such as the monsoon season and monarch butterfly migrations. Often it is the ethnic writers, the postcolonial writers, the indigenous authors, whose literary works tap into historical cultural formations that give greater credence to forms of human perception other than the rationally conscious, and frequently rely on forms of writing that cannot be aligned with Anglo-American Enlightenment realism.

The internationalization of nature-oriented-literature studies should not lead toward globalization of generic or aesthetic criteria, nor should it lead to a hierarchical ranking of the best the world has to offer. Rather, it should lead to that kind of balancing of similarity and difference, uniqueness and commonality, that remains so necessary in the cultural diversification of the American literary canon. If readers want nature to have a voice through representation of the nonhuman in literature, if readers want to see humanity decentered from its environmentally destructive narcissism and egotism, if readers want to see biological diversity represented aesthetically, and if readers want a reading and critical practice that enables the analysis and encouragement of such literary foregrounding of nature, then they must refine their sensibilities. One such act of refinement is to appreciate cultural diversity as a physical manifestation of biological diversity. Another is to redefine such things as ecocriticism and nature-oriented literature so that they are world inclusive in their perspectives and considerations. And one other is to remain always aware of the location, location, location of the reader and the text being read.

4

Ecofeminism and Postmodernism

Agency, Transformation, and
Future Possibilities

I n the preceding chapters, I have focused on the more general category of ecocriticism. Here I want to focus specifically on ecological feminism (more commonly termed ecofeminism) and its relationship to a category of literary analysis that ecocriticism has tended to avoid: postmodernism. Both of these isms need to be addressed to expand the purview of ecocriticism. By its name alone, postmodernism suggests a certain belatedness and reactiveness reflective of the 1980s and 1990s that tend to undercut militant political and social action. Yet ecological consciousness is very much predicated upon the possibility of informed, planned human change in relation to dynamic ecosystemic processes. In postmodernity, however, such consciousness often has difficulties positing a clear conception of the human possibilities and promise that breaks with instrumental reason and consumptive exploitation.

Many theorists and activists have suggested that feminism can provide an alternative conception and practice of agency. By extension, many others claim that a postmodern feminist conception of agency is incomplete without its integration with ecological consciousness, generating a postmodern ecofeminist theory and practice of agency. I want to emphasize, however, that a viable ecofeminist conception of agency will be rooted in the postmodern recognition of both the diversity of human experience and the reality that all analysis proceeds from situated knowledge and partial perspectives rather than being based on universalizing assumptions and androcentric generalizations.

Distinctions between Eofeminism and Postmodernism

In this chapter I presume that most of my audience is more familiar with concepts related to postmodernism than with those of ecofeminism. One reason for such a presumption is that since we are already living in the condition of postmodernity, I assume that my audience, for the most part, like myself, as educated professionals in a postindustrial nation-state, has been introduced to various ideas about postmodernism as well as critiques of it. Another is that postmodernist theories, critiques, and theorists have received more high-profile attention within the academy and from critics of the academy than has ecofeminism, its theorists, its practitioners, or the actions upon which it is based. A third reason is that none of us is yet living in any condition similar to that envisioned by ecofeminism. Indeed, that may be the most significant difference between any version of postmodernism and any version of ecofeminism.

Proponents of postmodernism—even those (including feminists) who resist that term but who rely nevertheless on a relatively narrow range of foundational white male theorists associated with it, such as Jacques Derrida, Michel Foucault, and Jacques Lacan—emphasize the ways in which postmodernist theory provides the mechanisms for a critique of the present, an evaluative description and critical interrogation of the current condition of many human beings in much of the world. Postmodernist theorizing focuses on what already exists in order to generate a comprehensive analysis in the form of a negative critique. That analysis is intended to explain how we have arrived at this present state of indeterminacy, relativity, interpellation, and economic constriction.

Ecofeminism is also concerned with such explanation, and ecofeminists generally welcome theoretical work that elucidates the contradictory conditions of being that generate tremendous short-term wealth for the few and intensifying oppression and misery for the many worldwide, at the same time that such conditions threaten the long-term viability of ecosystems for the continuation of many species, including the human. In contrast to postmodernism, which many see as locked in a negative critique of the present that may actually contribute to the extension of the postmodern moment, ecofeminism focuses on the future. Attention to the present serves to generate a level of understanding of our current condition sufficient for the goal of moving beyond it in very specific ways and as rapidly as possible. Resistance is not an end in itself but part of a process of radical transformation of the human condition, from the interpersonal to the political, from the economic to the psychical, to end all forms of oppression.

That movement beyond the present is predicated upon a belief in human agency according to which we can act in the world and effect cultural, political, and economic changes. Such changes will in turn open a different set of possible ways of living than are currently available in the configurations of global capitalism, homogenizing industrialization, and metropolitan cultural oppression of colonial and formerly colonial countries and indigenous peoples. From this distinction between ecofeminism and postmodernism, it follows that ecofeminism must make use of the beneficial aspects of postmodernist critique. The movement must not, however, allow itself to imagine that the discursive terrain of resistance is the primary site of struggle or that, because some of us are living in postmodernity, everyone else lives there as well.

The tendency of postmodernist theorizing to privilege the discursive terrain over the daily, physically engaged biospheric terrain can be seen even in the introduction to a book such as *Feminism/Postmodernism/Development*, a collection ostensibly about the linkages between lived experience and ideological formations. In "Exploding the Canon: An Introduction/ Conclusion," editors Jane L. Parpart and Marianne H. Marchand contend that "contributors have been encouraged to challenge each other's assumptions and to explore the limitations and strengths of postmodernist feminist thought for gender and development theory and practice." Yet the postmodernist bias toward the discursive is evident in their following remarks. Invoking the ideas of Michel Foucault and Judith Butler and stating that "individual subjects experience and 'understand' life within a discursive and material context," Parpart and Marchand immediately leave the "material" dimension of that "context" behind: "This context, particularly the language/discourse that 'explains' the concrete experiences of daily life, influences and shapes the way individuals interpret 'reality.' The self is thus not simply a reflection of experience (i.e., 'reality'); it is constituted in complex historical circumstances that must be understood and analyzed as such."[1]

A little farther in this same section they conclude that "postmodernist thinkers reject universal, simplified definitions of social phenomena, which, they argue, essentialize reality and fail to reveal the complexity of life as a lived experience."[2] Yet nowhere in these introductory remarks do they find the need to discuss the complexities of that "lived experience" and how they materially, as well as semiotically, overflow official conceptions of reality and exceed the explanatory capabilities of any discursive framework. Beginning the section subtitled "Postmodernism" with their disdainful phrase, "the self is thus not *simply* a reflection of experience" (emphasis added), they emphasize only the discursive and interrogative. Attention to the complexities of lived experience, particularly those that pertain to the relationship of self and community, are left to the sections addressing the theoretical work being done in the areas of gender and development.

Parpart and Marchand, despite their evident position as proponents of postmodernism, tend to argue for its benefits to gender and development as a supplementary form of analysis—as in their phrase "postmodern feminism"—one that provides "insights" and "interrogation" rather than one that proposes and develops explicit alternatives to what it critiques. In their introduction to part 4, "The Relevance of Postmodern Feminism for Gender and Development," they note that when the contributors from Barbados, Kenya, and India, "using their own experiences as a starting-point," evaluate the potential benefits of postmodernism for gender and development, two of the three "are less sanguine about the potential of postmodern feminism," and one of these two, the Kenyan Maria Nzomo, "criticizes postmodern feminism's overemphasis on discourse and representation at the expense of women's political and economic concerns."[3] Indeed, Nzomo concludes her essay—"Women and Democratization Struggles in Africa, What Relevance to Postmodernist Discourse?"—by stating that "it is postmodernism that needs to adapt itself to feminism and Third World conditions/knowledge if the former is to acquire significant and practical relevance for women, especially in the African context."[4]

Ecofeminists should utilize the insights of postmodernist critique, not only for its dissection of late-capitalist cultures and social formations, but also for its challenges to the limitations of ecofeminism itself, particularly ecofeminist theorizing—including, especially, my own, given my situatedness as a U.S. white male academic—arising from within postmodernity. At the same time, attending to Nzomo's cautionary words, ecofeminism must do so without accepting or being trapped by the limitations of postmodernist analysis. In "Postmodern Blackness," bell hooks observes that, "The critique of essentialism encouraged by postmodernist thought is useful for African-Americans concerned with reformulating outmoded notions of identity. . . . Postmodern critiques of essentialism which challenge notions of universality and static over-determined identity within mass culture and mass consciousness can open up new possibilities for the construction of self and the assertion of agency."[5] I think a similar argument applies to postmodernism and ecofeminism.

"Postmodernist thought is useful for" the development of particular aspects of the ecofeminist movement and can contribute to "open[ing] up new possibilities," but the "construction of self and the assertion of agency" will actually be developed beyond postmodernism. In particular such development will occur elsewhere because postmodernism is too obsessively focused on the idea of the individual and the construction of singular, even though fragmented and continuously reconstituted, identity, while the struggles of the oppressed around the world are much more concerned with the idea of maintaining communities and the conservation of culturally and environmentally relational identity.

As bell hooks argues, the "struggle for black subjectivity is the quest to find ways to construct self and identity that are oppositional and liberatory." And while the "oppositional" can be aided by postmodernist critiques of essentialism, the "liberatory" depends upon "emphasizing the significance of 'the authority of experience'" and a concomitant attention to community and people.[6] Such a position is widely emphasized in ecofeminism, particularly in relation to the struggles of indigenous, post-, neo-, and currently colonized peoples, and the so-called minorities in late-capitalist countries (especially as seen in environmental-justice movements), but too rarely are these groups the focus of attention within postmodernist theorizing except in terms of sweeping generalizations.

For instance, when we look at Drucilla Cornell's arguments in *The Philosophy of the Limit*, the problems of the focus on the discursive and the ignoring of the significance of lived experience in the formation of identity for individuals within communities becomes apparent. Cornell begins her philosophical meditation on deconstruction by arguing that "the 'postmodern' should be understood as an allegory and that, as such, it represents an ethical insistence on the limit to 'positive' descriptions of the principles of modernity" and that it "depicts the limit of institutionalized meaning and established communitarian norms."⁷ But in practice, Cornell seems to extend this "limit" to all kinds of "'positive' descriptions," including those of lived experience, by presuming that "institutionialized meaning" and "communitarian norms" can only be generated and held by dominating, oppressive cultures.

For instance, to understand the diversity of "communitarian norms" and the possible array of, and differences among, "'positive' descriptions" existing in the world today, we would need to study the actual practices of a broad array of cultures and peoples, not just the "principles of modernity." Cornell in her theorizing, however, is not actually concerned with the variety of women's experiences or human experience in general. Rather, she establishes a binary of modern and postmodern descriptions that ignores the possibility of any "'positive' descriptions" from any other ideological formations including various types of paramodern experience, such as the indigenous.⁸

Further, Cornell ignores the possibility that peoples in the world may be situated in economic, environmental, and cultural conditions quite distinct from the postmodern theorist's conception of either modernity or postmodernity, and that such situatedness generates very different types of "established communitarian norms" than the ones that interest her. For ecofeminists who recognize the necessity of diversity, it is a foregone conclusion that norms other than those of the United States and France exist. Further, in defense of maintaining cultural diversity as part of biological diversity, ecofeminists recognize that many of these other norms and the communities on which they are based need and deserve to be defended against postmodernity's transnational capitalism and cultural homogenization.

Cornell claims that her formulation of a "philosophy of the limit . . . helps us to think about justice and legal interpretation differently" and that "for marginalized groups, this is a difference that makes a difference," yet nowhere in her text are marginalized groups quoted, nowhere are they given a voice based on their own experience; rather, they are contained within the terms of Western European continental philosophy and capitalist jurisprudence (*Limit*, 12). No wonder that many African activists and theorists, such as Nzomo, remain skeptical of postmodernism's critical relevance; no wonder the editors of *Feminist Political Ecology: Global Issues and Local Experiences* found no need to include in their book an essay that addressed the concept of postmodernism.

Since Cornell claims to be concerned about making a difference for marginalized groups when addressing the limitations of "established communitarian norms," one would expect an analysis of various types of such norms and the limits of various community formations. Instead, she focuses on what she calls in the title of her second chapter "The 'Postmodern' Challenge to the Ideal of Community." Reflecting the tendency toward urbanophilia within postmodernist thought, Cornell begins this chapter by citing Iris Young, who counters "the very idea of community" with "a vision of a nonrepressive city" (*Limit*, 39). This vision obliterates the experience and value of community bonds shaped and shared by millions of rural and forest peoples around the globe, whose ways of life are often most immediately threatened by the physical expansion of cities and, more enduringly, threatened by the patterns of excessive consumption practiced by urban dwellers. Cornell reduces the concept of community to what she calls, in a subheading of chapter 2, "The Ideal of Communicative Freedom," ignoring entirely the experiential reality of community as a basic unit for human life, the production of human necessities, the conservation and evolution of cultural values and practices for the majority of the world's peoples (*Limit*, 56).[9]

Cornell engages in affirming a utopian Western discursive formation set against a dystopian postmodern urban cultural formation that represses the recognition of any possible eutopian (i.e., good rather than ideal) communities that might exist and need to be defended against encroaching modernity and postmodernity. From such a position it is not possible to even consider defending such communities for their ethical practices, which people living in postmodernity might want to emulate as part of their effort to move beyond postmodernity toward a liberatory culture. In her repression of the possible existence of defensible communities and her marginalization of the experiences of people outside the metropolis, Cornell denies the possibility that lessons for the future, that resistant and liberatory cultural practices, that mediations, subversions, and alternatives to the "gender hierarchy" that concerns her may already exist among the allegedly "marginalized." In short, she denies the possibility of agency in the present because her theorizing remains ungrounded in the richness of the diversity of contemporary lived experience.

Alienation and Agency

The issue of agency and our orientation toward its manifestations is crucial, forming a key distinction between much of postmodernist thought and every variety of ecofeminism. I am building this differential analysis of ecofeminism and postmodernism on Linda Hutcheon's claims in *The Politics of Postmodernism*. Hutcheon states in the beginning of her book that, "While the postmodern has no effective theory of agency that enables a move into political *action*, it does work to turn its inevitable ideological grounding into a site of de-naturalizing critique. . . . postmodernism works to 'de-doxify' our cultural representations and their undeniable political import."[10] Much of the orthodoxy that postmodernism seeks to "de-doxify" arose from Enlightenment beliefs, of which a crucial element is human alienation from the rest of nature. The Enlightenment formed part of the European entry into modernity, and modernism—although in crisis over the idealization of progress and linear development—embraced this belief in alienation and responded to it through a commitment to manipulation. Such manipulation was done through the control of fragmentation by means of formal experimentation. In science manipulation took the forms of social engineering and technological domination of every facet of daily life. In literature the threat of contingency and indeterminacy was deflected through the use of foundational myths as master narratives for new literary production, such as the *Odyssey*, the *Inferno*, and the Holy Grail quest.

Postmodernism has rejected any confidence in universalizing myths and master narratives, such as that of scientific progress. It has, however, been unable to shake the concept of alienation, because it continues to rely on an ungrounded and nonmaterial conception of consciousness and a commitment to intellectual commentary over transformative social action. As Albert Gelpi argues, some of the defining features of postmodernism in the United States have been "a deepening sense of the mind's alienation from nature and of the world's alienation from reality; an intensified experience of material randomness and temporal flux, of moral relativity and psychological alienation."[11]

In the last chapter of *The Politics of Postmodernism*, "Postmodernism and Feminisms," Hutcheon distinguishes feminist analysis from postmodernist critique, suggesting the role that feminism can play in advancing the negative critical project of postmodernism without succumbing to the limitations of postmodernism's ability to formulate a sufficient theory of agency and its surrender to alienation. Hutcheon claims that, "While . . . both feminisms and postmodernism, are part of the same general crisis of cultural authority, . . . there is a major difference of orientation . . . postmodernism is politically ambivalent for it is doubly coded—both complicitous with and contesting of the cultural domination within which it operates . . . feminisms have distinct, unambiguous political agendas of resistance."[12] Hutcheon goes on to argue that postmodernism disrupts and manipulates but does not transform signification.[13] She conceptualizes this reconstruction of signification largely in terms of desire and the establishment of the female as subject. She argues that early postmodernist literature and art continued the modernist practice of objectifying women.

What she does not address is the relationship of signification to reference, of desire to the physical body, in a larger framework of material, ecosystem semiotics. For desire in both modernity and postmodernity is bound with the alienated objectification of the natural world as a commodity, and the concept of the commodity is the foundation of consumer societies. Such societies in turn depend on a belief in unlimited technological expansion to create continuously new objects for consumption, a belief that depends on the myth of unlimited natural resources and the master narrative of human domination over the rest of nature. While postmodernism has challenged the concept of progress, the fascination of many of its theorists with technology and their denial of referentiality leave it disembodied. It is engaged only with the cultural manifestations of desire and seems utterly ignorant of the organic limitations on satisfying those culturally constructed desires. It also ignores the need to reconceptualize human desire ecologically in the context of biotic relationships. Thus we arrive at the need to use feminism to generate agency out of and beyond postmodernism and ecology to ground that agency in such a way as to make a break with the destructive economies of postmodernity.

While I would contend that neither postmodernism is as monolithic nor feminism as diverse as Hutcheon's opposition suggests, it is the case that postmodernist theorizing tends to rely on a much narrower range of European-based, predominantly white male foundational thinkers deeply affected by the phenomena of World War II. Feminist theorizing tends to draw on a much wider and far more contradictory range of thinkers, tends to be more inclusive of modes of theorizing beyond academic, formal philosophical practice, and is far more international in scope. This plurality within the feminist movement provides a basis for contending that ecofeminism, which is itself a philosophically and globally pluralistic movement, can play a key role in the further theoretical growth and enriched political praxis of women engaged in the struggle to end their oppression, eliminate patriarchy, and transform oppressive cultures. With its firm grounding in agency and transformative action and its clear vision of a different future, ecofeminism is strongly committed to international multicultural dialogue. To demonstrate the viability of my claim, I will now provide an overview of what I see as the defining features of ecofeminism.

Ecofeminism and Transformation

As Carolyn Merchant notes, "*Ecofeminisme* was coined by the French writer Francoise d'Eaubonne in 1974 to represent women's potential for bringing about an ecological revolution to ensure human survival on the planet. Such an ecological revolution would entail new gender relations between women and men and between humans and nature."[14] While most of the theoretical and critical articulations of the concepts, beliefs, and practices included under the rubric of ecofeminism have been produced by Western feminists, ecofeminist practice is a worldwide phenomenon. Significant ecofeminist actions, arising from the awareness generated by specific experiences rather than a theorized consciousness, take place in many countries. It is also important to note that many of these women's movements are conducted by women whose cultures and economies are neither postmodern nor modern, but often dependent upon subsistence gathering and farming. Neither totally isolated from nor fully integrated into the markets of global capitalism, and not fully homogenized by transnational postmodern mass culture, these cultures and economies might best be defined as paramodern. They come out of an indigenous, situated lifestyle to confront the political and economic incursions of multinational capitalism, which is intrusive, exploitative, and culturally destructive.

Ecofeminism, then, is first and foremost a practical movement for social change arising from the struggles of women to sustain themselves, their families, and their communities in the face of maldevelopment and environmental degradation. For the most part, those who set out to articulate the philosophy of this movement do so in the belief that such theorizing will assist the movement by increasing the self-consciousness of its participants and representing its beliefs to those who are open to considering its message. As Irene Diamond and Gloria Feman Orenstein note in their introduction to *Reweaving the World: The Emergence of Ecofeminism,*

> Ecofeminist politics does not stop short at the phase of dismantling the androcentric and anthropocentric biases of Western civilization. . . . ecofeminism seeks to reweave new stories that acknowledge and value the biological and cultural diversity that sustains all life. These new stories honor, rather than fear, women's biological particularity while simultaneously affirming women as subjects and makers of history. This understanding that biological particularity need not be antithetical to historical agency is crucial to the transformation of feminism.[15]

Transformation may very well be the single term to which all adherents of ecofeminism would assent. Starhawk—author of the ecofeminist novel

The Fifth Sacred Thing among other works—for example, defines the spiritual wing of ecofeminism as based on a goddess tradition, nature theology, indigenous spirituality, and immanence, adding that "ecofeminism challenges all relations of domination. Its goal is not just to change who wields power, but to transform the structure of power itself." In order to accomplish such a task, activists need to realize that "environmental issues cannot be intelligently approached without the perspectives of women, the poor, and those who come from other parts of the globe, as well as those of all races and cultural backgrounds."[16] For Starhawk and many others, then, ecofeminism is based not only on the recognition of connections between the exploitation of nature and the oppression of women but also on the belief that these two forms of domination are bound with class exploitation, racism, and colonialism and neocolonialism.

Such a belief does not require an adherence to any particular spirituality or mode of goddess worship. Rather, the spiritual wing of ecofeminism is linked to others, such as the radical and social wings, by means of a fundamental starting point, which Ynestra King defines: "In ecofeminism, nature is the central category of analysis. An analysis of the interrelated dominations of nature—psyche and sexuality, human oppression, and non-human nature—and the historic position of women in relation to those forms of domination is the starting point of ecofeminist theory."[17] King has provided the ecofeminist movement with an articulation of four basic principles that has been quoted extensively and generally embraced as a sound orientation. Her first tenet states that because industrialization subjugates nature, and therefore women, who are "believed to be closer to nature," ecofeminists must embrace all of the "life-struggles" of nature. Noting the human tendency of trying to project a hierarchy onto the "interconnected web" of natural life as a way to justify social domination, her second principle calls on ecofeminist theory to "show the connections between all forms of domination" and to remain antihierarchical. Her third principle concerns diversity social and natural, which is necessary to the health and balance of earth's ecosystem. In order to maintain such richness of life, "we need a decentralized global movement that is founded on common interests yet celebrates diversity and opposes all forms of domination and violence"; ecofeminism, she says, could be this movement. The final tenet maintains that in order for us to survive, we must come to a better understanding of nature human and nonhuman and we must challenge the "nature-culture dualism." The result of this challenge will be a "radical restructuring of human society according to feminist and ecological principles."[18]

Charlene Spretnak answers the question that might be posed by many postmodernists and feminists, "What is the purpose of cultivating ecological wisdom at this postmodern moment in human history?":

For the very first time in the modern era, there is widespread agreement that something is very wrong. The assumptions of modernity, the faith in technological "progress" and rapacious industrialism, along with the militarism necessary to support it, have left us very lost indeed. The quintessential malady of the modern era is free-floating anxiety, and it is clear to ecofeminists that the whole culture is free floating— from the lack of grounding in the natural world, from the lack of a sense of belonging in the unfolding story of the universe, from the lack of a healthy relationship between the males and females of the species. We are entangled in the hubris of the patriarchal goal of dominating nature and the female.[19]

Spretnak has enunciated the crisis, and Donna Haraway—clearly postmodern in her "cyborg" orientation—posits the role that ecofeminism can play in resolving that crisis: "ecofeminists have perhaps been most insistent on some version of the world as active subject, not as resource to be mapped and appropriated in bourgeois, Marxist, or masculinist projects."[20] While, according to Hutcheon, postmodernist theory has a difficult time assigning agency to anyone, ecofeminism is intent on assigning it to everyone who is human and also to the various nonhuman actors who share the world with us.

Such an extension of agency from the human to the nonhuman reflects the historical progression of the widening circle of living beings that come under the purview of moral considerability within Western thought. We find that a similar extension of agency is also common to indigenous thought and maintained as part of the metaphysical subculture within industrialized nation-states through situated belief systems, particularly religious and spiritual traditions with archaic roots. In many indigenous cultures' traditional beliefs, we find that nonhuman entities are not treated as alien "other" to the autonomous, individual self, but as relatives in a web of kinship. In matrilineal societies among the first nations, we find also that kinship is observed in terms of extended families, lodges, clans, and entire tribes, not nuclear family structures. As a result, it is more accurate to say that there are not others in such cultures, only anothers, that is, beings who are neither self nor other in any absolute dichotomy but are familiar, related, and connected with us. Rather than self and other, then, it would be more accurate to speak of we and another.[21] Such a notion of another is consistent with the ecofeminist ideas of healthy biological diversity and the view of life as an interconnected web, as a heterarchy rather than a hierarchy.

Usually, when humans ask "What good is it?" they really mean "What good is it to me or to my society?" Vandana Shiva has demonstrated the ways in which this question, when asked by the technological elite from the so-called First World countries, often leads to ecological disaster for people of the so-called Third World countries. Such destruction occurs because the "me" that the technologists treat as a universal does not fit the needs, perspectives, or environmental relationships of the indigenous peoples to which it is applied. Ecofeminism takes this critique further by asking a more complex question: "What good is it within its ecosystem, and what is the relationship of humans to the maintenance or degradation of that good within that system?" Using the health of the ecosystem as the fundamental criterion for judgment enables the recognition of diversity as a necessary dimension of individual species and ecosystem survival, with cultural diversity as one of the dimensions that enhances the survival of the human species. The appreciation of diversity is predicated upon the rejection of alienation as a permanent condition of being human and the acceptance of interconnection, which is the ontological basis for a "we and another" rather than an "I and other" orientation toward all life.

Postmodern Ecofeminism as Situated and Dialogic

The problem for ecofeminism within the condition of postmodernity is not the problem that many Anglo-European intellectuals face of finding

that there is only discourse and intellect and no ground or point of reference. Rather, it is the problem of knowing that the ground shifts. That is
to say, like the feminist movement from which it has developed and of
which it remains a part, ecofeminism is strongly antiteleological in its
recognition that its theories must be checked not only against its practice
but also against the realities and terrain upon which it is practiced. At the
same time, ecofeminism recognizes that reality changes, that ecosystems are
continuously in process and transformation. In ideologically shuttling
between the figure of practice and the ground of being, one must alternate
the criteria of self-conscious review, pivoting between the interacting
processes of cultured nature and natured culture, living the gestalt.

As postmodernist theorists have worked to oppose and reject the master narratives and universalizing theories of modernism, they have only
infrequently also managed to reject the displaced, ungrounded orientation
necessary for universalizing. As Spretnak noted of postmodern culture, it
tends to be free-floating and anxiety ridden, and likewise many of its theorists, particularly the males. Efforts to alleviate the anxiety have frequently
taken the form of humor and play, but often such playfulness seems strained
and desperate.

In contrast, ecofeminist theorists and literary authors have looked to
developments in feminist epistemology and feminist interpretations of the
history of science to posit a postmodern, antiuniversal ground from which
to act. One term for the ground in question, to be found in feminism,
ecofeminism, and postcolonialism, is that of situated knowledge. Nancy
Hartsock contends that "the point is to develop an account of the world
which treats our perspectives not as subjugated or disruptive knowledge, but
as primary and constitutive of a different world."[22] Such an account would
be one of process and participation, with the recognition that such knowledge, by always originating from a specific perspective, is necessarily situated and partial. *Situated knowledge* is just one term for a concept that has
been advanced by feminists and ecofeminists with various permutations,
such as N. Katherine Hayles's "interactivity" and "constrained construc-
tivism," as delineated in "Searching for Common Ground." The identification of situated knowledge, or some equivalent, as the appropriate locus
for truth is another manifestation of the recognition of the necessity of

diversity. It is also consistent with Starhawk's assertion that appropriate environmental solutions cannot be developed without including the differing perspectives of peoples from around the globe.

One of the limitations of postmodernist critique is the reliance on binary oppositions as the fundamental mechanism of analysis. As a result, the response to modernity can only be postmodernity, and everyone must respond to modernity because it is the dominant mode of economic, scientific, and cultural organization in the world. What is ignored by such oppositions is the continuation of a nonmodernity—including various paramodern formations—that cannot be defined by the parameters of postmodernism. Nevertheless, nonmodernity is a condition of worldwide postmodernity as a result of the political resistance of indigenous peoples to transnational capitalism and as a result of postcolonialism as a form of economic, philosophical, cultural, and, above all, political critique. That is to say that many cultures in former colonies and current colonies refuse to accept *modernity* according to the economic, political, and cultural models used by the United States and the former colonial powers of Europe. They also resist the teleological conception of progress that models of modernity embody. As a result, they may prefer to be nonmodern on their own terms rather than modern on someone else's terms.

Ecofeminist analyses, particularly by women of color, have demonstrated that postcolonial struggles and women's struggles, that postcolonialism and feminism, are interrelated issues. Corinne Kumar D'Souza makes the case that

> The movements for change need, today more than ever, to move toward developing conceptual paradigms born of a praxis that is rooted in the specificity of its social, cultural and political processes. . . .
>
> And to begin to move outside the universal, Eurocentric, patriarchal patterns, to search for new concepts that would touch and explain women's lives and experiences. . . . Feminism is, to the social sciences, a distinct paradigm shift, to the social movements, a distinct rupture.[23]

Shiva has shown that the maldevelopment under which the so-called Third World labors is the result of a model of progress and industrialization introduced during colonialism and continued into the present. This maldevelopment militates against the value of women's traditional and adaptive knowledge of agriculture, local production, and community participation at the same time that it destroys the local sustainability of the ecologies of the regions subjected to development.[24] As Rosemary Radford Ruether reminds "western ecofeminists," their "relations with nature . . . must be connected concretely with the realities of over-consumerism and waste by which the top 20% of the world enjoys 82% of the wealth while the other 80% of the world scrapes along with 18%, and the lowest 80% of the world's population, mostly female and young, starves and dies early from poisoned waters, soil and air."[25]

What I am trying to emphasize here is that the concept of diversity has many parameters and implications in ecofeminism, both in terms of the nonhuman world and in terms of human cultural and economic practices. Recognition of the necessity of diversity in nature leads ecofeminism to recognize the necessity of cultural diversity in humanity, which in turn leads to a recognition of the need for ecofeminism to be postcolonial and multicultural. Both of these positions on human societies are postmodernist in sensibility because of the rejection of Eurocentric universals; they also reinforce the concept of the diversification of agency. Such an ecofeminism is also, then, highly dialogical through its eschewing of ungrounded universal truth claims and master narratives and because it calls for including as many speaking subjects as possible in positing the truth of any situation and determining a healthy and sustainable direction for human-nature ecoregional interaction.

Implications of Ecofeminism for Literary Analysis

An ecofeminist literary analysis, cognizant of postmodernism, could certainly accomplish a great deal in negatively critiquing contemporary American literature, but to some extent such a critique would only reinforce the inertia and apolitical tendencies of much postmodernist criticism, particularly deconstruction, because it would become just another form of interpretation, another variant of close reading. Instead, some ecofeminist literary critics have emphasized the recovery of neglected works by women that display varying degrees of environmental awareness and sensitivity within the context of a gendered inflection of themes, descriptions, and narratives. Such has been the case, for example, with attention to Susan Fenimore Cooper, Mary Austin, and Charlotte Perkins Gilman. Other critics have focused on reconsiderations of canonical figures, such as Sarah Orne Jewett and Willa Cather, in light of ecological criteria, particularly the relation of place to culture and character.

When it comes to male canonical figures, ecofeminist literary critics are more likely to engage in readings that deconstruct a monolithic and monological masculinist interpretation of those authors' works and show the ways in which their sensitivity to environment often reflects a feminine, if not feminist, sensibility. At the first conference of the Association for the Study of Literature and Environment, for instance, in a paper titled "What if Wister Were a Woman?" Melody Graulich deconstructed traditional readings of *The Virginian*. Such critics emphasize the empowerment of ecologically conscious readers by showing the ways in which nascent and overt environmentalism has been lurking in the pages of American literature, waiting to be appreciated and appropriated for social transformation.

Most ecofeminist literary criticism, however, has focused on contemporary writing by women, with significant attention to works by women of color, and has shown a willingness to treat a greater variety of genres and cross-genre experiments than found in the bulk of nonfeminist ecological criticism.[26]

For example, the "new regionalism" paradigm has led to significant discussions of the ideas of an "erotics of place" and "narrative mapping" in the nonfiction works of such writers as Gretel Ehrlich, Linda Hasselstrom, Kathleen Norris, Terry Tempest Williams, Audre Lorde, and Gloria Anzaldúa, while Gretchen Legler has addressed such an erotics in both her creative and critical work.[27] It has led to consideration of the function of eutopian and dystopian literature, as in the works of Ursula K. Le Guin, Marge Piercy, Octavia Butler, Joanna Russ, Suzy McKee Charnas, and Starhawk. These works are eutopian because their future worlds are not finalized, blueprinted, programmed static sanctuaries, as is common in nineteenth-century male utopian writing. The very structure of these novels tends to reflect an ecofeminist sensibility at the same time that their con-

tent emphasizes the process of building a better society—the ongoing dialogue that must occur to resolve differences in a nonteleological and non-
dogmatic way, and the necessary transformation of gender and racial relations. They break with the pastoral utopian tradition of constructing
finished, static noplaces in which all struggles and all contradictions are
resolved to the satisfaction of the author's contemporaneous sensibilities.

Ecofeminist literary criticism from the start has been particularly attentive to centering not only the marginalized voices of women in general but
also the voices of women of color in particular, as can be seen in all five contributions to the spring 1997 *Ecofeminism/Ecocriticism I* special issue of
Phoebe: Journal of Feminist Scholarship, Theory and Aesthetics. Such attention
has been most conspicuous in relation to Native American and Chicana
authors, because their writing is so frequently explicit in developing the
relationships among place, culture, exploitation, and oppression. But
beyond merely providing ecofeminist readings of the novels of Leslie Marmon Silko, Linda Hogan, Edna Escamill, Ana Castillo, Alice Walker, and
others, ecofeminist critics have also generated a rethinking of genre definitions and nature-writing paradigms. In the spirit, but not necessarily in the
philosophical school, of postmodernism, many of these novels are written
in forms that break with traditional realism. They have been variously
labeled virtual realism, magical realism, supernaturalism, and fantastic, but
whatever the term, the criticism works up the relationship between the
mode of representation and the cultural specificities of the author and the
novel.

A tremendous amount of poetry is also benefiting from ecofeminist
critical analysis, from the writing of Paula Gunn Allen to that of Adrienne
Rich, from Lori Anderson to Audre Lorde, but this is the area where
ecofeminist analysis has developed most slowly. Owing to both the nonfiction tradition of nature writing and the emphases of ecological criticism,
women's nonfiction has received the most sustained attention, followed by
the novel. This situation also results in part from the fact that women who
are writing dissertations that engage in ecological and ecofeminist criticism
are mainly being trained by people specializing in the study of nonfiction,
and in part from the lack of new critical orientations for the study of
women's environmental poetry.

While many of the poems written by May Sarton and Mary Oliver, for example, are clearly nature poems in terms of their emphasis on accurate detail and close observation, that type of writing is not the dominant mode being practiced. Nor is there a strong romantic tradition at work, which would allow the transfer of critical apparatuses employed on the romantics and transcendentalists. Rather, this new poetry is far more participatory than observational, far more immanent and erotic than transcendental and intellectual. There is relatively little of the agonizing in solitude of romantic poetry, or even the individual-fronting-the-wilderness theme prevalent in much contemporary male environmental poetry. The poetry of Le Guin, Patricia Hampl, Luci Tapahonso, Joy Harjo, Anzaldúa, Hasselstrom, and Pat Mora is very much embodied and engaged, and the nature it engages is wild and domestic, farm and desert, rural and urban. Particularly among the women writers of color, the poetic engagement with nature is also an engagement with cultural preservation and the survival and liberation of a people. Because environmental poets want to emphasize the endless referral of human-nature interaction, relationship, and interdependence, we find relatively few traces of postmodernist stylistic experimentation, but such experimentation does exist, as in the work of Mei Mei Bersenbrugge, Patiann Rogers, and Lori Anderson.

Just as ecofeminism steps beyond postmodernism in its activism supported by a viable theory of agency, so too does ecofeminist literary criticism step beyond the limitations of postmodernist negative critique. Ecofeminist literary criticism, while developing a significant reappraisal of the traditional literary canon, also promotes literature that embodies and demonstrates ecofeminist principles and practices. It is helping to envision a future that provides for the possibility of a more natured culture in which biotic differences and gender differences are celebrated in their diversity and heterarchy rather than used as justifications for domination, exploitation, and extinction.

5

Anotherness and Inhabitation in Recent Multicultural American Literature

T HE PRECEDING CHAPTERS have been devoted to general and theoretical discussions of significant issues in the development of an inclusivist ecocriticism. In particular, in chapters 2, 3, and 4, I shifted the discussion from mode and genre to representation of speaking subjects, specifically the voices of women and of authors from around the world that would demonstrate a truly multicultural and international sensibility about nature-oriented literature. In the next several chapters, I want to shift from that more general approach to one more attentive to readings of specific literary works. This chapter will accomplish that transition through mixing a theoretical discussion of the concepts of other and another as they relate to conceptions of the self and the individual, and the impact such conceptions have on human-nonhuman interactions, with criticism applied to a set of American literary works.

Theory

The concept of the other has proven to be a valuable tool in psychoanalytic and feminist literary theory and criticism. It has been interpreted in various ways to provide stunning critiques of patriarchy, colonialism, capitalism, metaphysical linguistics, and Freudianism. This absolute other, founded upon notions of permanent incompleteness and prematurity, communicative incommensurability, and binary constructs, is, however, largely an illusion, and its continued acceptance is a dangerous reification that protects much of the Western dominant hierarchical power relations that its use has been designed to dismantle. Ecology and ecocriticism indicate that it is time to move toward a relational model of anotherness and the conceptualization of difference in terms of I and another, one and another, and I-as-another. My conception of the category of another, first introduced in *Literature, Nature, and Other*, is based on the writings of the twentieth-century Russian theorist Mikhail Bakhtin.

In *Toward a Philosophy of the Act*, Bakhtin claims three basic architectonic moments of human existence: "I-for-myself, the other-for-me, and I-for-the-other."[1] Later, in writing *Problems of Dostoevsky's Poetics*, he would demonstrate a clear distinction between two types of other. As Caryl Emerson notes, "Russian distinguishes between *drugoi* (another, other person) and *chuzhoi* (alien, strange; also, the other). The English pair 'I/other,' with its intonation of alienation and opposition, has specifically been avoided here. The *another* Bakhtin has in mind is not hostile to the *I* but a necessary component of it."[2] We need to introduce into English the concept of another as noun rather than adjective or pronoun, because the binary antonyms of self and other are fundamentally insufficient to represent the range of relational distinctions among entities existing in the world.

In both of his early texts, *Toward a Philosophy of the Act* and *Art and Answerability*, Bakhtin is concerned with "answerability," the responsibility of a participative thinker toward the rest of the world: "to live from within oneself does not mean to live for oneself, but means to be an answerable participant from within oneself, to affirm one's compellent, actual non-alibi in Being" (*Toward*, 49). An ethics of answerability presupposes a relationship of difference, a recognition of reciprocity across contradictions and dissimilarities, including the position of human beings and other entities within an ecosystem in relation to its conservation or destruction. Nothing human is intrinsically strange, but rather needs to be recognized as strange-to-me; that is to say, a difference of perspective or degree of recognition and identification rather than a condition of being. As Bakhtin observes, "Life knows two value centers that are fundamentally and essentially different, yet are correlated with each other: myself and the other. . . . One and the same object (identical in its content) is a moment of Being that presents itself differently from the valuative standpoint when correlated with me or when correlated with another" (*Toward*, 74). The enlightenment construction of the alienated, absolute other and the modern consignment of otherness to a category of psychoanalysis ignore the lived reality of world diversity from the multiculturality of an urban metropolis to the mutation of viruses. This construct is based upon and reinforces a universal interpretation of a fundamentally late-Western conception of the individual and the glorification of the idea of autonomy through the ideology of individualism.

Historically, one finds the self-other dichotomy being translated into the mind-body, male-female, and humanity-nature dichotomies, with both woman and nature embodied as the antithesis of spirit, mind, and culture.[3] These paired terms are not even actually dichotomous or dyadic but only indicate idealized polarities within a multiplicitous field, such as that of planet, thought, sex or gender, perception, and mind. These terms have never adequately expressed the range of human practices for working through the human-nature relationship—those who see humanity outside nature, those who see humanity as part of nature, and those who see humanity in a superordinate participatory position. What we find repeatedly is the construct of alienated other being used to repress or suppress the relationship, the anotherness, between groups in order to objectify and distance one group or culture from another in the service of some form of domination.

The changing depictions of Native Americans by European invaders, whether the "noble savage" or the "bloodthirsty savage," were designed to suppress the common humanity initially recognized. In order to steal a people's land or overthrow their form of government, it must be established that they are not equally human. I think it is unnecessary to detail the constitution of various sexual orientations as absolute others, except to highlight the degree to which certain segments of the population want to continue to depict AIDS as a homosexual disease. In this case, absolute constructions of otherness turn relatives into aliens.

Bakhtin claims that "an indifferent or hostile reaction is always a reaction that impoverishes and decomposes its object: it seeks to pass over the object in all its manifoldness, to ignore it or to overcome it" (*Toward*, 64). Such a reaction is precisely the practice in colonial discourses, of which the "taming of the West" in the United States was one. The threat of the indigenous, of other people living in relation to a particular place rather than re-creating it as some Edenic, idyllic, or previously familiar space, is precisely that such inhabitants remind the invading colonizers that they are actually the geopolitical outsider. In order to invert ideologically this relationship of inhabitants and invaders, and to suppress any recognition of relational, and therefore possibly nonhierarchical, difference and potential community of the different peoples coming into contact with each other, the colonizers can allow the subalterns to be viewed with familiarity and recognition only when depicted as exotics and primitives.

In opposition to what was perceived as Freudian psychoanalysis, V. N. Voloshinov's *Freudianism*, a book that many believe was written by Bakhtin, presents dialogical conceptions of the self, the psyche, and the "content of consciousness." His analysis initiates the recognition of the individual as a social-self construct developing within given social, economic, political, historical, and environmental parameters of space and time; the individual does not create his or her own self ex nihilo and is not given it intact in a transcendental soul. I participate in the formation of my self and others through such multiple subject positions as being a teacher, parent, spouse, neighbor, and inhabitant, while others participate in the formation of my self as son, ex-husband, stranger, and tourist. Voloshinov claims that "outside society and, consequently, outside objective socioeconomic conditions, there is no such thing as a human being."[4] Holmes Rolston III extends this point to the human as biological, and not just cultural, entity: "kept in its environmental context, our humanity is not absolutely 'in' us, but is rather 'in' our world dialogue."[5] That is to say, in order to be fully human, we need to have a healthy geopsyche. Or, according to Gregory Cajete, "There is an interaction between the people's inner and outer realities that comes into play as we live in a place for an extended time. Our physical make-up and the nature of our psyche are formed in direct ways by the distinct climate, soil, geography, and living things of a place.[6]

A dialogical orientation toward the human-nonhuman interanimation of both the human psyche and inhabited space will reinforce the ecofeminist recognition of interdependence and natural necessity of diversity, which I discussed in chapter 4. Such an orientation would require a rethinking of the concepts of absolute other and otherness. If the possibility of the condition of *anotherness*, being another for others, is recognized, then the ecological processes of interanimation—the ways in which humans and other entities develop, change, and learn through mutually influencing each other day to day—can be emphasized in constructing models of viable human–rest-of-nature interaction. Inhabitation as a dominant feature of much nature writing might, then, be emphasized over traveling-through, visiting, or going-out-to-experience-nature approaches. Henry David Thoreau, for example, did not inhabit Walden Pond in the way that the Native American poet Simon J. Ortiz hails from Deetseyamah, Arizona. Likewise, the walking tour as source of engagement with nature in nineteenth-century England might be rethought against what Terry Gifford has called the "anti-pastoral tradition" of poets like Patrick Kavanagh.[7]

The notion of anotherness has significant implications for teaching multicultural and environmental literature. To begin with, the notion of anotherness calls for a cross-cultural comparative analysis, rather than a comparative cultural analysis from the traditional center-margin orientation in which a tradition or canon or national literary style is used as the base against which to compare the other literature. Also, anotherness calls for close attention to the ways in which relationships and relational differences are portrayed or ignored in environmental literature, the ways in which an author situates him- or herself in relation to other entities. It would, for instance, provide the basis for thoroughly critiquing the mystique of the nonparticipant observer that we sometimes encounter in naturalist essays. Concepts of relational difference flow from and reinforce critical strategies of nondualist and multiplicitous subject constructions. These strategies in turn encourage the hearing of other speaking subjects and voicings—literary and critical, human and otherwise—of the silenced and the suppressed, whether those voicings come from the anothers in the world that many of us are just learning to recognize or from the anothers within our own selves.

My main concern is to argue not for the preceding theoretical constructions in the abstract or on the basis of their intrinsic value, but for their utility in facilitating the generation of a different paradigm for conceptualizing environmental writing, a paradigm that focuses on relational inhabitation as a fundamental worldview by which to analyze the efficacy of literary works. Existing paradigms do not seem to encompass the range of environmental literature or to be able to critique the diversity of expressions of human-nonhuman relationships, the generation of geopsyche, or the ecosystemic situatedness found in contemporary literature. I think that the notion of anotherness, with its attendant emphasis on relational difference, provides a significant mechanism for rendering ecocriticism a much more multicultural and international enterprise.

Writing

Let me now explore the implications of anotherness and inhabitation through brief readings of six texts demonstrating three different genres of environmental writing: essay, poetry, and novel. I will begin this section with a discussion of two works of environmental writing. The first is a collection by the Chickasaw poet and novelist Linda Hogan, and the second is a full-length prose journey-meditation by the white Mormon author Terry Tempest Williams.

Linda Hogan's dedication of *Dwellings: A Spiritual History of the Living World* reads: "For My Grandmothers, And For Grandmother, The Golden Eagle." The significance of the identification of an overarching, or generally embracing, grandmother as "The Golden Eagle" is explained in Hogan's preface: "[These writings] have grown, too, out of my native understanding that there is a terrestrial intelligence that lies beyond our human knowing and grasping."[8] The emphasis on "native understanding" and Hogan's self-identification as "an Indian woman" make explicit the point also made in Nora Naranjo-Morse's poetry (discussed in chap. 9): the writing, the knowledge, and the women's experiences cannot and must not be separated from the reality of native life.

Hogan's ecological orientation throughout *Dwellings* reflects not only the intertwining of multicultural and gendered experience, but also an indigenous heritage of teachings and practices that shape her life and the history that she shares with her reader. Hogan emphasizes throughout *Dwellings* that the "living world" still includes the "continuance," to use Simon Ortiz's term, of tribal peoples. That continuance constitutes part of her "spiritual history," which in turn proposes an ecocentric, rather than anthropocentric, vision of coinhabitation of all of the creatures that participate in the greater "terrestrial intelligence," something she explores in *Dwellings*.

Three key concepts orient Hogan's narratives, which some people would characterize as stories and others as essays: cultivating, nurturing, and listening. These apply equally to caring for injured raptors, interpreting observed events, and healing one's own body and spirit. These three activities are all based on a sense of answerability and a recognition of relational difference, and they require commitment over time, which in a sense is the most basic definition of inhabitation. While the first two are participatory, it is the third, listening, that guarantees the construction of the other as a mutually speaking subject, an another with whom we converse and from whom we learn and change. Such listening is also a form of decentering that helps keep the individual from placing oneself at the center and all others at the margins. Hogan, for instance, notes at the end of her second narrative, "The Bats": "What an enormous world. . . . It is all so much larger than we are," and then she goes on to ask, "How do we learn to trust ourselves enough to hear the chanting of earth?" Hogan contends here that we need to learn not to place the world in proper perspective but to place ourselves in the proper perspective that is the world. One of the ways that we engage in such placing is learning from the other animals that mutually inhabit this world, such as the bats who "are listeners who pass on the language and songs of many things to human beings who need wisdom, healing, and guidance through our lives, we who forget where we stand in the world" (*Dwellings*, 28, 27).

To receive what the bats would pass on, human beings need to learn how to listen to the world and also how to cultivate our relationships with our fellow inhabitants. In "All My Relations," for example, Hogan remarks that the title phrase is one spoken in a healing ceremony, and that in such a ritual "those words create a relationship with other people, with animals, with the land. To have health it is necessary to keep all these relations in mind." As is common among many Native American authors, Hogan fundamentally conceptualizes a multiculturality that is not limited to human cultures and languages; she defines culture as the practice of appropriate relationship among all the participants of the world. The ceremony Hogan depicts in "All My Relations" is a particular kind of cultural practice that is only fully realized in the continuance of healthy daily life, "when we take up a new way, our minds and hearts filled with the visions of earth that holds us within it, in compassionate relationship to and with our world" (*Dwellings*, 40–41).

"To" and "with" constitute distinct forms of relationship. "With" provides the insider status. "To" reminds the reader that humans are not always insiders to the rest of the world. There are places, events, and purposes that should not be treated as things-for-us, but as things-for-themselves. In "What Holds the Water, What Holds the Light," Hogan emphasizes the need for such a distinction because the dominant culture of the United States tends to define value only in terms of use-for-humans. "Wilderness," she believes, "is something beyond us, something that does not need our hand in it" (*Dwellings*, 45). "A different Yield," which immediately follows "What Holds," emphasizes that this alternative, intrinsic-value orientation is found occasionally within certain pockets of the dominant culture, as in Barbara McClintock's empathetic science, and throughout the healing traditions of "American Indians" and in earlier forms of tribal consciousness in human history.

In "Creations," Hogan contends that this other consciousness, which has been maintained in opposition to the dominant culture's attempts at global control, must be protected and strengthened, because "we have been wounded by a dominating culture that has feared and hated the natural world, has not listened to the voice of the land, has not believed in the inner worlds of human dreaming and intuition, all things that have guided indigenous people" (*Dwellings*, 82). Such an inhabitory consciousness that positions humanity in the perspective of the world, in participatory relationship with the other inhabitants, is humanity's hope and possibility. Through her faith in such a possibility, Hogan ends *Dwellings* emphasizing interconnection and relationship: "It is a world of elemental attention, of all things working together, listening to what speaks in the blood. Whichever road I follow, I walk in the land of many gods, and they love and eat one another. . . . Watch and listen. You are the result of the love of thousands" (*Dwellings*, 159). Hogan's conclusion culminates a book-length movement beyond a human-based concept of multiculturality toward, perhaps, a eukaryote-based sense of ecocultural interrelationship. The "love of thousands" likely does not refer only to human ancestors but to the "many gods" participating in that more-than-human "terrestrial intelligence," which is the "spiritual history of the living world," and, in Hogan's vision, our inhabitory future.

Linda Hogan speaks as an insider regarding the ecologically viable spiritual and cultural values of her native ancestors and contemporaries, positing such wisdom as a particular aspect of that greater world intelligence. In *Pieces of White Shell: A Journey to Navajoland*, Terry Tempest Williams speaks as an outsider championing the kind of indigenous continuance that Hogan embodies, a type of the cultural conservation that Pat Mora delineates in *Nepantla*, which I discuss in chapter 7. Williams does so because positioning herself explicitly as a cultural outsider enables her to recognize anotherness among humans themselves and between humans and other creatures in the world. In a sense, then, she can encourage thinking complementary to Hogan's vision, without needing to claim a personal history identical to indigenous continuity. In the prologue, for example, Williams draws out the similarities between the Navajos and her people, the Mormons, but she also notes that "there are major differences, primarily in the stories we tell and the way in which we walk upon the earth."[9]

Pieces of White Shell relates primarily what Williams has learned and wishes to bring home from the Navajo. She seems very aware of the dangers of cultural imperialism, and so she warns her readers: "Their stories hold meaning for us only as examples. . . . We must create and find our own stories, our own myths, with symbols that will bind us to the world as we see it today" (*White Shell*, 5). That is to say, her journey is part of a process of learning about ecologically sustainable inhabitation, a way of living that requires knowing intimately the place one calls home and then inviting others to hear the stories in order to learn their own ways, to find their own trails home, rather than pretending to be hermit crabs who can find new abandoned shells once they outgrow the old ones.

Throughout the text Williams interweaves a series of voices, letting inhabitants and visitors speak of place. Her own voice is quite distinct in the beginning but gradually blends with the voices of others who live in Navajoland. Mythic stories and geological history become interwoven until myth is recognized as an interpretation of a reality, and reality an experience shaped by the myths of the people who inhabit it. "The Navajo faith in the cyclic nature of things," Williams observes, "has come to them through their direct interaction with their physical environment," which is to say that myth and spirituality are components of the geopsyche of a people (*White Shell*, 44). As Williams learns, one participates in a place about which one tells stories rather than merely observing it passively or domineeringly.

Williams's penultimate chapter is "Storyteller"; in it she defines the purpose of storytelling and calls its existence an act of responsibility (*White Shell*, 130). In the ecological framework of the place-based subject construction of Navajo stories and their tellers, Williams defines herself as one who acts as I-for-another for the earth, in telling stories of its sacredness and preservation, and as I-for-another for the reader: "Story is an affirmation of our ties to one another." But Williams has learned that "one another" is much more than human multiculturality—it is also ecological diversity: "community in the Native American sense encompasses all life-forms: people, land, and creatures." Through immersion in difference, Williams becomes another teller of tales about the possibility of inhabitation. She does so first in terms of promoting the cultural conservation of indigenous ways of life, and second in terms of the kind of cultural regeneration that might enable exotics to become locals: "We have the power to rethink our existence, our time in earth's embrace, and step forward with compassionate intelligence" (*White Shell*, 130, 135, 136).

Poetry

In the United States, poetry is the literary genre most closely associated with nature writing after the "nonfiction" essay. What one notices in much contemporary poetry concerned with nature and environmental issues is the high degree of narrative structure, even in poems of lyric length, and concomitantly a strong resistance to solipsism and confession. Connection with other elements of the natural world, particularly the wild, predominate, but what seems rarely recognized is the multicultural character of such poetry. Here I will look at only two poets to demonstrate this point: Gary Snyder, the most widely acclaimed living white male ecological poet in the United States, and Simon J. Ortiz, a major Native American poet frequently cited by other environmental writers, such as Terry Tempest Williams, but not yet widely recognized among readers for his ecological vision. (Although many other poets could be invoked here, and some are in other chapters, these two serve as sufficient illustration.)

In 1992 Snyder brought out *No Nature: New and Selected Poems*, which reprints a generous portion of his previous collections and includes fifteen new poems. Of these, "Kušiwoqqóbɨ," "Off the Trail," "Word Basket Woman," "At Tower Peak," and "Ripples on the Surface," are of the most interest from an ecological perspective. They also demonstrate his sense of the necessity of an international recognition of multiculturality as part of an ecological practice. These poems repeat established philosophical positions and human-nature relationships found in Snyder's earlier poetry. "Kusiwoqqobi" and "Word Basket Woman" link contemporary inhabitory practice with a history of indigenous peoples and of one of Snyder's own ancestors. "Off the Trail" opens with the line, "We are free to find our own way," and later alludes to the *Dao De Jing* axiom that "the trail's not the way."[10] This poem can be read in conjunction with Terry Tempest Williams's warning to European immigrants to the United States, that they should not attempt to imitate its first-nation peoples, but rather to learn to construct new stories and myths that contribute to new forms of inhabitation, ones that will nurture the continuance of indigenous inhabitation as well.

In "At Tower Peak," Snyder contrasts the rejuvenating experience of mountain climbing with the increasingly urbanized world where "Every tan rolling meadow will turn into housing." But he does not let the poem sink into the kind of individualistic escapism that permeates American popular culture by ending with the illusion of the individual being able to separate himself from the rest of humanity through ascetic retreat to some pure, wild place. As he observes near poem's end, "It's just one world," and the contradictions must be worked through and from within.[11] He reinforces this one-world image in the volume's final poem, "Ripples on the Surface." He opens it with a quotation distinguishing different kinds of water ripples, and in mid-poem calls nature a performance, a "high old culture." He concludes by deconstructing the dichotomy of house and wild, of human and nonhuman.[12] His final line echoes the Buddhist image of the world as illusion. Or, in the words of *The Diamond Sutra*, a Buddhist text very important in Snyder's Zen training, "As to any Truth-declaring system, Truth is undeclarable; so 'an enunciation of Truth' is just the name given to it."[13] Stories are not experience but constructions of experience that shape the attitudes that people carry with them when they walk outside their houses and apartments. Like Hogan and Williams, Snyder is concerned that his readers understand the importance, and feel the sense of responsibility, of listening to the stories in order to learn how to contribute to the development of a more natured, more related culture than the one in which they likely live.

Simon J. Ortiz, the Acoma Pueblo poet, published in 1992 *Woven Stone*, which reprints three volumes of his poetry. The works elucidate an indigenous worldview that needs to become a key aesthetic text in the project "to Indigenize contemporary western education," the process of helping second Americans become, like the first Americans, inhabitory peoples.[14] Ortiz not only develops his worldview through narration and imagery but also indicates, through example and conception, methods by which a people can retain and recover their specific cultural constructions and balanced human relations to the rest of nature.

"Toward Spider Springs," one poem in the first section of the volume, begins:

> I was amazed
> at the wall of stones
> by the roadside.

The second stanza expresses the difficulty of the family that comprises the "we" of the poem:

> We were trying to find
> a place to start all over
> but couldn't.

And as a result of this apparent failure they trudge by the walls again and the teller remarks that

> The stones had no mortar;
> they were just stones
> balancing against the sky.[15]

A fundamental part of Spider Woman's wisdom is the knowledge of balance, which is often represented through images of weaving. The stones of the walls near Spider Springs are not cemented together but balanced in a woven pattern, which provides a lesson. The balancing stones require ongoing human participation; rather than starting fresh somewhere else— the paradigm of European colonization—this family needs to learn to continue and renew their relationship in their place.

Ortiz speaks throughout *Woven Stone* of a foundation based on situated knowledges and the determination of understanding through experience. Patricia Clark Smith makes the point that "the surface of the world has altered desperately and a person can feel overwhelmed by the loss of a vital culture, of the native Coyote-self. But despite appearances, Ortiz in his poetry . . . is saying that the old stories are more than cultural artifacts and childhood memories. . . . In remembering what is old, one can deal with what is new."[16] A case in point is the poem "The Significance of a Veteran's Day," in which Ortiz refines the power of remembrance and acknowledgment of the earth:

> we contemplated
> . . .
> the continuance of the universe,
> the traveling, not the progress,
> but the humility of our being here.

He concludes the poem: "I am talking about how we have been able / to survive insignificance."[17]

The insight that significance arises from partnership, that is, being one part of a relationship based on reciprocity, is repeated throughout *Woven Stone*, often as part of a storytelling poem such as "Canyon de Chelly." Here, Ortiz writes about taking his very young son to the canyon, and the boy, touching an ancient root, looks to his father "for information." Ortiz responds that it is a root, "and around it, the earth, ourselves."[18] Rather than treating the root as an object of naturalist attention and the scene as if devoid of human involvement, Ortiz locates root, place, and people in a single unifying context of mutual, interpenetrating existence.

While Ortiz's philosophy of "continuance" may sound simple, it must be terribly complex and difficult, or why else would contemporary American culture have so much difficulty with such simple things as respect, reciprocity, and humility? *Woven Stone* is both a retrospective and a visionary text, providing stories and images of a way of life that Ortiz is helping to recover and continue through representing its values and critiquing the destructive forces arrayed against it.

Fiction

When one thinks of ecofiction, the texts that most often come to mind are those like Wallace Stegner's *Angle of Repose* or Wendell Berry's *A Place on Earth*, works written in the form of enlightenment realism as defined in chapter 1. The appeal of such traditional realism is certainly its reinforcement of reader expectations of referentiality, that this fiction is about life in the world rather than the life of the mind. Yet, while such realism remains a mainstay of ecofiction, it is not the only strategy for environmental writing in this genre—something I have emphasized earlier in this volume. Here I want to discuss two novels practicing different types of fictional representation within the mode of environmental literature: Marnie Mueller's *Green Fires* and Ana Castillo's *So Far from God*. The first novel can be labeled first-person enlightenment realism and the second alchemical and situated realism, according to the definitions established in chapter 1.

Green Fires, Assault on Eden: A Novel of the Ecuadorian Rainforest chronicles the return to Ecuador in late 1969 of an American woman named Ana who had been a Peace Corps volunteer six years earlier. The crisis of the novel is generated by her and her husband's discovery that the government, with the complicity of various U.S. agencies, is bombing the villages of indigenous tribes to clear the way for multinational oil exploration within the rain forest. The novel details the indigenous way of life and clearly asserts a position in support of the continuity of those cultural practices, while emphasizing their degree of difference from the cultures of the other characters. It focuses its thematic attention, however, on the human-human relationships and the cultures they represent, rather than on the human-nature relationships, since these latter relationships are imperiled by the former ones. Responsibility and the embodiment of its implications become the key issue to be resolved, and Mueller allows different characters, each of whom has a different cultural distance or proximity to the indigenous peoples, to present conflicting interpretations of their responsibilities. All too often these interpretations make the indigenous people an object of attention, either for protection or exploitation, rather than a mutually speaking subject.

The dilemma is not resolved as the novel ends, and readers are encouraged to recognize that the events of 1969 are not past history but part of an ongoing process that is unfolding as deforestation of the Amazon and displacement of its indigenous inhabitants continue. The importance and the difficulty of establishing a sense of anotherness is highlighted as Ana attempts to avoid the pitfalls of both assuming too much similarity with the indigenous peoples and experiencing too great a sense of difference to see relatedness. Like Ortiz and Mora, Mueller emphasizes that recognizing the subordinated indigenous peoples is key to working toward new cultural formations that will discontinue global ecocide. And like Williams, she understands the significance of remembering one's position as an outsider even in the process of establishing relationships. Mueller never lets the reader forget that the wild jungle she describes is already well inhabited. She also indicates a significant dimension of the reader's responsibility toward others by having the main character realize that her assuming the role of I-for-another means returning home rather than remaining in the jungle.

In *So Far from God*, Chicana novelist and poet Ana Castillo addresses the threat environmental racism poses to Chicanos and other people of color and portrays the struggle against that threat as part of a worldwide struggle for environmental justice. One aesthetic device she employs to emphasize the difference between the native and Chicano communities of the southwestern United States and the dominant Anglo culture is to write in the type of representation that I call alchemical realism, and that Kamala Platt claims can best be defined as "virtual realism." Platt notes that, "Castillo situates environmental justice issues within the larger field of race, class and gender justice, thereby embracing the 'virtual realities' encountered by a Nuevo Mexicano community." As a result, she concludes that "Castillo's texts are therefore more adequately described as 'virtual realism': a realism that virtually encompasses lived experience, and propels it into postmodern fiction."[19] Part of this virtual realism consists of the alchemical depiction of miraculous and mythic events as part of the daily lived reality of the inhabitants of the community depicted. Castillo thus structures the realism of the text on the basis of the spiritual perceptions and practices of the people who are her subjects, rather than on the basis of the rationalistic reality promulgated by the dominant U.S. culture.

A significant component of this community's reality is a deeply spiritual and physical bond to the land in which they live. As a result, *So Far from God* has much in common in terms of ecological sensibility with Ortiz's *Woven Stone*. At the same time, like Ortiz but with greater emphasis, Castillo depicts the ways in which environmental pollution and racial exploitation of people of color destroy not only the natural environment of the region but its cultural environment and human inhabitants as well.

Unlike Mueller, however, Castillo does not stop with the presentation of a litany of grievances and outrages, but also depicts the development of community resistance to the environmental and racial injustices perpetrated against them. Since their relationship to the land is ongoing, the people of the community that Castillo portrays are able to develop alternatives to employment in plants that force workers to use toxic chemicals that pollute the larger environment and their individual bodies. The nature that concerns Castillo, then, is not a wilderness refuge or uninhabited sanctuary that one visits in solitude, but is an inhabitable place in which humans need to, and can, work out a balanced relationship. Like Mueller, Castillo foregrounds human-human relationships before human-nature relationships, but throughout *So Far from God* the possibility of healthy human-human relationships is predicated upon healthy human-nature relationships. Castillo pits the cultures of southwestern U.S. people of color against the dominant culture of white America in a battle of self against other and also shows the melding and productive interchange of the diverse native and Chicano cultures working out relationships based on mutual respect.

Conclusion

This discussion of just six literary texts can only highlight my argument for the use of inhabitation as a criterion for evaluating the efficacy of literature concerned with the environment and human relationship to the rest of nature. Even so, these texts do indicate the existence of a multicultural approach to environmental writing and the development of a corpus of ecologically sensitive literature. At the same time, I have sought here to demonstrate the benefits of a Bakhtinian approach to environmental literature, particularly in terms of the self-other-another triad and the issue of responsibility. For each of these writers, and a substantially larger body of U.S. writing, anotherness is a position of recognition and responsibility that many authors are attempting to gain and to depict. Anotherness also serves as an orientation for recognizing and distinguishing the diversity of environmental writing and its modes of representation beyond traditional realism and the naturalist essay.

6

The Worldly Diversity of
Nature-Oriented Prose Literature

VARIETY OF obstacles face the individual who attempts to survey any type of diversity within modern world literature. For one, the definition of modern varies from national literature to national literature. For another, it is impossible for any one person to know the literary history of more than a few national literatures or regions in any detail. For a third, unless the range of literatures is confined to a single language, such as writing in English from various countries, the survey is limited by an individual's ability to learn several languages well enough to read literature. Fourth, it is doubtful that even a person well versed in a specific national literature is really aware of that literature's actual diversity. This problem results from the limited access to texts due to publishing decisions, canon formation, and the opportunities for, and inclinations of, individuals to read works that range across all genres.

With nature-oriented literature, the situation is often even more challenging. For critics of most national literatures, nature or environment does not constitute a category of analysis, so one must start almost from scratch in defining the field of study, assessing what texts are available, and then determining where to start looking for texts that are no longer in print. Such has certainly been the case in Japan: there the discovery of a possible tradition of nature writing and of the ways in which environmental issues are represented in literature has fallen mainly on the shoulders of critics trained in American and English literatures rather than in Japanese literature. Narrow definitions of "nature writing" can further impede research in any national literature in that they can orient critics to look for types of writing that may not be found and to overlook other types of nature-oriented literature. As I work through the literary examples of this chapter, the issue of genre determinations and the demarcation of fiction and nonfiction will also necessarily come up.

Much of my sense of the diversity of nature-oriented literature in the world arises from having recently edited *The Literature of Nature: An International Sourcebook*. The majority of the chapters in that volume focus on prose, both nonfiction and fiction, and I suspect that what is discussed in many of the chapters constitutes only the bare beginnings of the delineation of the field. In many places critics are just starting the process of learning what works might be brought together to constitute a nature-oriented literary tradition in particular national literatures; they are far from determining whether those works that are currently available constitute a representative sample.

My purpose in this chapter is to provide something of the flavor of what is available in twentieth-century literature and to think about the ways that we need to define genre conventions, establish reader expectations, and work cross-culturally to understand a subject that is always heavily situated and culturally embedded: nature in literature.

German-Mexican Novels of the Jungle

I want to start with a person who could be defined as a cross-cultural author because he was born in Germany but eventually made his way to Mexico, where he wrote in German primarily about proletarian struggles and Indian oppression and insurgency in the Chiapas region. During his life he used various aliases, and for decades controversy raged over whether he was a German, an American, or a Mexican writer, even though he became a Mexican citizen and wrote mainly about Mexico. I am talking about B. Traven, who is known to American audiences mainly as a result of John Huston making a movie out of one of his novels, *The Treasure of the Sierra Madre*. In other words, a writer like B. Traven raises questions about the category of "national literature," just to add to the complexity of the issues at hand.

Here I will consider his Caoba cycle, six novels that form the bulk of what are known as his jungle novels, because they are all set in Chiapas. The novels of the Caoba cycle were published in German between 1931 and 1939, and until very recently only five of them were available in various English translations: *Government*, *The Carreta*, *March to the Montería*, *The Rebellion of the Hanged*, and *General from the Jungle*. The bulk of the criticism in English is therefore based on these five novels. The fourth novel in the series, *Die Troza*, was not translated into English until 1998 (published as *Trozas*).

These novels are filled with vivid descriptions of the southern jungles of Mexico, in particular the mahogany forests, which were being heavily exploited for export, particularly during the second regime of Porfirio Díaz (1877–80 and 1885–1911), the time period in which the novels are set. B. Traven documents at length the vicious exploitation and brutal oppression of the region's indigenous peoples, something still occurring in the 1920s when he arrived in Mexico. What sets the Caoba cycle apart from B. Traven's proletarian novels, such as *The Death Ship*, is that the former novels focus on the Indians of the region whose traditional ways of life are intimately bound with the natural world around them. In order to portray their dignity and heroism in opposition to the capitalist exploitation that B. Traven militantly opposes, he must paint a picture of both people and place, of the nature-based way of life from which the indigenous people are being torn by debt peonage. Through the course of the novels, B. Traven also finds that he must go beyond exposing the evils of comprador capitalism and neocolonialism to providing an alternative vision of a political future less exploitative and less environmentally destructive. At the end of the Caoba cycle, then, the peons become part of the greater Mexican revolution of 1910, as various critics, such as Robert B. Olafson would have it.[1]

But B. Traven goes beyond merely seeing the Chiapas Indians as part of that revolution. Rather, he views them as a political alternative to the direction the revolution quickly took in Mexico in the 1920s and 1930s. Heidi Zogbaum argues that "Traven's last novel [*General from the Jungle*] bears clear signs of resignation and disillusionment, as well as a heightened understanding of the complex problems associated with the restructuring of a society along revolutionary lines."[2] What the Caoba cycle, including its final volume, suggests is that B. Traven came to realize that attitudes toward exploitation of nature and oppression of indigenous people go hand in hand; an attitude towards nature is also an attitude towards humanity, a point that many of our contemporary environmental writers feel compelled to make. As a result of this recognition, the Indians' attempt at the end of the series, in *General from the Jungle*, to establish an autonomous communal village based on anarchist principles of social organization represents an alternative vision not only to capitalism but also to the course of the Mexican Revolution. In particular, it opposes the centralization of political power that occurred whereby the labor movement "was subordinated to the Mexican state."[3]

In terms of consideration of these novels as nature-oriented literature, it is highly unfortunate that B. Traven's travelogue about his trips to the Chiapas region, *Land des Frühlings* (1928), has never been translated into English, because it holds the key to understanding the shifts in his attitude toward revolution throughout the 1930s, from an urban anarchist proletarian revolt to one that I have previously labeled *anarcho-primitivism*, but that now I would perhaps call *indigenous-communitarian*.[4] As Friederike Baumann notes of *Land*, "Indians, landscapes, flora and fauna are seen through the eyes of an unusually perceptive and compassionate outsider, an unconventional anthropologist and naturalist."[5] Further, in terms of changes in B. Traven's thinking, Baumann asserts that, "It is a fascinating document of his philosophical, political, and historical reflections, growing out of his confrontation with revolutionary Mexico and his discovery of Indian community life, which, unlike the life in Western countries, seemed to him free from individual ambition and greed."[6]

A valuable point about B. Traven is that he did not set out to be a nature writer, nor did he maintain the kind of focus on nature that is found in the Caoba cycle. Rather, his political themes coupled with his keen observation skills moved him toward writing a type of environmental literature in this group of novels because the people he saw as heroes in that labor conflict had a strong agrarian connection with nature, one that many of them sought to reestablish through participation in the Mexican Revolution and subsequent revolts. In particular, that connection was communal rather than individual, which in turn required of B. Traven a rethinking of his urban and proletarian-based anarchist philosophy toward a more communitarian conception of heterarchical social life based on sustainable subsistence practices. In a sense, one could argue that B. Traven's work, at least in the Caoba cycle, represents a precursor of contemporary bioregional politics. *General from the Jungle* ends with one group working out its political independence in a particular place with a particular set of values without making a universal claim for the adoption of such values everywhere else.

This conclusion is foreshadowed in *Government*, which depicts two different Indian communities. The first, Bujvilum, is of the type that the revolutionaries at the end of the *General* seek to reestablish; although small and very poor, Bujvilum is an independent village with its own communal lands. For B. Traven, agrarian practices are the key to a peaceful society. Of the Bujvilum Indians he remarks: "They were not warlike. They were tillers of the soil, who are everywhere of a peaceable disposition as long as they are left to go their own way. . . . Agriculture rules out the warlike spirit. Fields and herds go to ruin if men have to be out on the warpath. . . . Agriculture is no nursery of adventure."[7] In *General*, B. Traven concludes that freedom fundamentally means freedom from the external imposition of political control and economic coercion so that individuals-in-community may work out their specific relationships with the environment, particularly through agriculture.

The Mexican revolutionary slogan, "Tierra y Libertad" (Land and Liberty), takes on a new meaning when people are placed in nature for the working out of their relationship with the land and through that their political relationships with each other: "the muchachos hoped that after they had won their battle for freedom they would be allowed to lead their lives in their own ways. . . . no longer to be dominated, no longer to be commanded."[8] While it might be easy to dismiss B. Traven's position as utterly utopian, it is instructive to remember that the Chiapas region continues to generate rebellions by Indians against the central government of Mexico, and that contemporary bioregionalists, openly influenced by writers such as Gary Snyder, are struggling to establish autonomous villages and cities in that area today.[9]

Bush Farming in the Caribbean

Moving a little east and south, I would like to turn to a Caribbean writer from Trinidad, Michael Anthony, and his third novel, *Green Days by the River*, originally published in 1967. This novel is related through the point of view of its fifteen-year-old protagonist, Shell, who has reached a turning point in his life. Due to his father's chronic illness, Shell must leave school and find a way to earn a living, which will likely determine his class and economic position for the rest of his life. Also, he appears to be on the verge of having to make a commitment to a young woman who will eventually become his wife. In both life-determining categories of his decision-making he finds himself at a crossroads, one in which two women and two modes of labor are intertwined.

Gareth Griffiths, in introducing the Heinemann edition of the novel, depicts *Green Days* as an allegory of entrapment, one in which the journey into adulthood for Shell means the loss of freedom at the hands of Mr. Gidharee, who seeks to induct him into an agrarian way of life.[10] But Griffiths ignores, I think, the point Anthony makes, which is that freedom is not an issue for a poor, young Trinidadian in the early postcolonial period. The crossroads is not set up as freedom versus enfetterment or being single versus being married; Shell will have to work for the rest of his life and he will get married. The question is, rather, which life of labor to choose, and that choice is intimately linked with deciding which woman he will marry. There is Rosalie, Mr. Gidharee's daughter, and a life of farming for himself with his own land on the one hand—a yeoman's life of cutting agricultural crops out of the bush—or a life of urban labor working for someone else and being with Joan, the girl from the city, on the other hand.

In brief, the plot unfolds in the following manner: Shell, his working mother, and his ill father, have moved from a beach area to an inland village, so that at the beginning of the novel Shell is dislocated and just getting to know the environment around him, including its people. Mr. Gidharee, whose daughter Rosalie is one year younger than Shell, befriends Shell and invites him to go along to his plot of land in the bush where he is growing various crops. Gidharee, in effect, introduces Shell to an alternative way of life in Trinidad, something different from the beach and the city, where the people of Shell's social class are servants and wage laborers. This way of life consists of living in the natural environment itself and the subsistence crop-growing that the environment makes possible. The interdependence of people and place in the bush holds the promise of an independence from the class legacy of colonialism. Gidharee's philosophy is expressed quite explicitly: "'I believe in land, boy,' he said. 'I believe in land and planting.'"[11] At the same time, Anthony repeatedly introduces personalities and economic and cultural aspects that remind the reader that he is not sketching out an Edenic way of life, a pastoral escape from hard work and poverty.

As the novel proceeds, it becomes apparent that Mr. Gidharee is evaluating Shell and his ability to learn to farm in terms of Shell's being a possible husband for Rosalie. But Shell, who is initially enamored of her, develops a crush on a friend's relative from the city who visits for a holiday, and at this point the tension in the plot begins to build. Anthony establishes a contrast between the two women, Rosalie and Joan, in terms of two different environments and ways of life for Shell, both of which he finds attractive. As the story progresses, the reader learns that Shell has a nose for fruits, a love of birds, and the abilities needed to make a good bush farmer, which Mr. Gidharee clearly recognizes. In contrast, Shell's father realizes that Joan is a city girl who is better educated than Shell, and he sees their social differences as a potential problem for any lasting relationship.

The climax comes when, after Shell has been sexually involved with Rosalie but is still thinking about Joan, Mr. Gidharee has his dogs attack the young man and warns Shell, "Perhaps they mean to tear you up unless you mean to get married to her."[12] While Shell is recovering from this attack, his mother receives word that his father is dying in a hospital in the same city where Joan lives. Upon hearing that he must go to the city to make preparations for his father's death, Shell realizes that to insure his future and to fulfill his responsibilities to his mother and to Rosalie he must marry her and not Joan. In so doing, he will also become a partner with Mr. Gidharee in his farming operations that now include cocoa acreage. As he looks toward the future, he begins thinking about the ways that he can reduce the waste that occurs on Mr. Gidharee's land because too many crops are grown without the surplus being adequately marketed. In the end, Mr. Gidharee has gotten rid of the dogs and has taken over fully as Shell's surrogate father, further educating him into the intricacies of farming and reassuring Shell that "everything will be okay."[13]

Anthony's novel contains many passages in which the land, the trees, the fruit, and the crops are described in great detail from Shell's point of view. Such passages could be used to make a case for *Green Days by the River* being defined as nature literature, as a novel about bush farming in Trinidad. But from another angle it could be read as an environmental fiction in which rural agrarian life is set against urban commercial life, with Anthony concluding that independent subsistence farming, with cash income from the sale of surplus crops, is the way for many Trinidadians to gain a measure of economic independence and stability. The land is presented as the ground on which Shell can build a different future than the one initially facing him in the novel, where his choice seemed to be either going to the city to try to find menial employment or staying in the rural area and becoming a plantation worker. Mr. Gidharee's philosophy of "land and planting" is presented not as a pastoral idyll or romantic escape but as a clear-eyed, practically minded understanding of how people can sustain themselves in accordance with the nature around them.[14]

Agrarian Inhabitation in Southern Africa

Having focused on two male writers of the Western Hemisphere, I would like now to cross the Atlantic and consider an African woman writer, Bessie Head. While various works by Head could be treated as nature-oriented literature, I will focus here just on her first novel, *When Rain Clouds Gather*, originally published in 1969. As the note on the author at the front of the 1995 Heinemann edition states, Head based this novel on the time she spent living as a refugee at the Bamangwao Development Farm in Botswana.

While there are strong women in *When Rain Clouds Gather,* the main character of the novel is a Zulu male fleeing South Africa into Botswana named Makhaya. Head provides an interesting commentary on this name that foreshadows the theme of inhabitation that will dominate the novel: "'Makhaya,' he said. 'That tribal name is the wrong one for me. It is for one who stays home, yet they gave it to me and I have not known a day's peace and contentment in my life.'"[15] The impossibility of Makhaya's staying home results not from his own psychological or educational problems, as he seems to suggest in the early pages of the novel, but rather from the brutality of apartheid, which prevents native people from inhabiting the land on their own terms. What Makhaya learns through the course of *When Rain Clouds Gather* is that being at home requires an active process of inhabitation, and that the agricultural and economic dimensions of such inhabitation must be developed sustainably in relation to the specific ecology of one's place. To enable Makhaya to learn such a lesson, Head sends him to an experimental agricultural village in Botswana.

Inhabitation, Head suggests, can only occur in a politically free country, not in a colonial, neocolonial, or apartheid state. Makhaya's process of understanding begins with his long walk from the border to the village where he will take up residence, connecting the political freedom of Botswana with its specific ecological characteristics: "As far as the eye could see it was only a vast expanse of sand and scrub but somehow bewitchingly beautiful. . . . perhaps he simply wanted a country to love and chose the first thing at hand. But whatever it was, he simply and silently decided that all this dryness and bleakness amounted to home and somehow he had come to the end of a journey" (*Rain Clouds,* 11). But while Makhaya may believe that he has found "home," learning to live at home will be a different matter for him; it is not simply a matter of learning local customs—he already speaks the language—and settling into a long-established traditional routine in some utopian return to a pastoral agrarian lifestyle.

Rather, through her depiction of the village of Golema Mmidi, where Makhaya takes up residence, Head thematically states that inhabitation in contemporary Botswana, a Botswana existing on the border of South Africa, surviving in a postcolonial world, and struggling in a global economy, requires the establishment of new techniques of sustainable agriculture and animal husbandry, the development of new gender and family relationships, and the generation of new traditions and customs. For Head, it is clear that the past may be built upon, but it is not where the living build their homes.

Fortunately for Makhaya, he has landed in a progressive village established around an experimental farm, which is being run by an altruistic Englishman and that has attracted individuals from all over Botswana who are ready to break with the negative aspects of tradition and forge a new life on the land. This decision to migrate to a farming and herding village seems to parallel the theme of Anthony's *Green Days by the River*. The standard neocolonial economic alternatives of plantation work and urban wage labor are rejected by the main characters of Head's novel just as they are by Mr. Gidharee and Shell.

Because of his having been educated in South Africa and because of his political experiences before seeking exile, Makhaya is taken on as an assistant by the English organizer of the farm, Gilbert Balfour. What Gilbert has realized, and what Makhaya is open to understanding, is that there needs to be a change in gender relations that will in turn alter the cultural assumptions about the relative value of stock raising and agriculture, which have traditionally been divided into male and female responsibilities respectively. Gilbert has the theories but he needs Makhaya to translate those theories into practical lessons for the villagers. To do that, Makhaya has to gain an understanding of local culture sufficient to enable him to teach the women agriculture and gain the men's acceptance of such educational and economic elevation of women's status.

As the novel follows Makhaya's growth into the position that Gilbert has offered him, his conflicts with the local backward chief, and his very gradual romantic relationship with the leading woman activist in the village, Head weaves in substantial information about the land and climate of Botswana. She also describes the innovations that Gilbert is attempting to introduce to reduce the depletion of the soil and water reserves through overgrazing and overplanting and to make the village's agriculture more productive in a collective effort. An important subplot of the novel, and a main plot in other works by Head, such as *Maru*, is the need of the Golema Mmidi villagers to overcome traditional prejudices against so-called inferior tribes who actually demonstrate better sense about the selection of agricultural crops in relation to soil quality and rainfall. As Juliana Makuchi Nfah-Abbenyi notes of the theme of *Maru*, "the message confirms the fact that the Bushmen, though looked down upon, are in a better position to be knowers."[16]

The significance of this point is demonstrated in two major ways in *When Rain Clouds Gather*. The wise chief of the region, Sekoto, takes in a woman to treat his own ailments who has been accused of witchcraft, but who defends herself by saying that she has learned herbalist healing techniques from "the people who live in the bush" (*Rain Clouds*, 47). It is also demonstrated through decisions about the appropriateness of growing millet rather than sorghum and maize. The problem, states Head, was that "year in and year out people had grown the exact same crops. Some where along the line they had become mixed up with tribal traditions," and such traditions prevented people from learning from other tribes (*Rain Clouds*, 38).

In an effort to make the Golema Mmidi villager's agriculture more sustainable through practices borrowed from the outside, whether from England or from allegedly "'inferior' tribes," Gilbert turns to another allegedly "inferior" group, the village women, to educate them in new agricultural techniques, with Makhaya assigned to be their teacher (*Rain Clouds*, 37). Head's narrator muses at this point, "Perhaps all change in the long run would depend on the women of the country and perhaps they too could provide a number of solutions to problems he had not yet thought of. Things could start in a small way with crops like millet, with talks, with simple lectures, and with some practical work done on the land" (*Rain Clouds*, 38).[17] And indeed, as the novel progresses, both Gilbert and Makhaya seem to function more as catalysts than protagonists, providing avenues for the women to revolutionize the lives of their families—to redefine the meaning of inhabitation in the arid land of Botswana, doing so one step at a time through an innovation a year in one small village of the great big world, trying to get right the work of being at home.

Decimated Nature and Impoverished People in Spain

Heading north to Europe I want to stop briefly on the Iberian Peninsula to consider a short text by the Spanish expatriate writer Juan Goytisolo. Goytisolo has been a prolific writer since the second half of the 1950s and along with his extensive production have also come major shifts in style and themes. The one work that I will treat comes from a period of artistic transition in the early 1960s and may serve to further complicate conceptions of the tenuous lines between nature writing and environmental literature, nonfiction and fiction. In the publisher's foreword to *The Countryside of Níjar and La Chanca*, which contains translations of two narratives published in Spanish as separate books, David Dayton first refers to these texts as part of "three non-fiction books. . . . documentary testimonies, whose narrator witness is the author himself." But later in the same brief foreword he remarks of *La Chanca* that, "Critics at that time [1981, when it was finally allowed to be published in Spain—nineteen years after its original date of publication] hailed it as a minor masterwork, praising the artfully employed narrative techniques which take the book beyond the realm of literary journalism and situate it in the nebulous border zone between autobiography and fiction—the prolific region Goytisolo returned to in his first innovative, truly major novel, *Marks of Identity*."[18]

The brevity of these remarks unfortunately makes it impossible to discern on what basis Dayton distinguishes nonfiction from fiction, although a key feature seems to be the inclusion of the "author himself" as "narrator witness." Yet this inclusion is certainly not a sufficient criterion, as various postmodernist works have demonstrated, as narratology has been at pains to clarify through both theoretical and applied arguments, and as the history of the Japanese literary genre of the "I-novel" would indicate. It is likely that today critics and even publishers might very well label both *The Countryside of Níjar* and *La Chanca* as autobiographical novels, which relegates them to the realm of fiction in the binary terrain of fiction-nonfiction genre analysis.

I would place *The Countryside of Níjar* in the realm of fiction, specifically in the genre of environmental fiction, because narrative as drive rather than narrative as service determines narrative and aesthetic decisions for the

construction of this text. In particular, because Goytisolo insists on inject-
ing political explanations for the current ecological impoverishment of the
Almería region of Spain, the environmentalist theme dominates aesthetic
decision-making in a way that a more nature-observation orientation might
not require. We also have the complication here, as in many other countries
on different continents, that the need to circumvent censors if one wishes
to be published in one's own country and remain out of jail requires various narrative compromises over the realistic representation of actual experience. As Dayton notes in regard to Goytisolo's writing, "it is obvious, from
reading *La Chanca*, that Goytisolo wrote *The Countryside of Níjar* in the
manner he did so that it could be published in Spain."[19]

Dale Pratt and Barbara Gordon associate these two texts by Goytisolo
with a movement known as "*libros de viajes* or travel narratives produced
during the late 1950s and 1960s" practiced by Goytisolo, Jesús Fernández
Santos, Antonio Ferres, and others, which "reported the abhorrent conditions of rural Spain." With these narratives the emphasis is not on factuality in terms of only writing descriptions of the interaction of nature and culture based on actually, personally observed scenes, but rather these authors
"presented an objective way of observing, contemplating, and exploring the
forgotten villages of Spain." And yet, the degree to which the word "objective" is appropriate here depends upon the degree to which a person accepts
the idea of partisan objectivity, for, as Pratt and Gordon emphasize, "these
authors write to decry the poverty and inhumanity of the social hierarchy
exploiting the peasants. They seek to show, not tell, that the environment
is not that of a nineteenth-century Romantic novel, but the harsh reality of
a raped land."[20]

Let me now turn to the actual content of *The Countryside of Níjar*, which
begins in the city of Almería, on the southern coast of Spain in southeastern Andalusia, home of the slum named La Chanca that will be the focus
of the book by that name. In *Countryside*, the first-person narrator quickly
leaves urban life behind as he heads northeast by bus from Almería toward
the town of El Alquián. As he rides by bus he observes the surrounding
countryside, which "is at the complete mercy of the sun," and carries on a
conversation with a local man about experimental gardens and innovative
farming techniques, such as using sand to hold in heat so that "the vegeta-

bles grow faster and you get 'em to market ahead of time," as well as an irri-gation system by means of which "the intense evaporation common to the area is reduced."[21]

While the narrator sometimes expresses a certain nostalgia for this area in terms of places and cultural practices, he does not turn the land into a scape through idealization. Rather, he gradually brings in a sense of history and a critique of national efforts to redress past ecologically destructive practices. In particular, he emphasizes the difficult task of the National Forestry Service to grow trees in the region in order to bring rain and reduce the conditions of desertification encouraged by drought: "MORE TREES, MORE WATER. It's the slogan of the National Forestry Service. . . . In Almería there are no trees because it doesn't rain, and it doesn't rain because there are no trees. Only a tenacious effort on the part of engineers and tech-nicians, and a generous amount of capital, will one day be able to break the vicious circle and give this poor land a future with both water and trees" (*Countryside*, 9). Shortly after this description the name of Franco is invoked and the region's gold mine is introduced into the story.

By such means Goytisolo establishes an oblique criticism of the gov-ernment. The gold mine could provide "a generous amount of capital" for the region, but like the other kinds of mines in the mountains, the ore from this one is trucked away to other places along with the profits, while the miners are left with low wages and silicosis. Readers may infer that the area actually contains within its borders the resources necessary to make the agriculture and the land sustain the human population, but exploitation by the central government intensifies its impoverishment.

Another resource that Goytisolo suggests is being squandered is the human population of Almería. Throughout the description of the narrator's trip to Níjar and his visit to that town, Goytisolo repeatedly describes the agricultural experimentation, both grand and small, underway. Vignettes about men who have emigrated from the region in search of work are inter-spersed. For example, Goytisolo begins chapter 4, "The village is sur-rounded by barren land, but human effort has harmoniously transformed the landscape. Cultivated terraces scale the mountainside. Fruit and almond trees intermingle across the ochre hills, and olive trees plunge down the steepest slopes like runaway sheep" (*Countryside*, 24). The word *harmonious* is key to this description, suggesting that the local people understand what needs to be done and how to do it, if, like B. Traven's founders of the independent village of Solipaz at the end of *General from the Jungle*, they are free from external coercion and exploitation (as is also the case with Goytisolo's description of crop rotation later in the narrative [*Countryside*, 50]).

In addition to this possibility of developing a sustainable life in such an arid area, Goytisolo also explores the contradiction between the grinding poverty that residents in the various villages repeatedly discuss with him and the tendency of many people to stay put or else to return after working elsewhere. Like Makhaya in Head's *When Rain Clouds Gather*, it becomes evident that such seemingly barren land has a certain beauty and starkness that gains a lasting grip on its inhabitants. For instance, Goytisolo opens chapter 6 with these words: "Between Cabo de Gata and Garrucha lies a hundred-mile stretch of arid, isolated coast, beaten by the wind in winter, beset by the sun and heat in summer, and as astoundingly beautiful as it is unknown" (*Countryside*, 49). But the beauty does not in itself provide a livelihood. Garrucha, a once prosperous mining town, stands in ruins along with other villages that relied on lead mines owned by foreign companies. As with the gold mine, the wealth here has been siphoned off, the land ruined, and emigration for work become a way of life.

If the inhabitants of the Almerían coast cannot afford to remain in place to appreciate the land's beauty, there are others, Goytisolo informs his readers, who appreciate that beauty and intend to render it profitable through the promotion of tourism. Don Ambrosio is one such entrepreneur, but his development plans are in no way intended to benefit the local people. Rather, he purchases an entire village with the expectation of evicting its long-time residents. As with the mining operations, tourist-related economic development is also not intended to promote inhabitation. And, indeed, toward the end of this short narrative, Goytisolo remarks that "deforestation and emigration transformed its old landscape into today's desert. . . . A saga of incomprehension and neglect kept it cut off from all the vital movements of change that arose in Spain" (*Countryside*, 67).

And yet, as the narrative ends, Goytisolo repeats words overheard in a bar where men speak "in a monotone as if chanting a litany" of the beauty of the region and what a desirable place it is to live (*Countryside*, 77). Such men, Goytisolo apparently believes, would make a home of the region of Almería and the countryside around Níjar, learning to work with the forces of nature, if only the forces of politics and economics would allow them.

Two Views of Nature in Early Twentieth-Century Japanese Fiction

Since I have emphasized in the preceding examples works of environmental fiction, I want to treat two Japanese fictions from 1917 and 1922, respectively, that are clearly more nature literature than environmental literature. Like Goytisolo's *Countryside*, these two texts are very autobiographical, but they are nevertheless considered in Japanese literary studies to be works of fiction, suggesting that the very definitions of nonfiction and fiction may be at least to some degree culture bound rather than universal.

The first work is a very short story called "At Kinosaki" by Shiga Naoya.[22] Not only is "At Kinosaki" of interest in its own right, but it is also important for understanding the second work, "Love of Mountains," by Uno Kōji. Uno is influenced by the style of Shiga's story but is also parodying it. What interests me in particular about Uno's story is the question of whether, or how, a work of parody can also be a nature-oriented text. Shiga's straightforward realist story, then, sets the stage for consideration of "Love of Mountains."

Elaine Gerbert, the translator of "Love of Mountains," says of Shiga's "At Kinosaki" that it was "the ultimate achievement in this 'inner state' *shishōsetsu* [first-person fiction] tradition," a tradition in the early decades of the century in which authors wrote thinly veiled autobiographical fictions, particularly in the vein of what Gerbert calls "literary naturalism."[23] Within this tradition, there are various stories, such as Shiga's, that pay close attention to the natural world with detailed descriptions, and yet the focus of critical concern has been on the "inner state" of the narrator rather than the outer state of the world depicted that gives rise to the inner meditation. Ecocriticism may need to revisit this literary trend in Japanese literature and flip the critical attention from inner to outer. Nevertheless, in so doing it would be a mistake to construct arguments on the basis of nonfiction versus fiction, or fact versus imagined detail, since they are inextricably intertwined. At the same time, useful comparison can be made between Shiga's story and American and English authors' *essays*, such as Virginia Woolf's "The Death of the Moth" and Lewis Thomas's "Death in the Open," especially since "At Kinosaki" is also a story of learning about life through observing death.

In Shiga's story, the first-person narrator has gone to the Kinosaki hot springs to convalesce because he has been hit by a commuter train and is in danger of developing potentially fatal "tuberculosis of the spine." This brush with death initiates the narrator's meditation of "lying face up under the ground in Aoyama cemetery." He first encounters a dead bee and his observations of it induce in him a sense of both loneliness and tranquility, to the point that he considers changing the point of view in a long novel he is writing from that of the murdering husband to that of the murdered wife—thus looking at life through the eyes of the dead. He also observes a drowning rat and then inadvertently kills a water lizard that he was attempting to frighten by tossing a rock at it. Here at story's end the role of chance in both his own living after his accident and the lizard's dying after its accident becomes his meditational focus, in which he concludes, "I who had not died was walking here. I knew I should be grateful. But the proper feeling of happiness refused to come. To be alive and to be dead were not two opposite extremes."[24] Real events in the natural world inspire the narrator to think about the naturalness of his own life and death with respect to the larger processes of the world that encompass all of the events narrated, including his own accident.

Uno in "Love of Mountains" shifts from the attention to minute particulars that dominates Shiga's story to sweeping vistas of the Nagano mountain region (now visually known worldwide as a result of the winter Olympics held there). Gerbert in her introduction to this story emphasizes its literary antecedents and influences as well as the kind of Japanese writing against which Uno was reacting, such as Shiga's literary naturalism. She also points to the European romantic literature that Uno read and enjoyed, as well as some of the more grotesque literature, such as the writing of the Russian author Nikolai Gogol, that he fancied. It is also useful to know that mountain climbing had just become a popular sport in Japan in the early twentieth century, having been introduced by Europeans, and that the industrial and economic success of the Meiji Restoration, Japan's victorious war against Russia, and other factors contributed to urban Japanese having more money to spend on such leisure activities as going to spas and resorts in the mountains.

Combining these literary influences, combating literary trends with which Uno disagreed, and expressing a self-critical attitude toward his own fascination with the mountains in terms of an aesthetic sublime, Uno's "'Love of Mountains' lightly parodies the romantic novelist's search for a 'dream woman,' [just as] it gently spoofs the *shishōsetsu* writers' engagement with landscape through a playful interrogation of reality that critiques the reliability of perception."[25] No doubt, much of the aesthetic and intertextual subtleties of this story are lost in translation. Nevertheless, the parodic tone of the narrator comes through in part because Uno frequently alternates the sublime with the silly, the romantic with the pragmatic, and the idealized with the vulgarized.

The story is written in the first-person form of the Japanese I-novel, with the narrator being a writer who lives in Tokyo and travels frequently by train to a particular hot-springs resort in the Japanese Alps. His reasons for doing so are apparently twofold: he loves mountains and he loves a geisha who works in the spa town. But just as he often cannot ascertain the exact name of a particular mountain he is looking at, so too he does not consummate his love for this geisha but marries another one from the same place instead. Likewise, at story's end, the narrator and two friends undertake a trip to the mountains ostensibly to provide them all with a new year's vacation. In actuality, however, one friend is evading his creditors, the other is evading his lack of a job, and the narrator is evading the contradictions of his own married life. And yet he greets the mountains from his train with genuine enthusiasm—that is, once he is able to clean the frost from his glasses so that he can actually see them.

Most fascinating about "Love of Mountains" in regard to the issue of defining nature-oriented literature is the degree to which Uno himself cannot escape becoming enthralled by the mountains that provide the setting for his story. Their descriptions frequently take over scenes, episodes, and perhaps the entire plot, even as he pokes fun at local villagers who cannot identify specific mountains and urbanites who think they know the mountains because they have learned the names of various peaks. Uno thereby accomplishes two tasks that at first may seem contradictory but in the end are complementary. He deepens the reader's appreciation for the mountains of the Nagano region and repeatedly invokes their relationship to the past through the choice of outdated place-names, implying a certain cultural and historical alternative to urban Tokyo life. The romantic depictions of the mountains, even when written tongue in cheek, are appealing and evoke strong emotions in a reader. At the same time, his self-critical, ironic, and parodic writing practices cause the reader to become more self-conscious about his or her reactions to the sublime and romantic word-pictures that Uno paints.

In the end, readers do not reject the affects of the sublime, the picturesque, and the romantic that they have felt, but they are left reflecting on why Uno's depictions evoke such reactions and wondering why they feel the way they do. Even as readers realize that the train trip out of Tokyo can provide no lasting escape from the economic and emotional problems that the characters are experiencing, readers nevertheless feel the same sense of exhilaration and emotion of freedom-to-breathe as do the characters in the final scene of the story:

> Next we tried the door on the right. It was as difficult to open as the other one had been, but as it opened there stood Yatsugatake, deep blue, yet covered from its peak down with snow that looked like granulated sugar.
> "We're here at last!" I cried. "Wonderful!" cried Ichiki.
> And the train sped on to Shinano . . . Shinano. . . .[26]

Conclusion

In providing an excursion through works from various continents and national literatures, I hope this chapter has suggested the diversity of nature-oriented fiction developing out of a wide range of literary traditions, in some cases (Uno and Shiga) nature fiction and in others (B. Traven, Anthony, Head, and Goytisolo), environmental fiction. Further, some of these works are written in the first person and need to be treated as autobiographical fictions, while others are third person and clearly fictional from start to finish, even though accurate in their depictions. Some are told in a straightforward manner without any self-consciousness, while at least Uno's is highly self-conscious and to some degree self-reflexive. With B. Traven's novels, the environmental themes are overtly political, while the political commentaries of Head and Goytisolo are much more nuanced.

Though few in number, these works clearly indicate the need for eco-critics to be more self-reflective about genre categories and assumptions about literary and critical traditions, particularly in relation to the fiction-nonfiction category problem, and they suggest the value of looking more internationally for study examples and teaching texts in order to demonstrate that environmental concerns and nature appreciation are not just American or English fads or luxury attitudes spawned by the affluence of those national economies. The majority of these works, although I did not select them for this reason, suggest the need to be more attentive to the agrarian dimension of nature-oriented literature, internationally and domestically. They also reveal the benefits of a comparative analysis that does not attempt to conflate differences but does attempt to appreciate diversity.

7

Conserving Natural and Cultural Diversity

The Prose and Poetry of Pat Mora

AVING RANGED ACROSS texts by half a dozen authors in each of the previous two chapters, I would like to focus here on the work of just one author, Pat Mora. Rather than treating prose and poetry separately, a problem I raised in regard to another multigenre talent, Wendell Berry, I will instead read Mora's prose and poetry in relation to one another. A study of Mora's writing enables me to continue emphasizing multicultural diversity while at the same time focusing on the interrelations of race, gender, and, to a lesser extent, class as they are addressed by this author.

Nepantla

Mora writes in *Nepantla: Essays from the Land in the Middle* that the United States "has both the opportunity and responsibility to demonstrate to this world of emerging representative governments that nurturing variety is central, not marginal to democracy." The use of the word *nurturing* seems in no way fortuitous because she recognizes natural and cultural diversity as integral threads of the life-web labeled humanity, which is one thread of a much larger life-web labeled earth. As a result, she calls for emphasizing cultural conservation with the same enthusiasm with which some movements labor for "historical preservation" and "natural conservation."[1] This recognition of the interrelationship of natural and cultural diversity and emphasis on the nurturing practice of cultural conservation are found throughout her poetry in *Chants* (1985), *Borders* (1986), and *Communion* (1991), as well as in *Nepantla* (1993), of which she says, "The essays are about my encounters with my world."[2]

Pat Mora is a Chicana who began writing around 1980; she has won awards for both her adult poetry and her children's books. Born in 1942, she grew up, raised three children, and worked in El Paso, Texas, before moving in 1989 to Cincinnati, Ohio. She has taught at the high school, community college, and university levels and served in various administrative capacities at the University of Texas at El Paso from 1981 to 1989. Of those years, Mora remarks that "I was fortunate to work on issues of outreach to women and to the local Mexican American population. . . . For those of use committed to extending the opportunities of the university to our community, it was a frustrating but exciting time to participate in that gradual transformation" (*Nepantla*, 4). *Nepantla* is a Nahuatlan word meaning "place in the middle," and Mora makes it clear that she recognizes herself as having come from such a physical place, the Tex-Mex borderlands, and also from such a psychic and cultural place, a Mexican American. Mora seeks in her writing, as well as her life, to conserve the generative tension of the dynamic plurality that is borderland existence. "I am in the middle of my life, and well know," she declares, "not only the pain but also the advantage of observing both sides, albeit with my biases, of moving through two, and, in fact, multiple spaces" (*Nepantla*, 6).

One danger of a segment of the natural conservation movement is its focus on the recovery or preservation of a small section of a larger ecoregion. Tourists can then visit that parcel and experience nostalgia for the rest that was allowed to be destroyed. The same danger is evident in urban historical preservation, particularly in historically ethnic areas being crowded out by skyscrapers and highways. In both cases too much is destroyed for what remains to have any integrity or self-sustaining viability, while their continued existence depends on the economies of tourism. As Tey Diana Rebolledo and Eliana S. Rivero observe in the introduction to *Infinite*

Divisions, "since many freeways in large urban areas were built in the barrios, the freeways often run along Chicano/a residential areas. In addition, they may have also destroyed much of the older sections of the barrios, thus destroying traditions."[3] In such urban renewals-removals, one often sees that the buildings preserved as representative of a particular cultural heritage are ones that are of interest to tourists and tourism promoters rather than to inheritors of the culture.

Mora is well aware of this danger of token wilderness preserves and Potemkin-village *mercados* and warns against any idea of recovering the Mexican-American heritage as curio or artifact: "a true ethic of conservation includes a commitment to a group's decisions, its development and self-direction" (*Nepantla*, 30). Just as the ecology movement warns that biological diversity is crucial to biotic survival, Mora warns that cultural diversity is crucial to human survival, since it actually helps to maintain general diversity: "Pride in cultural identity, in the set of learned and shared language, symbols, and meanings, needs to be fostered not because of nostalgia or romanticism, but because it is essential to our survival. The oppressive homogenization of humanity in our era of international technological and economic interdependence endangers us all" (*Nepantla*, 36). Human diversity can be maintained only by means of the cultural conservation being practiced by the marginalized and subordinated groups who defend and recover their heritages in order to generate their futures. Many of the essays in *Nepantla* focus precisely on the issue of cultural conservation even as they embody such a practice. Mora rightly emphasizes the conservation of Chicano/a and Latino/a cultures but does not stop there. She also addresses the need to respect and be aware of other cultures internationally, and the differing degrees and kinds of effects that dominant U.S. culture has on subordinated cultures within the United States and worldwide.

Chants

Mora's first book of poetry, *Chants*, demonstrates some of the ways by which the recovery-of-heritage dimension of cultural conservation may be realized. Part of such recovery requires retelling the old tales and untelling the old interpretations by people outside one's own culture. For southwestern Latinos, one such untelling involves embracing the Indian heritage of the mestizo/a in opposition to the imposition of the "Spanish" heritage as the primary cultural determinant. Mora opens *Chants* with the poem "Bribe," in which she retells the story of the "long ago" practices of "Indian women" to seek inspiration for their weaving arts from "the Land." She then claims those traditional practices as part of her own heritage through ritual imitation:

> Like the Indians
> I ask the Land to smile on me, to croon
> softly, to help me catch her music with words.
>
> (7)

But it is not only an imitative relationship of artistic practices, weaving and writing, that she claims; she claims a parallel relationship with the personified "Land" through identifying both the women weavers' practice and hers as being efforts to represent the earth's creativity through artistry. She thus claims and images an inheritance and continuation of a human cultural relationship with the rest of the world in which respect, honor, and humility define human-nonhuman interaction.

Another part of such recovery of heritage consists of reaffirming the situatedness of culture, the relationship of values, beliefs, practices, and character to place. As Mora notes, "Many Mexican American women from the Southwest are desert women" (*Nepantla*, 53). This is not merely anecdotal, but a delineation of identity and a source of pride as well as a claim about historical residence.[4] Mora, for example, opens "Desert Women" in *Borders* with the lines, "Desert women know / about survival" (80). Survival must be understood not as a minimal condition of existence but as an achievement against odds and concerted efforts, not by nature but by other cultures. Survival is thus not some passive form of endurance, but an ongoing practice of resistance and self-education. "Mi Madre," the third poem in *Chants*, celebrates "the desert" that is a "strong mother" (9), because the skills necessary not only to survive but also to flourish there are part of what defines the culture Mora celebrates. The use of Spanish here differentiates her own cultural identity of Mexican heritage from the precontact heritage of desert Native Americans. She uses turquoise to define a commonality without conflating the difference between the native and immigrant cultures sharing and struggling over the same terrain through generations of inhabitation.[5]

Several poems that follow "Mi Madre" elaborate the desert's "strong mother" role. For example, "Lesson 1" and "Lesson 2" emphasize the desert's power to reassure and emotionally heal the speaker. "Lesson 1" consists of three stanzas, with the first focusing on the desert's return to balance after a thunderstorm, the second depicting the speaker's seeking the desert when "shaken, powerless" with "sadness," and the third stanza imparting the lesson. Knowing she is the *"Mi'ja"* of the desert mother, the speaker feels free to express her emotions while not surrendering to disempowerment and learns to "cry away the storm, then listen, listen" (*Chants*, 10). "Lesson 1" begins with rain pounding the land, and the lesson of the poem derives from the desert's rapid recovery from this downpour. "Lesson 2," on the next page, also begins with water, but this time it is rising from the river through the evaporative power of sunlight. Here the desert again speaks a lesson about overcoming sadness, but Mora has added an interesting dimension. In the first lesson, she emphasizes imitating the solidity of the land to weather sadness and the life storms causing the emotion. In the second lesson, she emphasizes imitating the fluidity of the water, rising above her river of troubles, strengthened, transformed, and active. Mora moves from the desert mother's instruction to "listen" to her challenge to "dance," recognizing that both solidity and fluidity are processes of a single dynamic system.

A third part of recovery of heritage, particularly for building a future, is to critique the oppressive and exclusionary elements of one's heritage: "to question and ponder what values and customs we wish to incorporate into our lives, to continue our individual and our collective evolution" (*Nepantla*, 53). In *Nepantla* she critiques, for example, dominant Mexican culture's suppression of indigenous peoples and languages (28–29, 40). In *Chants* she critiques the sexual oppression of women enforced through the virgin-whore dichotomy by depicting the fear of two brides-to-be in

"Discovered" and "Dream." In the first poem, the speaker fears that she will be denied a dignified wedding and ostracized by the community if her loss of virginity is discovered; and also, perhaps, that "her lover" will see her as a "whore," that is, a sexually active being, rather than as a wife, a supposedly sexually passive being. This speaker remains firmly subjected to cultural oppression. In the second poem, the bride-to-be has the same wedding-day fear of public censure but relishes the sexual awakening she enjoyed the night before and speaks to her groom as someone who understands. Here the speaker breaks free ideologically of cultural restrictions and "Mexican superstitions" and asserts a relationship of equality with her lover. Interestingly, this speaker seeks assistance from the flowers for her hair—a symbol of nonhuman, uncultured nature—to keep her secret through the wedding (13, 15).

Mora returns to this topic of gender oppression and sexual inequality in *Borders* with "Diagnosis," which treats a Chicana's anguish over being informed that she needs a hysterectomy because "She fears her man / will call her empty" (25). She also addresses it in *Communion* with "Perfume," in which a man kills his wife in a jealous rage; and with "Emergency Room," in which the woman declares that her jealous husband "clothed me in bruises" (45). As with "Discovered" and "Dream," the woman in the second poem is stronger, is a survivor who has learned something about her culture and her oppressed condition.

Mora more forcefully repudiates the sexual oppression in her heritage, however, through diverse affirmative images of empowered women in *Chants*. The *bruja* of "Bruja: Witch" is depicted positively, as a seeker of freedom and a champion of other women, for exacting retribution for a male's infidelity and double standard:

My work is done. A frightened husband
will run to the wife who paid me
three American dollars

    . . . . . .

    Beneath white
    stars, I dance.
       (16–17)[6]

The mother in "Plot" reveals a deep determination and lasting anger in planning to protect her daughter from the same degradation she experienced on her wedding night when her husband discovered she was not a virgin:

> I'll arm my daughter with a ring
>
> .   .   .   .
>
> . . . She must use the ring.
> I don't want to split his throat.
>
> (20)

"Curandera" emphasizes the healer's strength drawn from her integration with the environment, a particular kind of cultural empowerment. This female tradition is explicitly linked to a dynamic relationship with the mysteries of the natural world that empower this woman:

> The *curandera*
> and house have aged together to the rhythm
> of the desert
>
> (26)

And, in "Aztec Princess," the young woman thwarts her mother's traditional efforts to enforce her domestication through choosing the "rich earth" and "moonlight" over "the home for happiness" (28).[7] Such empowered women appear throughout *Borders* and *Communion* as well.

Borders

While *Chants* may focus more on recovering and affirming heritage, the early poems of *Borders* address the difficulty of maintaining and legitimating one's heritage and communicating it across the borders existing in the United States. The title poem, with its epigraph from the feminist psychologist Carol Gilligan, emphasizes the gender border; but Mora also ties it to the divisions created by language. Communication is always a translation of "like but unlike," in which the differences cannot be effaced in order to understand the other's desires, needs, culture, heritage (10). When one culture claims universality and dominates the lands and the lives of another culture, translation breaks down.[8] Mora has several poems emphasizing such breakdowns, like "Unnatural Speech" and "Bilingual Christmas." In "Echoes" Mora recognizes that language alone is not the culprit; class divisions serve as well. The speaker of "Echoes" is a guest of a white woman with a Mexican maid; feeling kinship the speaker tries to bridge the chasm of class with Spanish, but it is insufficient. Then she hopes "to hear this earth / roar" in retribution for the maid's oppression, but realizes the responsibility lies with her. "Perhaps," she thinks, "my desert land waits / to hear me roar" (*Borders*, 23–24). Only through voicing the common ground of their heritage, not just speaking a recognizable language, can the speaker overcome the class division that places her on the side of the oppressor against others of her own heritage.

Perhaps because of her concern over class divisions, Mora places the eulogy "Tomás Rivera" after the title poem in *Borders*. Rivera represents someone who rose from the fields to a position of prominence that carried class status, yet his hands remained always outstretched to others and a reminder of his own history. Significantly, Mora emphasizes the initial difficulty Rivera had in developing his own literacy:

> Those hands clenched in the dark
> at *víboras, víboras* hissing
> > we don't want you, you people have lice
> as the school door slammed
> but Tomás learned
> and his hands began to hold books
> gently, with affection. . . .

Beyond personal literacy, Rivera advanced Chicano/a cultural literacy:

> He searched
> for stories about his people and finally
> gave their words sound, wrote the books

he didn't have, we didn't have.

(13)

He is therefore a model to emulate for his own achievements and his bridging of class divisions, and also for his efforts to encourage others with similar experiences to build a better life by revaluing their shared roots and place in the world rather than leaving them behind.

Remaining connected with the people rooted in the land is what provides strength, as Mora testifies in "University Avenue." These first generation Chicano/a university students, a population with whom Mora had extensive contact in her university years as student, teacher, and administrator, know that "Our people prepared us / with gifts from the land" (*Borders*, 19). While Mora addresses many subjects in *Borders*, her poems return again and again to the relationship of people and land, particularly toward the end of the volume.

In "Miss Doc at Eighty," Mora speaks in the persona of an octogenarian who was an herbalist, or *curandera*. Her morning ritual of working in the garden reminds her of and connects her with the restorative, healing qualities of plant life:

> . . . sharp smell
> of plants on my fingertips
> where the facts once were
> so my patients said.
>
> (48)

Later, in "Secrets," Mora elaborates on the importance for cultural conservation of healers such as Miss Doc. In the first two stanzas she describes "Felipe, the Tarahumara, guiding / my great grandfather." In the third stanza Mora expresses her desire

> for such a guide, a woman,
> teaching me the art of bending
> close to the land,
> silent, listening, feeling the path.
>
> (86)

In "Mi Tierra," the speaker addresses the land directly, indicating that *Mi Tierra* in its generative essence is also *Mi Madre*. Through going bare-foot the speaker can feel the earth move: "through me, but in / me, in me" (*Borders*, 79). The speaker is part of an entity and part of a system, with the relationship depicted as participatory and processive.

While "Mi Tierra" emphasizes an individual woman-earth relationship, "Desert Women" extends that relationship to a community. Here the women become like the desert because they are a part of it, knowledgeable "about survival" in extremes, with "deep roots . . . to hide pain and loss by silence." These lines remind the reader of "Lesson 1" in *Chants* about learn-ing the silent listening strength of the desert. The conclusion of "Desert Women," however, reminds the reader of "Lesson 2." In that poem the speaker accepted the desert's challenge to "dance," while in "Desert Women" she exclaims: "Don't be deceived. When we bloom, we stun" (*Bor-ders*, 80). In "Success," the final poem of *Borders*, the speaker, both as poet and cultural activist, wishes "To be of use / like *hierbabuena*" (88), healer from the desert. But Mora knows that through writing this poem, as with all of her others, she is already useful to those who share her heritage and to those who seek to understand and respect another's heritage. Poetry serves as both a healing agent and as a repository of the knowledge neces-sary to know how to "steep leaves patiently" (88). In *Nepantla*, Mora defines the sense of responsibility behind her writing: "I write because I believe that Mexican Americans need to take their rightful place in U.S. literature. We need to be published and to be studied in schools and colleges so that the stories and ideas of our people won't quietly disappear. . . . deep inside I always wish I wrote better, that I could bring more honor and attention to those like the *abuelitas*, grandmothers, I write about" (139).

Communion

Communion is filled with the stories of such people and ideas that must be preserved, and repeatedly these are tied to the land. "Gentle Commu-nion" opens the first section, "Old Bones," with a tribute to "Mamande," who the speaker says "came with me from the desert" (11). As a symbol of resistance to assimilation, she remains, even though "long-dead," a source of reassurance and comfort. This comfort is imaged as peeled grapes, and the pleasure of their taste depends upon the same patience required to steep leaves for tea. The desert that opens the poem is linked with a fruit, and Mamande is linked with both, indicating the nourishment to be derived from a "natured culture," one generated and maintained in the place from which it arose. The heritage Mamande represents is one not so much built as grown and nurtured through generations, a heritage that survives and may flourish despite changes, difficulties, and the barriers of languages.

Similarly, the three poems "Divisadero Street, San Francisco," "Desert Pilgrimage," and "Don Jaime" link the preservation of traditional knowledge embodied in the stories and lives of *abuelas* and *abuelos* with maintaining their rootedness in the land. The woman of "Divisadero Street" lives in the city but reminds the speaker that we are "*Lost without dirt,*" without connection to the soil that is the source of the wisdom and healing power handed down from one *curandera* to another. This woman seems very much a younger version of Miss Doc found in *Borders*. Mora notes that her gardening affects the people around her. As the flowers reflect the sunshine, ". . . light dazzles / until we too shimmer" (*Communion*, 17). In the final stanza Mora equates growing these urban flowers with cultivating the next generation.

"Desert Pilgrimage" reinforces the generational importance of *curanderas* as the first-person narrator recounts all of the arts she practices that have been learned from a woman like the one on Divisadero Street. Such a woman's voice remains with her, guiding her in the way that she would want to be guided, as expressed in "Secrets" in *Borders*. The power of herbal healing is also celebrated in "Don Jaime," which immediately follows "Desert Pilgrimage." Here, a male is depicted as *curandero*, perhaps like "Felipe, the Tarahumara," but Mora does not nostalgically memorialize a lost art; she celebrates its continuation as "the lame healer and his grandson" gather "branches and bark, / with *botón de oro*" (*Communion*, 21). Other poems in the volume also pay tribute to such individuals, with "Strong Women," the penultimate poem, providing a generalized celebration and invocation for ongoing learning. This connection to the land that Mora believes must be maintained even in the cities, as indicated in "Divisadero Street," can be understood in terms of a strategy for survival against assimilation and disenfranchisement and a basis for reestablishing and preserving community. As Rebolledo and Rivero note, "the city, shining land of opportunity, signals only struggle and often destruction for [Chicanas], their families, and their culture."⁹

Having introduced *curanderas* in *Chants*, Mora returns to them in *Communion*, as in the poems previously mentioned, and clarifies their importance in *Nepantla* in the essay, "Poet as *Curandera*." The traditional healer is a part of Mora's heritage, providing her with a name that defines her own artistry as an act of healing through "witnessing" her culture. In that first poem of *Chants*, "Bribe," she identifies her writing with the land and with the most ancient elements of her heritage, embodying what she has come to understand by the time of writing "Poet as *Curandera*": "learned wisdom, ritual, solutions springing from the land. All are essential to *curanderas*, who listen to voices from the past and the present, who evolve from their culture" (*Nepantla*, 126). The people and the land interweave in Mora's conceptions of cultural conservation and the word-healing of poetry. In "The Border: A Glare of Truth," Mora defines the origin of her being as poet-curandera:

> When I lived on the border, I had the privilege accorded to a small percentage of our citizens. I daily saw the native land of my grandparents. I grew up in the Chihuahua desert, as did they, only we grew up on different sides of the Rio Grande. That desert—its firmness, resilience, and fierceness, its whispered chants and tempestuous dance, its wisdom and majesty—shaped us as geography always shapes it inhabitants. The desert persists in me, both inspiring and compelling me to sing about her and her people, their roots and blooms and thorns. (*Nepantla*, 13)

Conclusion

With that view of both sides of the river, Pat Mora opposes any national monoculture because she knows that place is not determined by national boundaries. A culture can and must cross political boundaries to remain true to its own place of existence. The Chihuahua desert and the lifestyles of the peoples who have lived there have mutually evolved over time. They were divided in an instant by a border, but their roots remain a tapestry woven beneath the surface, crisscrossing—as the people continue to do today—the Rio Grande. She opposes any national monoculture in the United States and elsewhere, second of all, because there exists an implicit ecological sensibility of multiculturality (the existence of multiple cultures existing within geopolitical boundaries) within her concerns for the cultural conservation of Latina heritage. Even her decision to use "Latina" and "Latino" more frequently than other labels reflects her sense of this multiculturality, because it seeks to unite "Puerto Ricans, Cubans, Mexican Americans, Central and South Americans," whom she defines as interrelated, but certainly not identical (*Nepantla*, 7).

In labeling Mora's sensibility an ecological multiculturality, I conceptualize *ecological* here in two related ways. One, I see it in terms of ecosystem as metonym and metaphor for a set of necessary human-land relationships. As Mora contends, "because humans are part of this natural world, we need to ensure that our unique expressions on this earth, whether art forms or languages, be a greater part of our national and international conservation effort" (*Nepantla*, 25). Only if a person understands and accepts what a *curandera* does will that person then appreciate the plants upon which she relies for her power. Two, I see it in terms of environment as a component of cultural heritage and continuity. As Rebolledo notes, for "Hispanic writers . . . the southwestern landscape . . . meant a long tradition of families not only tied to the land but nourished by it. . . . Recent writers have looked to the rich and varied heritage of the past to find a regenerative and transforming sense of identity in the present and for the future.[10]

The very concept of *la mestiza* that Mora raises, referring in *Nepantla* to the work of Gloria Anzaldúa—as a cultural melding occurring in a specific region that need not efface difference between peoples, but that recognizes multiplicity within the individual, the community, and the communities of the region—also forms a component of an ecological multiculturality. When Mora refers to herself as a "Texican," that too is a manifestation of this multiculturality characteristic of borderlands and the dynamic tension that resonates across the desert. It also recognizes, however, that Texas is not California, and the experiences of cultural conflict and preservation remain varied. As Mora emphasizes, her desire is "to be one of the many voices and not *the* voice, for we know the grand variety in our community, *and we want others to recognize this human wealth*" (*Nepantla*, 45).

Mora's voice is one of many speaking out against what she labels "the safety of uniformity," the antiecological pursuit of a national monoculture that would diminish the world by diminishing its biological and cultural diversity. As Mora and others warn, these two are not unrelated: "the inheritors of culture [are] those who remain in contact with nature and tradition," in all their diversity (*Nepantla*, 121). She encourages a cultural conservation through the cultivation of the rich roots of her Chicana heritage. She also reminds us that other voices are speaking out for the necessary preservation of cultural diversity. To all of these heretofore marginalized and suppressed voices we must also attend.

8

Ishimure Michiko

The Price of Pollution and the Presence of the Past

*I*SHIMURE MICHIKO is the most famous living environmental writer in Japan, frequently referred to as her country's equivalent of Rachel Carson, the American author of *Silent Spring*. Like Carson, Ishimure set her formidable literary talents to work exposing environmental pollution, specifically methyl mercury poisoning. In part through Ishimure's efforts as both an activist and an author, Minamata disease has become well known around the world. Even though two of her full-length prose works have been translated into English—*Paradise in the Sea of Sorrow: Our Minamata Disease (Kugai jōdo. Waga Minamata-byō*, 1972) and *Story of the Sea of Camellias (Tsubaki no umi no ki*, 1976)—she remains relatively unknown in the United States in literary circles.[1]

Several factors may account for this phenomenon. One, the translations, although in English, were published in Japan only in hardcover and not aggressively marketed in the United States. Two, the translation of *Kugai jōdo*, *Paradise in the Sea of Sorrow*, was not published until 1990, decades after the first cases of Minamata disease were reported in the mid-1950s and nearly twenty years after the first governmental determination of the Chisso Corporation's pollution as the cause of the disease. Three, most American ecocritics in the late 1980s and early 1990s were paying little attention to works written in languages other than English, even when translated. Four, *Paradise in the Sea of Sorrow* does not fulfill the literary expectations of those suffering from a nonfiction prejudice. As the translator, Livia Monnet, notes, "part imaginative biography, part mystical confession, part investigative journalism and part historical document, *Kugai jōdo* transcends established literary genres to create a new form."[2] As such, it does not fit the common definitions of nature writing, although it contains many of the features that are included in those definitions. Rather, *Paradise in the Sea of Sorrow* is clearly a work of environmental literature that draws heavily on nonfictional and historical elements as well as direct observation and scientific details, but it does not limit itself to the narrow requirements of a nonfiction genre. It is a text that would benefit greatly from evaluation through the analytical lens of the environmental-justice movement.[3]

The extent of the neglect of Ishimure's *Paradise in the Sea of Sorrow* in the United States is surprising, considering what a tremendous example it is of literary writing by an activist that is directly tied to changes in social awareness and environmental legislation. I learned of the existence of this translation of *Kugai jōdo* only because I went to Japan in 1997. The neglect of *Story of the Sea of Camellias* is, however, not so surprising. Written as an autobiographical memoir, it depicts the life of a poor village in the Minamata area in the 1930s, when Ishimure was a young child (she was born in 1927). Although a work of nature literature, *Story* emphasizes human community rather than the kind of solitary exploration of wilderness that is preferred in many studies of nature writing. It is full of philosophical and religious meditations about the nature and causes of human suffering in the world and the beauty of the natural world in which such suffering takes place. *Story* also depicts social changes produced by technological developments and the way socially determined gender roles are intertwined with these changes. As a result, *Story* does not have the political force of the first book or its tremendously moving first-person testimonials of the Minamata disease victims. Nevertheless, *Story of the Sea of Camellias* is a beautiful work worthy of attention.

Following the translation dates of the two books, 1983 for *Story* and 1990 for *Paradise*, and given that a move from nature prose to environmental prose would seem more likely (as in the case of Marcia Bonta's two books that I discussed earlier), most American readers would probably be surprised to learn that *Paradise* was written and published first. Ishimure has stated that she turned to a memoir of her childhood as a literary and emotional break from her multiyear, multivolume writing and activism on behalf of the Minamata disease victims (Monnet, preface to *Story*, iv). I have found that one's interpretation of *Story* differs depending on when it is read in relation to *Paradise*. If the two books are read in the order of the publication of the translations, many minor themes, events, and even descriptions in *Story*, such as the arrival of the Chisso Corporation and the building of a road through the town, take on a much more sinister hue than if one has no knowledge of *Paradise*. For that reason and because of its prominence of place in modern Japanese society, I will treat *Paradise* first and in greater detail than *Story*.

Paradise in the Sea of Sorrow: Our Minamata Disease

Like Carson's *Silent Spring* in the United States, *Paradise in the Sea of Sorrow* had an immediate and tremendous impact on public awareness in Japan. Unlike Carson's book, it was also recognized as a literary masterpiece. Monnet notes:

> It was awarded the Kumamoto Nichinichi Cultural Prize (1969), the Oya Sōichi Prize for Non-fictional literature (1970) and the Republic of the Philippines' Ramon Magsaysay Prize (1973). Ishimure turned down the first two awards, saying that she could not accept any honors as long as the demands of the Minamata Disease victims were ignored. The book's impact was enormous: noted writers and critics referred to it as the most important literary event since the end of World War II; many readers gave up their studies or professions and went to Minamata to help the patients in their struggle for survival. Ishimure's book has also given great impetus to various regional conservationist move-

ments . . . and is now part of the literature curriculum in senior high schools. (Preface to *Paradise*, iv)

Paradise focuses mainly on three separate years in the long struggle to determine the causes of Minamata disease, to stop the pollution known to be the cause, and to gain reparations for the victims: 1959, the year of a political demonstration and riot by fishermen; 1965, the year Ishimure interviews various disease victims; and 1968, the year the government officially identifies the cause of the disease. The story does not, however, unfold in a linear time line; Ishimure weaves together memories and events from different times to deepen the emotive effect on the reader. She begins in the year 1965, then moves back to 1959, and concludes with 1968, with flashbacks of various duration added throughout.

Chapter 1, "Sea of Camellias," for instance, opens with a timeless kind of description of a small fishing village, with Ishimure using the vague phrase "in those days" to signal some past age perhaps more mythic than historical in its significance. Two pages of geographical description of the village of Yudō and its location end with a matter-of-fact paragraph: "The area with the most numerous cases of Minamata disease extends from Izumi City in Kagoshima Prefecture to Minamata in Kumamoto Prefecture, including the villages lining National Highway No. 3: Modō, Fukuro, Yudō, Detsuki, Tsukinoura. The Minamata plant of the Chisso Corporation discharges its wastewater into Hyakken harbor" (4). The journalistic style of the contemporary world of industrial development and discharged wastewater clashes with the poetic, rhythmic, and almost mythic, language used to describe the village of Yudō.

Having set the scene and introduced the antagonist, Ishimure turns to a story about one of the village children with congenital Minamata disease, Yamanaka Kuhei, based on a visit she made to this village in 1963. Although blind and with one arm half-paralyzed, the boy attempts to play baseball by himself, and Ishimure watches him silently before calling out his name. The scene is significant not only for the reader's introduction to the effects of Minamata disease on those who live with it—rather than, or before, dying from it—but also for Ishimure's establishing the degree to which she has come to identify with both the victims and the natural environment in which they live and in which their fishermen families have always labored:

> Intent on his pantomime of a baseball player, which he performed like an esoteric ritual, Kuhei was the only dynamic element in that still scenery. He moved about in a sheath of light. Still standing motionless on the same spot, my breath merged with the breath of the grass, the trees and the stones. I was one with the boy's movements. . . .
>
> This was my first encounter with Yamanaka Kuhei. He was roughly the same age as my son. (9)

Ishimure, through introducing her own son and the connection that she as a mother would feel for Kuhei, draws the reader into close proximity with the Minamata disease victims. Using Kuhei and his family as a pivot, Ishimure discusses the treatment of disease victims by the public health department, the sincerity of village leaders, and the utter ineffectiveness of the medical profession and the government in addressing the crisis. But always she returns to Kuhei, an individual who embodies the disease itself and is a symbol of the suffering industrial pollution imposes on the innocent.

Ishimure follows this highly emotional first section of chapter 1 with "Dr. Hosokawa's Report," a dry, clinical analysis of the outbreak of Minamata disease filed with the Ministry of Health and Welfare on 29 August 1956. This report is followed by Ishimure's own dry, clinical-style description of the first recorded Minamata disease patient, with excerpts from an interview with Dr. Hosokawa. Kuhei's mother's voice then replaces this clinical objectivity in Ishimure's telling of her conversations with the mother about the death of Kuhei's older sister, Satsuki, from Minamata disease. The mother relates both the strength and beauty of her daughter fishing in the Shiranui Sea and the ugliness and terror of her daughter's death from the disease. This part, too, is in turn alternated with another clinical description of the disease, which is taken from an academic article in the *Journal of the Kumamoto Medical Society* that indicates that as early as 1957 medical practitioners suspected industrial pollution as the cause of the disease. Despite this, another eleven years would go by before the government was

willing to draw the same conclusion and force the company to take action—
even though the first Minamata disease patients were admitted to the company's own hospital.

Chapter 1 closes with a section titled "Funeral Banners," which focuses on the death of one of the oldest men of Tsukinoura village, Old Sensuke. The slow decimation of his body by methyl mercury poisoning affected everyone around him: "As they witnessed Sensuke's gradual physical and mental degradation, the villagers began to feel that something in their lives, too, was slowly coming apart" (40). Sensuke and other fishermen embody an ancient way of life practiced in this area, subsistence fishing and farming, that is being eaten away. Minamata disease becomes a synecdoche not just for all forms of industrial pollution, but for industry as pollution.

In chapter 2, "The Shiranui Fishermen," Ishimure provides a little more information about the way of life that the Minamata disease victims represent. In particular, she relates a history of Minamata in which she includes several long quotations from various historical records. One of these, from the eighteenth century, claims that "remote, backward country places are often repositories of many a valuable treasure of the past, which should not be allowed to perish" (106). Here Ishimure reflects her own attitude toward the fishermen of the Shiranui Sea through a voice long dead. As the fishermen die off, the traditional life dies with them along with a series of values and relationships with the natural world that are not replaced by modernization. Thus, for Ishimure, Minamata disease is both a tragedy in itself and a symptom of a larger tragedy, which is modern Japan's loss of traditional ties with the natural world.

By shuttling back and forth temporally, Ishimure shows the ways in which events are related linearly, in time, and also philosophically and commercially across different periods. As the Chisso Corporation becomes a dominant factor in the money economy of the Minamata region, researchers and villagers avoid trying to lay responsibility at its factory doors. Industrial production is seen as the future, while subsistence fishing is seen as a vestige of a past to be forgotten. Hence, as Ishimure shows, many residents of the Minamata area also try to forget about the Minamata disease victims, viewing them as anachronisms. In contrast to this sentiment, Ishimure portrays the disease victims as valiant, heroic people who worked hard at fishing and work hard at overcoming their illness. They are also portrayed as holding timeless values that cannot afford to be forgotten if the world in which both fishermen and factory workers live is to be saved from developmental destruction.

Chapter 2, however, primarily focuses on the failure of local and national governments to respond adequately and rapidly to the Minamata disease crisis. It also depicts the callous disregard of the Chisso Corporation for the residents of the area around the factory discharging methyl mercury and other pollutants. This chapter opens with a description of a demonstration held on 2 November 1959 by the region's fishermen to greet a delegation from the Diet, Japan's national legislature. This demonstration comes six years after the fishermen first became concerned about strange events in Minamata Bay and three years after all fishing in the bay had ended due to the outbreak of the disease. Beginning peacefully enough, the fishermen's demonstration spontaneously turns into a riot against the Chisso factory, which Ishimure describes in great detail.

Chapters 3 and 4, "What Yuki Had to Say" and "Fish of Heaven," in contrast, reduce attention to the political dimensions of the Minamata disease and once more look closely at two of its victims. In these chapters, readers find the most developed descriptions of the relationship of the fishing communities with the natural world and their sense of the human–rest-of-nature bonds that guide their working and living behaviors. Ishimure tells of visiting Sakagami Yuki in May 1959, a few months before the fishermen's demonstration and riot. The latter part of Yuki's chapter is a section titled "I Want to Be Human Again," in which readers hear Yuki's story of the life she led on the sea with her husband, her contracting the disease, her struggle against being destroyed by it even when confined to the hospital, and, finally, her desire to be reincarnated as a human being again: "I've spent all my life on the sea. Perhaps I'll come back as a fisherwoman. My heart is overflowing with love, so I'll surely come back as a human being" (174). Chapter 4 comes forward in time to 1964 and shares the story of an extremely poor fishing family in which several members have been afflicted with Minamata disease. While not as emotionally moving as Yuki's story, the story of the Ezuno family reveals even more about the simple values and virtues of the people whose livelihood came from the Shiranui Sea, in particular their mixture of animistic and Buddhist religious beliefs.

Before bringing the story up-to-date in the year of 1968, Ishimure includes two other chapters, "Fish on Land" and "Tonton Village." The former treats mainly the ways in which other people in the region reacted to the onset of Minamata disease, in many cases blaming the fishermen for their problems and defending the corporation. But in this chapter Ishimure also provides some of her most overt philosophical statements, such as the following two comments: "In our modern world of progress and civilization we have long forgotten what it means to live in keeping with the laws of nature; we have become deaf and blind to the vibrant soul of all things surrounding us" (236) and "Minamata Disease is a fundamental issue in our time, a finger pointed accusingly, as it were, at the philosophy and morals sustaining modern civilization. In the Minamata fishermen, the first victims of the mercury poisoning, we can still behold the original shape of humanity. They show us how our ancestors lived ages ago, in unbroken communion with nature" (239).

In the "Tonton Village" chapter, having earlier established how the disease victims could be seen as human sacrifices before the god of progress for the benefit of the rest of the nation, Ishimure depicts the exploitation and discrimination against the fishermen as a form of internal colonization. She then links that depiction with the history of Japanese colonization of Korea. There, too, Chisso Corporation set up a factory in which an entire fishing and farming village was destroyed for the benefit of the company. Not only did this village provide a site for the factory, but it also provided laborers who were now available for factory work because they had lost their traditional livelihood. Thus, the international dimensions of capitalism are brought out, increasing the environmental-justice critique that Ishimure has been developing all along. Ishimure also links Minamata disease with other major incidents of industrial pollution of rural Japanese areas, such as "the Ashio Copper Mine Pollution Incident, the first instance in modern Japanese history of the systematic annihilation of a traditional farming community by private capital" (295). In fact, near the book's end, Ishimure depicts the Minamata disease victims as reincarnations of earlier peasant victims of industrial pollution.

Paradise in the Sea of Sorrow ends with the year 1968, in which the government declares Chisso Corporation responsible and the company president drives around to apologize to families with Minamata disease victims.

What is perhaps most distressing about this chapter is not the belated and limited acceptance of responsibility on the part of the company executives, but the degree to which other people in Minamata continued to resist the idea that the company was at fault because they feared losing their factory jobs and the local taxes paid by the corporation. Clearly, part of the explanation for this phenomenon is the degree to which traditional fishermen and farmers had come by the late 1960s to be seen as some kind of dispensable anachronism, rather than as vital bearers of a cultural heritage of more intimate relationships with the natural world.

In part, this view is based on an arrogant belief in the linear progress of industrialization and the mistaken assumption that human commerce and production are not dependent on the rest of nature. It also indicates the rapidity with which people come to believe that the way they live now is the only possible way to live, no matter how apparently destructive to the world around them, including their fellow citizens. Ishimure's poignant and angry depiction of Minamata disease and the destruction of the traditional fishing economy of the western coast of southern Kyūshū reminds me of poems in Simon Ortiz's *Woven Stone* about native land being turned into a "national sacrifice area," supposedly for the benefit of the rest of the United States.[4] *Paradise* shows that environmental justice is not just a racial issue, but rather that internal colonization and the oppression of economically distinct groups are necessary results of capitalist development, and that such colonization and oppression always entail environmental as well as cultural destruction.

Story of the Sea of Camellias

Ishimure has indicated that writing *Story of the Sea of Camellias* was supposed to provide some relief from her intense focus on Minamata disease and the struggles of its victims for just treatment by the Chisso Corporation and by the local and national governments. But it is not an escapist or nostalgic reminiscence even so. Although it does clearly contain strong moments of nostalgia, these are undercut by Ishimure's Buddhist-based belief that this life consists of suffering and that the main wheel of that suffering today is capitalism. It also, however, indicates through its vivid and extended descriptions of the natural world that there was great joy, value, and ethical conduct, even in the midst of extreme poverty, in the traditional ways of life of the farming and fishing communities that have been almost completely extinguished by Japanese modernization, particularly after World War II.

Two elements that appear briefly in *Paradise* are major intertwined thematic features of *Story*: narrative identification with others and reincarnation. Ishimure relates *Story* as a first-person autobiography told by the child Michiko, in the tradition of poetic diaries that date back to the Japanese medieval period (Monnet, preface to *Story*, vi). The time frame is limited to the years before she turns seven, the age when a Japanese child is considered to have become fully human.[5] Thus, it is a period in which Michiko stands in a liminal state between the natural and cultural worlds, and we find her frequently rejecting the confusing world of adults and their culture for the natural world and its creatures, both mythical and material. In this liminal state, Michiko frequently identifies so closely with plants and animals that she imagines herself transforming into them, such as a white fox cub in chapter 7 and a dragon's gem plant in chapter 8.

This intense degree of psychic transformation that she records is closely aligned with her Buddhist belief in reincarnation. As a not yet fully human child, she can easily identify with other creatures, and even plants, because she may have existed as such in a previous life. Likewise, she relates a long, involved dream in which she visualizes her insane grandmother, O-Moka-sama, as a crab in chapter 8. Indeed, with both her material and dream experiences of phenomenal nature and the ultranatural, Michiko recognizes that the natural world and the cultural world are in conflict. She even attempts in chapter 9 to choose the former over the latter by throwing herself into a fast-flowing stream produced by floodwaters near the temple of Kannon (283). It seems unlikely that it is purely coincidental that Kannon is the god-goddess of compassion and mercy. In the next chapter, Michiko reflects on her mother's summer agricultural work and how the mother and the mother's sister are more at ease in nature than in town (296), because in nature they are spared the ridicule of other people—who lack compassion—as a result of having an insane mother (Michiko's grandmother).

Michiko's immersion in the floodwaters near Kannon's temple, then, appears to be a turning point in *Story;* she has attempted and failed to reject the cultural world. Michiko then describes her mother's and aunt's field work and in doing so depicts a way of life in which the natured and the cultured may be balanced in relation to one another. Such balance includes the joys and the sufferings and the benefits and the hardships that both worlds contain.

As a result, in the final chapter (chap. 11), Michiko focuses on helping and showing compassion for her insane grandmother, O-Moka-sama, through taking her grandmother to see the first blooming of the lotus buds, symbols of knowledge of the natural world and the mysteries of the dharma realm of the Buddha worlds:

> In the palm of the round, large leaves sailing quietly on the pond rested, sunk in prayer or meditation oval, opalescent buds. Only the small aperture at their upper end afforded a glimpse into the crimson depths of their silent world.
>
> The sun lay behind the mountains. I snuggled against O-Moka-sama. (347)

At this moment, Michiko has an epiphanic experience in which she composes her first poem, a poem about her grandmother in which natural and religious images—both Buddhist and animist—intertwine and the mundane is transformed into the mythic.[6]

Story of the Sea of Camellias, then, can be read as the story of a child coming into consciousness, becoming fully human, who in doing so accepts the vocation of being a poet, a writer, whose task it is to reintegrate the natural and cultural worlds in accordance with her Buddhist and Shinto beliefs while showing deep compassion for human suffering and assisting those who are from the exploited and outcast social classes. Not only does the child Michiko show compassion and empathy for her insane grandmother, but also for a family of lepers, local prostitutes, the man who cremates the poor, and fishermen—especially those from her ancestral home of Amakusa island—who have been forced by the economic depression of the 1920s to leave their fishing villages and roam the land seeking work as laborers. Throughout the course of *Story*, she also lavishes detailed description on the natural world of the area and the positive characteristics of subsistence farming and fishing, as well as the values embodied in local animistic beliefs and practices, such as various festivals, ceremonies, and rituals.

Conclusion

With the foregoing in mind, a reader can easily interpret *Story of the Sea of Camellias* as an explanation for why Ishimure has dedicated so much of her life and her artistic creativity to the Minamata disease victims. Whether viewing this dedication as her karma or her ethical obligation, or seeing these two as one and the same thing, a reader can understand Ishimure's deep commitment to remembering through her writing ways of life more in tune with the rhythms of nature. Readers can also understand her defending the outcast and the exploited as the working out of her own path to salvation through a relentless expression of compassion. Such compassion must be extended not only to humans but to all other entities, a perspective that one might argue could serve as the foundation for any approach to environmental justice. Compassion, by various names, also often serves as a defining feature of both nature literature and environmental literature. Perhaps that is why the subtitle of *Paradise in the Sea of Sorrow* is "*Our* Minamata Disease."

In these two works by Ishimure Michiko, American readers can see some of the variety of nature-oriented literature as it is being written through the lens of other cultural perspectives. In particular, we can see the ways that similar themes can actually be expressed in two different types of work, one that is decidedly environmental literature, *Paradise in the Sea of Sorrow: Our Minamata Disease*, and one that is basically nature literature, *Story of the Sea of Camellias*. While *Story* only occasional uses documentary material—historical reports of visits to the Minamata region, for example—*Paradise* is replete with such materials. It also contains other kinds of documentary materials, such as medical reports, academic studies, and newspaper articles, but presents them within the framework of a Japanese literary tradition that blurs the boundaries of fiction and nonfiction.

Such a technique is not postmodern and should not be confused with such usages; it does not call into question the factuality, accuracy, or truthfulness of any text in a way that a Western postmodern work might thematically do through using such material. Rather, Ishimure's usage within the context of Japanese tradition emphasizes the truthfulness of the imagined as well as the recorded within her texts. Coming out of a different cultural perspective and literary tradition, such nature-oriented literature calls on American readers to rethink our stylistic, structural, and generic criteria of evaluation in appreciating not only these two texts, but others produced outside the Anglo-American nature-writing tradition. Appreciation of *Paradise* also encourages more attention to the ways that themes of environmental justice may be surfacing in world literature in response to the ongoing industrial poisoning of the planet and the beings who live on it.

9

"The Women Are Speaking"

Using Women's Literature to Extend and Critique Ecofeminism

N THE EARLY months of 1996, the presidential caucuses and primaries had just gotten under way and Patrick Buchanan was scoring victories with a message attacking multiculturalism, international dialogue, immigration, and sexual diversity; espousing a single religious tradition as informing all that is truly *American*; and promising a return to family values based on a singular image of what constitutes a family. In other words, he was attacking the kinds of ideas and values espoused by virtually all of the writers I have discussed in the preceding chapters. Such rhetoric had been building for some time, and the other candidates, including Bill Clinton, responded by blasting Buchanan's extremism but adopting modified versions of many of his platform planks. Such attacks have not lessened in the intervening years (and in early 1999 Buchanan announced another run for the presidency).

Is it coincidental that such attacks on cultural diversity have occurred at the same time that the United States is experiencing a backlash against environmentalism, environmental regulations, and long-range environmental planning, at the same time that Congress, for instance, tried to place a gag order on any governmental discussions of global warming? I think not. Efforts are continuously being made to separate conceptions of nature and decisions about environmental problems and planning from cultural constructions and the relationship of cultural practices to environmental effects. It would seem that, as education and research begin to make increasingly apparent the linkages between the values that shape how we live and the shape that such living imposes on the land, the rhetoric depicting a static, perpetual, true America becomes more shrill and intense. Yet many people know better and have found someone else to whom to listen because the women are speaking: of gender, of nature, and of culture.

Ecofeminism from its inception has insisted on the link between nature and culture, between the forms of exploitation of nature and the forms of the oppression of women. While these linkages have been most fully explored in philosophy and practiced through a variety of means in the streets and forests, an increasing body of literature identified as ecofeminist has emerged, as has an even larger number of works recognized as demonstrating or containing significant elements of a feminist ecological sensibility, as I suggested in chapter 4. But anyone working with theory has to guard against the danger of trusting the theory and only testing the practice, whether that practice consists of acts of civil disobedience, behavioral changes, or the production of literary works. With literature, readers need to constantly ask themselves what the texts in their hands can offer to enhance the theories that shape their lives.

For that purpose I have chosen two works labeled nonfiction by Sallie Tisdale and Jane Brox, but which I will call *writing* to be consistent with my opening taxonomy, and two volumes of poetry by Lori Anderson and Nora Naranjo-Morse. All works are by women, but they are not necessarily all feminist works, either in terms of an authorial self-expressed ideology or a position easily definable as such by a reader. All of them demonstrate a significant awareness of the interdependence of women's oppression and environmental degradation. They also tend to emphasize the relationship of cultural diversity and natural diversity, the kind of ecological multiculturality that I introduced in my discussion of Pat Mora's writing. In the next two sections of this chapter I want to focus on these works in terms of how they raise questions about, or help us extend, certain theoretical issues and activist concerns.

Writing

The literary nonfiction essay is the prose genre that has come to define nature writing in the United States, in part because it appears to combine a personal voice with factual and accurate description. The poles of the generally accepted Enlightenment binary construct of subjective-objective seem to meet in a blend of the best of each. Belief in such a blending justifies the presentation of universalizing general philosophical statements that are often based on an author's very specific and relatively minute experiences. For the most part, such nonfiction has been written by white males yet treated as if it were speaking for everyone—and while women have always participated in this genre, their numbers have been underrepresented, when not totally ignored, in critical discussions and anthologies. Increasingly, however, white women and women of color have taken up writing in this genre and in doing so have increased its potential for discursive variety and broadened the voices expressing the freedom to evaluate natural and cultural phenomena.

Sallie Tisdale's *Stepping Westward: The Long Search for Home in the Pacific Northwest* chronicles the efforts of Anglo-European immigrants to create culture by attempting to determine how to live in this particular region of the United States. A first point to note is that Tisdale continuously refers to the numerous tribal peoples inhabiting this region prior to the slow but inexorable onslaught by easterners and new immigrants. She emphasizes the diversity and locally appropriate inhabitory practices of the various native communities and criticizes the racism to which they have been subjected historically and contemporaneously. The organicism of their diversity becomes an ideal that Tisdale holds up in her hopes for the possibility of a contemporary settlement that is ecologically viable, economically sustainable, and inclusive of the Native Americans who continue to inhabit the region.

Another point to note is Tisdale's gender-balancing of examples of individual lives and authorities. Where in another text of this type one would expect a reference to a male pioneer or scientific authority—because that is how most of these books are written—Tisdale is more likely to refer first to women, such as Mary Ellicott Arnold and Mabel Reed, who in 1908 "were among the first white women to appear in Karuk country."[1] Here Tisdale does not simply provide the reader with female examples who conform to masculinist stereotypes of pioneer women but also provides counterstereotypic examples: Arnold and Reed "had come west looking for adventure of some undefined kind, knowing only that settling down into marriage and motherhood had to wait until more of the huge world had been seen" (*Stepping*, 32). She often follows such a presentation with an example of the male frontier stereotype, destructive, ecologically insensitive, and bent on subduing the land and the natives to his own designs.

Still, Tisdale does not limit herself to male stereotype versus female counterstereotype; she also provides frequent examples of male counterstereotypes, whose ideas and actions align them more with the values of the pioneering women than with the gold rush, timber harvest, exploitative men (see, for example, the contrast between David Douglas and Frederick Weyerhauser, *Stepping*, 165–75). In these accounts, Tisdale demonstrates along cultural and along gender lines what rancher-writer Linda Hasselstrom philosophizes: "we have tried to change nature to fit not only our needs and desires but our whims. We should seriously consider a period of adapting ourselves to nature's laws, before our damage is irreversible" (quoted in *Stepping*, 197).

Tisdale makes a poignant case for the necessity of an ecoregional orientation toward inhabitation. If those who have migrated to the Pacific Northwest, displacing its first human inhabitants, are ever going to be able to settle down and make a home, rather than just a profit or loss, they will have to create a culture adapted to the region's characteristics rather than continuing to render the land in the image of some other place. Through her repeated calling forth of women from the past to speak of the wilderness in which, and of which, they made their homes, she demonstrates the necessity for any regional, ecologically responsible agenda to be an ecofeminist one, to include the true diversity of human experience of habitation through insuring that the women who have been speaking are now being heard. She also, by implication, demands of ecofeminism that it further articulate its position on regionalism as an agenda and organizing principle, that its practitioners and theorists continue to define and redefine their conceptions of community-in-place.

On the opposite shores of the United States, Jane Brox has engaged in *Here and Nowhere Else: Late Seasons of a Farm and Its Family* a very different type of writing from *Stepping Westward*. It is a frequently meditative narrative, written not so much for its audience as for the author and then shared with others. While Tisdale treats a large, sweeping region of the United States, Brox focuses on a single family farm in Massachusetts. She too addresses its regional ecological particularities, doing so in the context of the passing of an agrarian way of life, many of the values of which need to be preserved even as the historical means of practicing them continue to be plowed under by agribusiness. While *Here and Nowhere Else* does not read as if written to be a feminist polemic, or to be particularly gender emphatic, it nevertheless weaves themes of nature, gender, and culture into a single fabric that the reader feels compelled to appreciate by looking at it and also by feeling its texture and reflecting on its frayed ends.

In her narrative, Brox makes it clear that she feels compelled to return home. She is pulled homeward by the appeal of place, the memories of childhood, the rewards of working with her hands in addition to working with her words. But the compulsion comes from the plight of her parents as they try to maintain their agrarian, homesteading way of life in the face of suburban sprawl, economies of scale, their own aging, and, most important for Brox, the incapacity of their son and heir to the farm. Of her siblings only her brother has remained to practice the arts of farming, but he is a drug addict incapable of full participation in the work or the family, and so she returns home, moves into an abandoned house on the property, and once more takes up helping with the farm. Hers is no nostalgic trip home, although there are nostalgic moments of memory and common labor. Rather, she feels the contradictory demands of her own desires and life work, the expectations of being a dutiful daughter, and the obligations of a descendant through whom the traditional family farm lore must pass or become extinct.

The strength of Brox's narrative, in addition to the sensuous beauty of her precise, descriptive prose, lies in the tension and anguish that she records. She recognizes that there is no simple separatist or autonomous decision to be made. She perceives the obligations of family tradition and continuity, of lineage and heritage, as real ones, not to be shrugged off so that she can pursue her personal dream. But she also recognizes the need to avoid being trapped by traditional gender roles, by the image of the dutiful daughter who will become mother to her parents and brother.

In the end, she continues to live in her house on the farm but withdraws from the farm's daily operations, realizing that becoming the head of the farm is not the life that she must lead: "I can still feel that my returning here has only delayed what was inevitable, and that we've all returned to our old places. . . . Still, I can't imagine this place as anything other than a farm."[2] Brox knows that the issue is not inheriting the land but inheriting a working farm and a specific way of life, one that she respects but is unable to pursue. That inability does not come from weakness, however, but from difference and unwillingness to accept the paring down of her own possibilities that would be required as part of inheriting the farm. In a sense, Brox's dilemma is that the culture needs to be preserved, but it cannot be continued without change. In this case, the impossibility of breaking down traditional gender roles within this specific environment precludes her inheriting the farm's way of life, which in turns places the future of the land at risk. Community needs are set against individual growth. Brox makes a choice but does not imagine that it is without cost, knowing that interdependence rather than autonomy defines her identity.

As a result of Brox's personal anguish and her recognition of the price of her decision, *Here and Nowhere Else* is strongly elegiac in tone, particularly in her recording of her meditative walks through the woods. During these walks she develops a philosophy of change and continuity based on the second-growth processes of the previously cleared but long abandoned farmland-returned-to-woodland. She finds an ancient oak standing alone surrounded by second- or third-growth trees, threaded by collapsing stone walls of forgotten fields: "Maybe spared by sentiment or reverence, this one outlived them all."[3] This line is, of course, appropriate for the family farm as well. Her hope lies not with the new trees, but with the very process of succession itself: clear-cutting giving way to second growth, softwoods giving way to hardwoods, abandoned fields reaching toward mature forest stability.

In such hope Brox reveals that she does not have the answers to the larger cultural questions that her meditations provoke: What is our obligation toward the protection of sustainable family farming in lieu of a viable alternative at this point in time? Can the gender roles of traditional family farming be transformed, or must we wait for the second growth following the catastrophes attendant upon agribusiness and exploitative extraction, which Tisdale catalogs and warns against, to try anew? What structure can replace the nuclear family that will support the liberation of women from gender oppression and maintain or renew community and mutual responsibility? While a significant body of literature by women on and in agriculture and ranching is developing, ecofeminist theory and literary criticism have not yet addressed such literature to any significant degree. This gap suggests that critics have not yet thought through the complexities that writing such as Brox's raises in regard to agrarian ways of life in industrialized, agribusiness-driven countries, but that they need to do so—and soon—with the same intensity that others have practiced in addressing women and agriculture in the countries of the so-called Third World.

Some ecofeminists, however, have attempted to address at least part of the problem depicted in *Here and Nowhere Else*. Linda Vance, in "Ecofeminism and the Politics of Reality," addresses the dilemma Jane Brox faces in necessarily contradictory ways. Vance states that while ecofeminists cannot expect to see "huge demographic transitions within our lifetimes," they can "make the need for responsible cooperation with the land known, and use our own lives to model the possibilities."[4] Brox undertakes the first of these actions by describing in detail the example of her family's "responsible cooperation with the land" but finds that she cannot "model" its continuation because of the limitations of gender roles that have developed along with that cooperation. Brox does experience what Vance says women have learned historically: "a type of attentiveness that allows us to move back and forth between seeing the needs of an individual and seeing the needs of a larger community," but the attentiveness does not enable Brox to generate a solution that mediates those needs. Instead, she feels compelled to choose and undertakes something else Vance calls for: "to take on the challenge of exploring our own reality as free as possible from the constraints of masculinist ideology."[5] But that will mean letting the farm die, letting the lone example of an alternative to creeping suburbia in her locale go under the blades of the bulldozers.

It must be remembered, however, that while the protagonist's father is a good farmer, he is still a patriarch, and it is the role of patriarch more than farmer that his son wants to assume. All the good farming in the world will not be good enough within that logic of domination. When Vance uses "we," she refers only to ecofeminists who are women concerned for, and identifying with, what Brox and those like her must endure, address, and transform. Men in ecofeminism and men who are willing to read ecofeminist criticism and women's literature with ecological and feminist sensibilities must avoid a convenient identification with the victimized, the protagonist and the farm, and admit instead the degree of identification between our lives and behaviors and the male antagonists of this text. Men with feminist consciousness have a special responsibility to work out the implications of how we can persuade and transform the men who are the culture-bearers of the oppression that ecofeminism is committed to transforming.

Brox assumes the responsibility for choosing her freedom from familial patriarchal domination at the likely cost of local agrarian tradition, but only because she cannot refuse to be a victim and at the same time protect the farm from victimization. Why? Because the men will not change; because her brother will not relent or enter into recovery; because her father cannot turn over the farm to anyone other than his son, no matter how unfit. The elegiac tone of *Here and Nowhere Else: The Late Seasons of a Farm and Its Family*, then, results not from the protagonist's limitations—although she engages in some self-blame—but from the resistance of men heavily invested in patriarchal ideology and traditional male-dominant behavior.

Poetry

As I have discusses in earlier chapters, contemporary critics have tended to align poetry addressing humanity's relationship with the rest of the natural world with British romanticism and American transcendentalism. Further, the *I* of poetry is generally identified as no more fictional than that of the naturalist essay, while both are treated as qualitatively distinct from the *I* of prose fiction. Proceeding from these bases and relying on many of the attributes for which nonfiction nature writing is praised, critics often place significant emphasis on solitude, meditation, nonparticipant observation, accurate detail, ego dissolution or expansion, and personal epiphanies.[6] The two poetry volumes I will discuss here, both published in 1992, do not work along those lines.

As the title of Lori Anderson's collection *Cultivating Excess* suggests, the poems tend to be short on most of these attributes and long on attitude, action, and immersion. Nora Naranjo-Morse's collection *Mud Woman: Poems from the Clay* combines poetry with color plates of her sculptures and pottery, which aesthetically and thematically reinforce each other, as they indicate that narrative is more semiotic than linguistic. In both poems and art, symbol and metaphor articulate the weight of cultural mediation of environmentally immersed and self-aware personal experience, but eschew any nostalgia for, or idealization of, unmediated interaction with the rest of nature. Indeed, Naranjo-Morse celebrates the cultural enrichment of individual interaction with the natural elements.

Gretchen Legler notes that *Cultivating Excess* "asks readers to challenge traditional notions of nature, of nature writing, and of human relationships with other humans and with the natural world. In this collection, Anderson deliberately, and excessively, works to turn the binary oppositions in language and philosophy upside down and inside out."[7] *Cultivating Excess* is divided into four sections: "Excess Jesus," "Silviculture," "Civilculture," and "Excess Isis." Here I will focus on the first three, but before doing so I want to comment on the book's title, which signals the kind of word play to be found throughout the book, as when the "Excess Jesus" section ends with the poem "Exegesis and her Song." *Cultivating* signals the environmental orientation of much of the book, as well as suggesting images of caring and nurturing, practices depicted in patriarchal thought as being natural for a woman, but Anderson ruptures such an easy and oppressive identification in two ways. She weds *cultivating* with the word *excess*, establishing an inversion of expectations that rescues *cultivating* from its patriarchal domain and sets it loose on the terrain of sexual politics. The understanding of the word *excess* itself is also gradually reversed for readers. Anderson is not referring to something that is actually excessive as in too much or more than appropriate, which is frequently a relative rather than an absolute condition and a cultural rather than natural limit. Instead, *excess* can be understood as meaning exceeding, as in the transgression of norms.

In the "Excess Jesus" section, one sees the practice of binary inversion that Legler identifies in the five-stanza poem "Fish in Air," which may be read as a pun on *visionnaire*.[8] In the opening stanza the speaker identifies herself and an unnamed "you" as "new lovers," who are visiting a park named "Eagle Something," while the second stanza reveals that both lovers are women. As Greta Gaard has observed in a personal letter about the poem, the phrase "new lovers" "can be read in two ways: newly in love, or newly out," as in first admitting one's sexual orientation. The first stanza ends "long after," suggesting that the events of the rest of the poem happen some time after the characters' sexual initiation. In the second stanza, the "you" character recoils from the lesbian identification established in stanza one and calls on

> . . . a holy host
> of others (your Father, your Friends)
>   male trinity ensuring we
>   only look for eagles. You all
> agree on one I cannot
>   see then tell a tale:[9]

The holy patriarchy's story is about an eagle who grabs a sturgeon too large to haul into the sky and then allegedly drowns through the sin of covetousness. The "eagle" dies for overreaching itself for an allegedly unnatural satisfaction of its appetites, which could be understood as lesbian sexual desire. As if the triteness and convenience of the story might not be enough to cast doubt on its veracity, the use of the word *tale* signals that this story is taking place in the mind of the teller rather than in the air over the river.

This eagle allegory wielded against the speaker of the poem is a stereotypical animal story, in which the other's existence is anthropomorphically expropriated for human edification. But the speaker of the poem decides that she can play the game of allegory as well and renames the eagle "she" and redefines the eagle's dive as a quest for transformation:

> But how else would eagle ever enter
> water to such depths save
> by an anchor of flesh? Maybe
> her longing is as ours is:
> fish in air, bird under
> water, man off earth (woman in
> heaven) ((heaven down under))
> flesh needing flesh to rise
> to delve to depths beyond/above
> our allotted home.
>
> (*Excess*, 10)

How often when the "eagle" is deployed as symbol do readers or viewers consider it a female? How often is the use of "unnatural" deployed as a term to conceal the hierarchical value attached to a cultural construction of difference, particularly sexual difference?

The poem concludes with an inversion that identifies the "you" as a sturgeon with an eagle in her mouth, in sensual repartee rather than devouring hierarchy, and another inversion is suggested. Whereas the events of the second, third, and fourth stanzas portray the "you" of the poem as denying her own sexual identity and internalizing the homophobia inculcated in her by "Father" and by "Friends," the final stanza's allusion to the "you" character's "new lover" as also a woman indicates that she has in the end accepted the naturalness of her sexuality. The speaker is thus successful in reversing and refuting the patriarchal rhetoric of the dominant culture's compulsory heterosexuality that would attempt to define both what is natural and what is in excess.

In the "Silviculture" section of *Cultivating Excess*, Anderson critiques the use of mathematics and fragmenting technical vision in the poem "Self Portrait Eye to Eye with Clinometer & Prism" and then reinforces that critique in the following poem, "Berm."[10] A clinometer is used to measure a slope or, more for Anderson's sexual ecological politics, an inclination. It is the erotic inclination throughout the poem that chafes against the commodification of the forest as timber, because, when the erotic asserts itself: "Trees about us no / longer commodities our body taking us for ride" (*Excess*, 35). But the clinical detachment of the clinometer reasserts itself and insists on the logic of human domination over the forest and over the erotic impulse, in much the same way that the "tale" of "Fish in Air" was designed to tame lesbian desire. Out of frustration, the speaker in "Berm" offers the path of a deer trail in opposition to the straight-line, bushwhacking of a forestry agent who is measuring off land for a timber sale. In her anger she would like to leave him behind forever.

Anderson, however, in "Reclaiming Slashburns," informs the reader that marking timber for sale is not nearly as painful as clearing the land for commercial tree farms. With bitter irony, she contrasts the work of the slashburn crew with popular culture's idealized image of pristine forests in *The Sound of Music*. Where theater and television audiences see the singing family hiking through unspoiled mountain vistas, Anderson images the reality of clear-cutting and subsequent tree farming that not only destroys the mountains and their forests, but also poisons women and children downstream:

> Pre-replanting, these chemicals leached
> down into the water
>
> where women drank and bred
> and miscarried.

Invoking Isis and edelweiss in opposition to the film's von Trapp mythos and the trap of commercialism, the poem's speaker sings of her own "entrapment" in the "understory" of our mountains and forests. The "understory" here is both literal and metaphoric; the former in terms of the slash that is being burned off, left behind from the clear-cutting, and the latter in terms of the subversive critique that Anderson writes in opposition to our cultural illusions and corporate disinformation. As Legler observes, this entire section "echoes work done by Susan Griffin in *Woman and Nature*, where Griffin juxtaposes scientific and institutional language with the language of desire and the language of women's spirituality."[11] By placing such discourses on equal terms, Anderson validates the gender inflection and difference of vision that can be heard in women's speaking, particularly in regard to revisioning the nature-gender-culture interrelationships.

This more general critique of the forest industry in the context of American popular culture prepares the way for the poems in the third section of *Cultivating Excess*, "Civilculture." The first poem, "If This Quilt of Names Were Made of Fire," initiates an attention to AIDS that is continued throughout the section. This poem is not just about mourning, but like the previous sections emphasizes action and transformation: "Navigation / charted, as always, by the shape-changers" (*Excess*, 57). From an ecological perspective, "You Better Remember Your Own Immunization" provides the most powerful poetic expression of the interconnections between cultural perceptions and conceptions of nature, and the disastrously wrongheaded depiction of nature as something out there beyond the human, rather than a process and system throughout the human body within the world body. Through this poem, Anderson traces the history of the post–World War II belief in immunizations and immunity from the illnesses of the world (as a casual review of newspapers reveals, all kinds of diseases thought eradicated are returning and various new superviruses have been born from their allegedly eradicated ancestors), through the collateral belief in antibiotics, food additives, herbicides, and pesticides. Anderson uses the cultural mythos of Cold War immunization as a warning against those who imagine that they are "immune" if they are not homosexuals or drug addicts, who imagine that AIDS is the only new plague on its way.

From "Fish in Air" through "You Better Remember Your Own Immunization," Anderson links the chemicals in the forests to the chemicals in our water, food, and bodies. She relates these to cultural preconceptions and misconceptions that define the domination of nature as scientific and therefore progressive, and as unnatural and therefore perverse, desires that unleash feelings of identification and connection, reciprocity and renewal, between human beings and between human and other beings of the world.

In a sense, Anderson promotes a journey into excess to get out of commercial monocultural cultivation. In contrast, Nora Naranjo-Morse promotes cultivation, but of a very different kind—the cultivation of inhabitation, which is an act of spiritual and psychological survival. Such cultivation is necessary for cultural evolution, which groups of people must undertake each generation in order to remain viable societies. Many southwestern writers of various ethnicities are today engaged in this cultivation of inhabitation. As I argued in my discussion of Pat Mora's writing, cultural diversity should be understood as a form of biological diversity. It should also be recognized as a component of human evolution in terms of the interactive dynamics of somatic change generating genetic change, and the way that all people can be said to have a geopsyche, to once again employ Gregory Cajete's term.

The tradition of American nature writing as it has been codified to date remains too much a monocultural monologue about the right ways to relate to nature from an already alienated position. Such alienation is reinforced particularly in its emphasis on going out to wilderness areas to experience "nature" through recreational activities, to participate and, unavoidably, to intervene, and the emphasis on observing seasonal cycles rather than, say, working on a local farm or feeding oneself through organic gardening. This tradition has not yet succeeded in entering into dialogue with natural diversity as manifested in the plurality of human cultures and represented in the art and literature of such native writers and artists as the Pueblo sculptor-poet Nora Naranjo-Morse.

Naranjo-Morse's *Mud Woman: Poems from the Clay* opens with a preface that intertwines environment, culture, and art. The environment, "veins of colored earth run along the hillsides of New Mexico," gives rise to a history of integration with that place: "For hundreds of years Pueblo people have treasured their powerful relationship with clay."[12] Without the clay there would be no pueblos. As Naranjo-Morse notes, "subtle lessons from Clay Mother awaken my appreciation for daily rituals, connecting me to the Pueblo world view" (*Mud Woman*, 10). The clay is neither a possession for proprietary claim nor located in a secret place so that it may be hoarded. Rather, it is part of the community, and community is reaffirmed through a relationship with it: "Even today, when a vein is located and uncovered, a prayer is offered to Nan chu Kweejo (Clay Mother). . . . This prayer continually renews our relationship to the earth, her gifts, and Towa" (*Mud Woman*, 9).[13]

Naranjo-Morse's beginning her sentence with "Even today" makes clear that maintaining these rituals and continuing the Pueblo worldview involve a complex process of engaging and resisting the Anglo-dominated world. Typical of many remarks about Native American languages is Naranjo-Morse's observation that Tewa has no word for art; "there is, however, the concept for an artful life, filled with inspiration and fueled by labor and thoughtful approach" (*Mud Woman*, 15). While a sculpture might become a commodity, art is not a profession but part of a community practice of inhabitation. The artful life is set within the inhabitory framework and unfolds in relation to it, both through received inspiration and through the cultural continuity expressed by means of artistic representation, yet the pressures of the dominant society's values work against this community spirit and attempt to introduce and idealize individualism even in collectively evolved artistic expression.

While objects for sale may be made, it is questionable whether art can be practiced under such pressure, because the conditions and relations of production within the dominant society contradict the worldview behind the artistry, which is spiritual, communal, and ecological. As Naranjo-Morse believes, "Plant, animal and human life cycles, nurtured and guarded, are held equally in a larger vessel called earth. The symmetry of earth's vessel depends on our respect for earth's balance and our caretaking of these cycles. Gathering this knowledge as I do clay, I am impressed by the spiritual strength of these lessons" (*Mud Woman*, 10).

Mud Woman is organized into four sections: "Mud Woman," "Wandering Pueblo Woman," "Pearlene and Friends," and "Home." In the first section the author establishes herself as an artist, which means becoming "Mud Woman" as a result of her immersion in the earth that inspires her creativity; Naranjo-Morse lives reciprocity. But by the fifth poem, the world of art has become complicated by the marketplace. Even so, at the end of the day in front of the museum wall, what counts is not the sales made but the relationships established between Mud Woman and the sculptors, jewelers, and artists from other pueblos and tribes. Such relationships help sustain her through the next few poems as the sculptor runs the gamut of the white-dominated art marketplace and loses her "innocence."

The "Wandering Pueblo Woman" section begins with a poem about how Mud Woman will return home after she has assimilated various urban sights for future art. The next poem focuses not on the individual but the history of her people before "change disrupted night's mystery," and it ends with the evocation of a tribal birthright. This birthright reassures the wandering woman in the next poem, "Two Worlds," that even far away in Hawai'i she "will always be a Towa" (*Mud Woman*, 50). Yet, Naranjo-Morse closes this section with the poem "Sometimes I Am a Sponge," in which she stakes out her place as a particular kind of Towa, "someone not afraid to stare" the kind of artist needed to represent the complex realities of these unnatural times (*Mud Woman*, 54).

"Pearlene and Her Friends" addresses the generation gap, if you will, in the Santa Clara Pueblo between more traditional "Tewa matriarchs" and modern young women. Here Naranjo-Morse, with poems about Pearlene, Moonlight, and Coyote, suggests that the temptations of modernity and dominant popular culture are trickster manifestations, to be countered by the artist as trickster and tribal matriarchs as tradition bearers. These poems are followed by the section "Home." Its first few poems are about Mud Woman's mother and sisters, and the fourth is about home as a vessel and a relationship, built and shared "one adobe at a time." It is built from and on the clay of the earth, and will return to it, just as Mud Woman has arisen from and is made of this earth. Her place on this earth is assured her by her father, who says, "it goes in beauty" (*Mud Woman*, 106).

The volume ends with this beauty being realized in a new work of art, a fired bowl, created within the tradition but also rendered fortuitously as a variation of it. The bowl becomes proof that the ancient art remains alive, nourishing and replenishing. This "old, new medicine bowl," like Mud Woman, inhabits the present as a representation of the Pueblo worldview, which inhabits the present in a particular place and with a specific balance and continuity that needs to be artfully realized.

Gaard makes an extremely important point in "Ecofeminism and Native American Cultures": "Ecofeminism and Native American cultures have many values in common. To avoid cultural imperialism, however, ecofeminists must resist the urge to import 'convenient' pieces of Native American cultures, Middle Eastern cultures, or any other cultures to construct a mosaic of theories from varying cultural sources. Such a theory would lack the regard for context that is the common goal of all authentically feminist theories."[14] With such a warning in mind, one must first admit that Naranjo-Morse describes a particular interdependent relationship of life, art, and place, through the clay of soil, home, and pottery that is rarely experienced in the United States today, whether in terms of food, shelter, or usable art. Non-Tewa people may buy both poetry and pottery yet remain outsiders, but being outsiders does not necessarily require being alien or other to Naranjo-Morse's philosophy, aesthetics, and life, a point that Tempest Williams worked to make in regard to the Navajo in *Pieces of White Shell.* There remains the possibility of being another, but how is that to be accomplished? Not by imitation, as Naranjo-Morse indicates, since one must be born into the world that she inhabits—imitation would only generate sterility and a parody of the attempt to renew viable cultural practices, because the shallowness of the roots of the imitators would be revealed. By emulation and parallel practice one may come into a similar sensibility.

How do people experience an organic relationship with their habitats and theorize the significance of such relationships? Who sees images of the Exxon Valdez oil spill when looking at vinyl siding thinly covering the wood siding that sustained a house for one hundred years? Who sees the flooding of the first nation Canadian lands of James Bay for hydroelectric power when they flip a light switch in New York City? Activists of various orientations have taken significant steps to bring factory farming and food processing before the eyes of U.S. consumers as they stroll the supermarket aisles, whether it be from the feminist-vegetarian position enunciated by Carol J. Adams or the organic cattle raising perspective of Linda Hasselstrom, yet the true costs and the actual natural sources of the fabric of houses and apartments, transportation, and energy continue to go largely unnoticed. Often individuals are presented with abstract data on such consumption, but rarely is it posed in terms of the alteration and destruction of the habitat of other beings, human and nonhuman. How many of

Naranjo-Morse's readers can name the materials that constitute the vessel of their homes and visualize the materials' preprocessed states, and how little of it comes from their own locale? (Every new two-by-four I purchased during the composition of this book came from Canada.)

As ecofeminism continues to expand its articulations of the interdependencies of the molecular and energy pathways of daily lives on this planet, its practitioners need to learn from Naranjo-Morse and others like her how to depict and image these lineations with the elegance and balance expected of a well-crafted poem, of an aesthetically rendered serving bowl, of a formula in physics, of the touch of a lover's hand. Let me suggest, then, that Naranjo-Morse's art, which reminds her readers of the role of story in the continuity of culture, indicates that, just as spirituality is realized in ritual, theory needs to be realized in symbol and image. That is one of the lessons that the literature I have discussed here, and all the other texts deserving attention that I could not cover, can teach about extending ecofeminist theory and the ecofeminist movement.

More Work to Be Done

With the many trends in ecofeminist literary theory and its application, critics often compare its development to that of feminist literary theory and criticism: First, feminist critics reread canonical works and criticized their gender bias. Second, in extending that criticism to the entire canon, they began to recover suppressed, neglected, and lost works by women writers. Third, they began to criticize the representations of women and to uncover feminist themes in works by women. Ecofeminism, then, has come into literary criticism as the influence and continuation of an activist movement. As a result, the recovery of works by women demonstrating ecological sensibilities and protoecofeminist and ecofeminist themes has been given high priority, particularly in women's studies and women's literature courses. Along with this work has come intense debate about the degrees to which some of these recovered authors are feminist or ecological or ecofeminist, as with Rachel Carson, Willa Cather, and Charlotte Perkins Gilman. Works by men who had been held up as candidates for the nature-writing canon, such as Henry David Thoreau, Ralph Waldo Emerson, and Edward Abbey, have also received ecofeminist critical attention.

An area yet to be studied in depth is the degree to which contemporary male environmental writers, who have had the opportunity to learn about ecofeminism as a consciously articulated movement, are beginning to integrate ecofeminist theory and practice into their creative works, as well as responding negatively to ecofeminism. In which category, for instance, would one place Tom Robbins's *Even Cowgirls Get the Blues*? This task may be the particular responsibility of male ecofeminist critics. I would think that in such work we would especially look for the depiction of prominent female characters who act as speaking subjects for women's consciousness and difference and display both the awareness and the action upon which ecofeminism is based as a movement. How, for example, would I react to and account for Wendell Berry's insistent romanticized, traditional depictions of farm women in his fiction? And what would I or others make of the ecologically devastated landscapes and totally artificial environments in cyberpunk fiction by male and female writers alongside their frequent depictions of strong, independent female characters? In other words, we need to ask whether the male authors have been listening to the women who are speaking, and reflecting those voices in their own work, even as we continue to promote the women who are speaking and encourage other women to give voice through literature to their beliefs and values.

More narrowly, but nevertheless part of the transformative goals of ecofeminism, critics need to demonstrate, as feminist theory and criticism have done, that ecofeminist literary criticism is a necessary component of literary studies. Such critics need to develop further, and display through critical practice, an understanding that a multicultural ecofeminist literary criticism brings the nonhuman actors and characters into prominence alongside the human ones from every ethnicity and nationality.

10

Commodification, Resistance, Inhabitation, and Identity

The Novels of Linda Hogan, Edna Escamill, and Karen Tei Yamashita

WHEN CONTEMPORARY American women writers from oppressed minority groups suffering from racism, economic exploitation, and dislocation from the land turn toward writing about nature, they rarely do so in the narrow, traditional sense of nature writing. Rather, their work is more likely to consist of environmental literature that combines concerns about nature with issues of race, class, and gender. As a result, in order to discuss novels by three such writers, I find it necessary to couch my readings in terms of commodification, resistance, inhabitation, and identity. These terms link human relationships with nature, and human relationships among people. Before engaging in the literature, then, let me define these four key concepts.

Commodification, Resistance, Inhabitation, and Identity

Commodification is generally associated with the rise of capitalism and one of its most recent manifestations, American post–World War II consumer culture. It functions ideologically and economically to deny subject status to other entities and also to encourage conceptions of other entities, including humans, in terms of their monetary value in the circuit of exchange rather than in terms of intrinsic value or even use value. For example, reference to the trees of a forest as "board feet of lumber," though including a vague image of use value—that wood can be used for building—defines those trees in terms of the basic unit of timber-products exchange, with a price tag already attached, and the intrinsic concept of forest as a biotic system effaced.

It is interesting to note that when I presented this idea at a conference, a young man attending the conference disagreed with me. He remarked that if we don't call it "board feet of lumber," how can we build our houses? Indeed, if we redefined lumber by a series of more discriminating categories, Americans might just begin to change the way we approach housebuilding. For instance, what would happen if two-by-four bins at the lumber yard were labeled "studs from an old-growth forest," "studs from tree farms," "studs salvaged from razed buildings"? Such naming would counter the homogeneity generated by commodification that obscures origins and defines all dead tree parts as wood products. Consumers would be able to reduce their consumption of old-growth forests even as they continued building. The continuous reminder that they were destroying forests might even cause some individuals to reconsider their remodeling projects or to reconsider following the trend in building styles that has doubled the average size of a house in the United States since the end of World War II. By making everything appear to be a product, commodification encourages the conception of the world as dead things and focuses attention only on ends rather than means, on objects rather than processes and relationships.

Resistance used in relation to contemporary U.S. multicultural literature refers to different aspects and types of actions by visibly ethnic peoples to oppose racial and cultural oppression and their concomitant exploitation. Increasingly, resistance has included positive efforts to defend and cultivate cultural particularities, such as family relationships, rituals, agrarian habits, and languages and dialects, often in association with specific places and claims to land and community relationships with such land.

Resistance, then, is often coupled with insistence on difference, historical continuity, tradition, and ritual. While successful resistance may eventually entail a revolution to sweep away the opposition—the oppressive system that threatens the peoples and their ways of life that resistance seeks to defend and protect—its practices are frequently highly conservative. For example, the struggle to maintain a daily community language distinct from the dominant, official language—or sometimes even just the effort to maintain a local dialect—often causes resistant individuals to learn that language more completely, to read the literature written in that language, and to engage in historical study of the cultures identified with that language. African American interest in African languages and religions in the 1960s and 1970s, for instance, or the recovery of Japanese by *sansei* (third generation) and *yonsei* (fourth generation) children of parents who were taught only English, even though their parents spoke Japanese at home, did not involve critiques of these culturally formative languages.

Similar recovery and adoption-adaption of rituals, clothing, and foods often become small yet highly significant contributors to resistance by helping to transform a political-racial-nationalistic course of actions and protests into an alternative way of life. That process of transformation flips resistance from a negative action to a positive mode of thought and behavior.

Inhabitation is the establishment of a multigenerational community-based relationship with a particular place, with mutual interaction between cultures and biomes. In much nature writing by white authors there is an emphasis on learning how to inhabit a place in opposition to the frontier-tourist-development orientation of dominant American culture, a subject that Sallie Tisdale addresses in *Stepping Westward*. In some writing by visibly ethnic authors, reinhabitation—the relearning of traditional practices that have been suppressed or half-forgotten—is emphasized.

Both inhabitation and reinhabitation, then, become acts of resistance because of their function as an alternative mode of behavior. Like the consolidation of resistance through language and other cultural dimensions of daily life, reinhabitation grounds the maintenance of difference in a generative and continuity-producing practice. New readers of bioregionalist manifestos, essays, and interviews may view the practices of first-generation reinhabitants as utopian, impractical, and idealist, but their continuation through successive generations demonstrates that they can become a form of normal daily life. As such, they establish a strong counter to the commodification rampant in contemporary consumer culture.

Finally, *identity* is a concept often confused with autonomy, separation, and atomistic selves. Arising from the capitalist philosophy of individualism and its politics of singular-votes democracy, identity in the U.S. requires everyone to agree to be different, and the brokering of a majority of individual votes is privileged over the achievement of community consensus. This dominant culture places emphasis on the illusory goal of unique identity on the basis of separation from alien others, rather than on relational identity through identification with kindred others. In the resistance writings of oppressed people, especially women, as well as in the writings of those seeking to practice reinhabitation, the search for and the struggles to establish an individual identity contribute to a process of going toward, or returning to, relationship and connection through community, language, culture, and extended family. The search for identity occurs as a resistance to separation, isolation, and disconnection at the hands of the dominant culture's homogenizing oppression and exploitation. It results in an identity-with rather than an identity-from. Reevaluating and appreciating the former has been one of the struggles waged by feminism in order to voice the particularities of women's distinct identities from the male dominant norms.

The novels of Native American poet and novelist Linda Hogan, Chicana author Edna Escamill, and Japanese-American novelist and playwright Karen Tei Yamashita demonstrate the diversity of contemporary multicultural fiction on the one hand, and the frequency of concern over ecological and inhabitory issues in such fiction on the other. They also exemplify how departures from Enlightenment realism can intensify the themes found in environmental literature: Hogan and Escamill demonstrate that forms other than traditional American realism can provide extensive accurate depictions of the environment, while Yamashita shows how the defamiliarizing practices of postmodern representation can cause readers to attend more carefully to the natural world around them. While giving attention to the differences among these writers, I want to emphasize the commonalties of their writing strategies through reading their works by means of commodification, resistance, inhabitation, and identity.

Mean Spirit

In Linda Hogan's *Mean Spirit*, it is the 1920s and genocide is under way against Oklahoma's Osage Indians, who have the misfortune under the Dawes Act of being required to choose individual allotments on oil-rich lands in the face of profit-driven murder, eviction, and financial fleecing. Hogan depicts a range of Osage reactions and self-defensive maneuvers against the oil boomers through a multiplotted novel with a large number of major characters. No one character, however, can be defined as the individual hero or the singular protagonist. The novel is structured by accretion and accumulation, so that without careful attention to the process of community consensus-building, the reader may judge the mass exodus at the end of the novel to be purely reactive rather than resolute. Since the novel stops with this exodus of the most-discussed set of characters, the reader is left considering the significance of the action itself rather than its results.

The reader experiences a resolution only insofar as she or he is willing to evaluate the extratextual implications of the novel in terms of the history of Native American survival since the 1920s. Hogan demonstrates in *Mean Spirit* how a people survive serial killing, reclaim and remember the community base of their cultural continuity—in opposition to a culture based on commodification of everything—and decide consensually to depart in order to fight another day.

The Osage depicted, with a balanced attention to both male and female characters, renew their sight and insight, which had been temporarily blinded by a brief blizzard of trinkets, houses, and vehicles bought by oil revenues, commodities procured through the illusion of ownership rather than earned through the nurturing of the earth. The imposition of a commodity-based relationship to the land by means of the Dawes Act, which initially showers them with a wealth so great they have difficulty spending all the money, separates them from their own work ethic and also from the sustainable and reciprocal land-community practices that had been their economy. This older economy of inhabitation is maintained in the novel by the Hill People, with the Blanket and Graycloud families serving as the link between the old ways of the Hill People, who remain as removed as possible from white encroachment, and the urbanized Osage, who become completely caught up in it.

At first the Osage react in piecemeal fashion to the murders and disenfranchisement that individuals and families experience, but gradually their spiritual leaders, who themselves must regain vision and find a way through the economic blizzard, remind them of a tradition of resistance. This tradition is the resistance to assimilation through recovery of their roots, particularly in terms of spiritual values versus commodity values, and remembering that cultural identity and environmental identity are one and the same. As Joe Billy remarks early in the novel: "It's more than a race war. They are waging a war with earth."[1]

From the lessons of the Hill People, from the knowledge of the keepers of the fire, from the shamans, and from their own family histories, the survivors regain their sense of right relationship to the land, which is the basis for their identity as a people. The concluding consensual group exodus results from the reassertion of community identity, which will gird them through decades of wandering. It is precisely this sense of identification with their heritage, based on resistance and a rejection of commodification, that provides the possibility for their descendants to reinhabit the land as native peoples. Hogan's conclusion of the narrative reinforces this claim: "They looked back once and saw it all rising up in the reddened sky . . . the life they had lived, nothing more than a distant burning. . . . They carried generations along with them, into the prairie and through it, to places where no road had been cut before them. . . . The night was on fire with their pasts and they were alive."[2]

The commodification of the lives of the Osage is depicted early in the novel in significant detail, while the resistance is shown to grow gradually and to be practiced unevenly by different tribal members. Hogan demonstrates the ubiquity of what they must resist through a variety of situations and characters, to the point where the reader becomes unsure of the roles of some characters. Are they dupes of capitalist interests, turncoats in league with profiteers, schemers for their own financial advancement, or just ignorant individuals caught up in a system so diffuse that no individual can command it? By refusing to grant the reader a simple dichotomy of innocent and good versus evil and corrupt, Hogan encourages recognition of the complexity of the systems of domination on the one hand, and the diversity of forms of resistance and levels of awareness on the part of the oppressed on the other.

Resistance builds as the characters begin to reconsider what is valuable, which is not only individual life but the larger life of the community, a life built on practices of inhabitation. Reconsideration leads to increasing awareness, which leads to a growing sense of disidentification with white society and a concomitant renewed identification with tribal society. Hogan seems to imply in her conclusion that if the survivors know who they are, they will be able to relearn how to live and determine where and how to make that place home.

Daughter of the Mountain: Un Cuento

Edna Escamill's bildungsroman *Daughter of the Mountain: Un Cuento* depicts the resistance through inhabitation practiced by a Chicano community, especially one of its biracial young women, Maggie. Set in the border area of southern Arizona in the 1940s and 1950s, the novel focuses on Maggie and her increasing maturity and understanding as she faces the evisceration and urban removal of her maternal culture, not only its language and customs but also its communal, agrarian economic base. At the front of the novel, Escamill provides a map of "El Pueblo," Arizona, which shows the predominance of the Spanish language in the area and its community organization around "El Barrio Central," "Las Rancherías Chiquitas," and "La Milpa," agrarian-based communities. A table at the top tells the story by the numbers: in 1940, 6,000 people, mainly mestizo and Indian, lived in this place; by 1959 the population had swelled to 130,000, almost all of them Anglo settlers.

The post–World War II invasion of Anglos and this rural area's rapid urbanization are depicted as a process of commodification of the desert, farmlands, ways of speaking, homes, and kinds of work. The communal backbone of the community is broken through the dispersal of common lands into individual hands, resulting in the parceling out of the desert into tract housing with privacy fencing, and the closing off of public lands into leased grazing allotments. As the narrator notes in telling of a sudden moment of recognition for Maggie, "The whites were committing injustices against her people, against Grandmother's people, against the desert and the mountains. They were taking away the wildness. They made only logical decisions that crushed the feeling needs of others. This was how they made progress. This was how they ate the face of the earth."[3] In opposition to such economic, cultural, environmental, and spiritual annihilation, *Daughter* portrays the rise of mestiza Maggie's spiritual unity with the land of her birth, tribal ancestry, and cultural continuity as means of resistance and as hope for future inhabitation.

In the world of Anglo domination, education becomes a vehicle for assimilation and class segregation rather than cultural continuity and community responsibility, as English forcibly replaces Spanish and the realities of local history are subsumed under the abstractions of national mythology. In the face of this cultural decimation, even as she learns what she needs to know to get into college, Maggie enacts an educational resistance through following in the footsteps of Adela Sewa, her Yaqui grandmother who is also a *curandera*. Under her tutelage, Maggie becomes ecologically and spiritually literate. By reclaiming her enculturated and situated identity through becoming a "daughter of the mountain," Maggie lays claim to the continuity of place-based culture in opposition to the transitory and likely short-lived invasion of desert cattle-grazing and suburbanite housing, which cannot be sustained without large, constant infusions of water and electric power.

Chapter 1 introduced the reader to Adela Sewa as a drunk living on the street who went up to the mountain pass to face death and be spiritually and physically cleansed. Near the end of *Daughter*, Adela chooses the day that she will die; in chapter 29 of the book's thirty-one chapters, after Maggie has matured sufficiently to continue on her own, Adela goes up to the mountains again. This time she ascends La Madre to pass physically, not from but into the earth, while her spirit lives on. Adela Sewa's own journey from the gutter to the mountain prefigures Maggie's own ascension into a geopsychically based, culturally continuous spirituality.

At the end of the novel, Maggie climbs from Las Tinajas (the earthen jars, vessels needed for storing the essentials for sustenance and healing—an image of home) toward La Madre and meets with Adela Sewa's spirit to consolidate her understanding of how to survive in the white-dominated world by embracing her heritage, its knowledge of how to live with the land rather than against it, and the promise of its spirituality.

Gary W. Rogers, in studying Frank Waters's *People of the Valley*—a work with which Escamill's favorably bears comparison—quotes both Donald Worster and Margaret Mead. Both quotations seems as pertinent to *Daughter.* Worster remarks that "when both the identity of self and of community become indistinguishable from that of the land and its fabric of life, adaptation follows almost instinctively"; regarding a lifestyle like that of Maggie's people, Mead contends that their villages "belong to people who depend on one another for their livelihoods and their diversions." Rogers quotes Waters to emphasize the distinction between the historical mestizo culture of the Southwest and the Anglo culture overwhelming it: "Fulfillment is individual evolution. It requires time and patience. Progress, in haste to move mass, admits neither."[4] In the end, Maggie understands the necessity and the value of both "time and patience" and has been educated into a female-based geospiritual tradition that wields both in the interests of survival.

By subtitling *Daughter* "Un Cuento" rather than "a novel," Escamill emphasizes that this is a folktale, a community story of common people. Maggie's story is largely a quest for identity in the face of oppressive deculturation and racism. While the suburbanite invaders practice urban renewal on a semirural community, they make no attempt to integrate the residents into the American dream, attempting rather to intensify their economic exploitation by displacing them from the means of subsistence and stripping them of the wisdom and practical knowledge that would enable them to maintain community autonomy. Thus, in order for *Daughter of the Mountain* to be a tale of individual triumph, it must also be a tale about cultural preservation. By having Maggie's spiritual meeting with Adela Sewa on the slope of La Madre take place prior to her leaving for college, Escamill indicates that the epiphany of spiritual union is a preparation and protection for a much longer travail, one just as ongoing as the resistance to it.

Through the Arc of the Rain Forest

Karen Tei Yamashita's *Through the Arc of the Rain Forest* is a postmodern novel set in contemporary Brazil. Unlike the two novels just discussed, this one does not specifically concern the resistance and inhabitation of an ethnic American group, although it does address the concept of national multiculturality within Brazil and the oppression of postcolonial countries by global corporations. *Through the Arc* is a comic, cautionary tale about the destruction of many communities, and, by extension, virtually any community, by multinational capitalism's ubiquitous commodification of objects, peoples, practices, and beliefs.

The novel details the difficulties of resistance to such ubiquity. From the ability of a Japanese person with an alien ball floating in front of his head to detect rail-line abnormalities, to a peasant's knowledge of the use of feathers for therapy, to the religious beliefs of an innocent pilgrim, to a man's infatuation with carrier pigeons, every action that an individual in this novel undertakes for personal gratification or self-sacrifice becomes a moneymaking proposition. Throughout the novel, then, commodification breaks down the identity of the individual by turning that person into a marketable commodity using media objectification and promotion. Yamashita also depicts how the financial success attendant upon the selling of the individual's gift results in that person's alienation from his or her original community, and how restoration of community only occurs after material success has vanished or been destroyed.

Unlike *Mean Spirit* and *Daughter of the Mountain*, *Through the Arc* does not contain any heroes who self-consciously resist oppression or who understand the forces that would destroy their identities and their forms of inhabitation. Rather, Yamashita's novel demonstrates the degree to which common people attempting to live simple lives are almost inextricably enmeshed in the machine of commodity production, consumption, and environmental destruction. Not only do they not seek the outrageous patterns of consumption and resulting wealth when they initiate their small personal venture, but they never envision the excessive and unsustainable outcomes toward which they are driven.

Yamashita, however, informs us that it is only "almost inextricably enmeshed" that these people live. Many resist their total absorption by capital through the emphasis of their lives on love, empathy, generosity, and other personal attributes, that is, on those qualities that define subject-to-subject relationships rather than subject-to-object domination. For example, Batista and Tania Aparecida Djapan lose everything their carrier-pigeon enterprise had given them, something Batista had begun as a hobby, but they regain each other and renew their loving relationship at novel's end. Kazumasa, Lourdes, and her children take up fruit-farming after Kazumasa's alien ball disintegrates and drops from its position in front of his forehead.

While there are many subplots of commodification of individuals and their talent other than those just mentioned, the main plot revolves around the *Matacão*, an unknown plasticlike substance discovered in the midst of the Amazon rain forest that a multinational corporation seeks to exploit by every means possible. An entire economy and tourist center develop around it, and virtually all of the major characters are somehow caught in its exploitation or gravitate toward its location. Some are destroyed in the process, but all are threatened, as is the rain forest itself, which must be cleared to get at this new commodity.

In the end it is a mysterious natural bacteria, which evolves in response to the commodification of the *Matacão*, that saves the rain forest and many of the characters, because the bacteria eats this strange substance and eliminates it as a commodity. *Through the Arc*, then, is structured by means of a comic plot, in that many of the characters survive their commodification into moneymaking machines and the rain forest survives its corporate onslaught as a result of the adaptability of the biosphere and the adaptability of many of its organisms, including human beings. But the novel is highly cautionary in that it shows the facility with which commodification can load people's arms with goods while robbing them of their inhabitory awareness and place-based identity.

In Yamashita's vision the rain forest will survive, but the debits on the ecological balance sheet may never be canceled out:

"On the distant horizon, you can see the crumbling remains of once modern high-rises and office buildings, everything covered in rust and mold. . . . The old forest has returned once again, secreting its digestive juices, slowly breaking everything into edible absorbent components, pursuing the lost perfection of an organism in which digestion and excretion were once one and the same. But it will never be the same again." The novel ends: "Now the memory is complete, and I bid you farewell. Whose memory you are asking? Whose indeed."[5] The complicity of the reader in the absurdity of quotidian environmental degradation is made explicit through such direct address. It demands a response to the utterance of the novel, perceiving it not as a postmodern fantasy so much as a vision provided by the ghost of Christmas future. After all, this strange plastic-like substance is fundamentally no different from "discovered" natural materials, such as uranium, or the synthetic products manufactured from natural materials, such as asbestos, polyvinyl chloride, or fluorocarbons, which threaten environments and their human inhabitants. Nor is Yamashita's postmodern scenario significantly different from the destruction of mountains in the American Southwest to provide the pumice for making stonewashed jeans.

Conclusion

These three environmental novels by visibly ethnic U.S. women writers attend simultaneously to the destruction of natural environments and the natured cultures that have existed within those environments. All three do so through departures from the traditional Enlightenment realism that would reinforce the cultural status quo as the atemporal reality of human life. Cultures that have practiced an interdependent economy of nurturance are depicted as being simultaneously decimated and surviving, and in those forms of survival lie hope for a continuing resistance to commodification and a renewed exploration of the necessity of inhabitation. They also call for rethinking identity at the gendered personal, community, and species levels, even as they remind us of the necessity to redefine continuously our conception of nature literature from multicultural and multiformal perspectives.

Perhaps, then, *Mean Spirit, Daughter of the Mountain,* and *Through the Arc of the Rain Forest* serve also to remind us that particular ways of thinking and received ways of perceiving reality can also be forms of cultural and economic commodification that need to be resisted whenever they promote an alienated mode of identity and a negation of inhabitation. Thus for writers such as these, the decision to use a situated realist, an alchemical realist, or a postmodernist narrative strategy is not simply a matter of aesthetic taste nor an abandonment of an intention to represent the material world that includes but exists beyond human consciousness. Rather, each provides an alternative form of representation that encourages readers to resist the imposition of the American status quo as reality and to consider what other realities may exist or be brought into being. Read together, Linda Hogan, Edna Escamill, and Karen Tei Yamashita also remind us that identity, community, and culture are intertwined, with identity generated and sustained through the communities formed by healthy, generative, nurturant cultures. The development of such identities is itself a form of resistance, since they are not for sale.

11

The Tremendous Power
of a Quiet Nudge

Birch Browsings in the Seminar Room

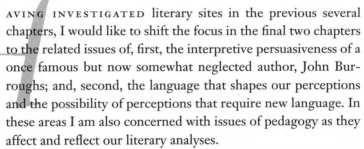

AVING INVESTIGATED literary sites in the previous several chapters, I would like to shift the focus in the final two chapters to the related issues of, first, the interpretive persuasiveness of a once famous but now somewhat neglected author, John Burroughs; and, second, the language that shapes our perceptions and the possibility of perceptions that require new language. In these areas I am also concerned with issues of pedagogy as they affect and reflect our literary analyses.

Some readers may find it curious that I include a singular discussion of Burroughs, one of America's preeminent nature writers, in a book that emphasizes the need to resist the nonfictional prejudice that privileges the genre of nature writing. I take up Burroughs here in part because I want to indicate that my criticism of the narrowness of ecocriticism to date does not mean that I think we should suddenly focus only on fiction and ignore nonfiction and literary essays, whether nonfictional or fictional nature writing or environmental writing. As demonstrated in previous chapters, my approach to redressing the bias toward the nature essay is to use examples drawn from the genre of the novel, that of poetry, and that of the essay. (In the future, I intend to add examples from the genre of drama to my arguments.[1])

I also include Burroughs here because I think some of his work demonstrates my contention that much of what readers find of interest in traditional nature writing consists of the afactual portions of such texts, those speculations, opinions, meditations, and claims that may be suggested but cannot be verified by observation and scientific experimentation. These are the philosophical and political components of such writing that shape readers' own views of nature beyond whatever they may learn from an author's observed or imagined descriptions. Finally, I include Burroughs to remind myself and others that, even though I believe environmental literature deserves emphasis over nature literature in the current global environmental crisis, the most vehement or polemical voices are not necessarily the most persuasive ones.

Burroughs in Relation to Muir and Austin

In recent years western American wilderness writers have gained the most attention from teachers of nature writing and ecological critics, with John Muir overshadowing Burroughs in popularity and critical investigation. In their own day, however, Burroughs was more famous over a longer period of time. Even in terms of popularity we notice a signal difference: Muir gained notoriety from large-scale political battles over the protection and preservation of massive tracts of wilderness lands; Burroughs, to the degree that any aspect of his fame could be described as notoriety, gained his through a stubborn fight over accurate depictions of animals. Muir fought against the destruction of Hetch Hetchy; Burroughs against misrepresentations of the behavior of squirrels and birds. Both have their place, or as Bill McKibben puts it in his Introduction to *Birch Browsings*: "we need them both."[2] But Muir's brand of nature writing and his fascination with western wilderness have attracted so much contemporary attention not only because of the need to preserve wilderness areas but also because his writing appeals to the romantic and the sublime, to the masculine and the individualistic. Burroughs's appeal stems more from his resistance to the romantic and the sublime, his attention to the not-yet and not-quite do mesticated and the intermingling community of the human and nonhuman along the margins. McKibben is very much on the mark when he refers to Burroughs as "midwife," a nurturing, domestic, and usually feminine term unlikely to appear in any discourse on Muir.[3]

My attention here to Muir is not simply for the sake of establishing a comparison through which to provide Burroughs with a better image at another writer's expense. Rather, it arises from having had to scrutinize Burroughs to develop a reading list for a graduate seminar. Then, as now, I included him precisely because of his antiromantic, antisublime, nonindividualistic, and proximate approach to the wild. He, Muir, and Mary Austin became the three opening authors for the class "Topics in American Literature since 1870," which focused on prose nature literature.

A reading of Austin consolidated some of my impressions about Burroughs being in polarity with Muir because, while, like Muir, Austin writes of the western United States, she writes of the desert more than the mountains and her sensibility is more akin to that of Burroughs. Without Austin I would have only the polarity, but with her I have the index mirror to gauge an arc of difference and an arc of similarity. To extend the sextant imagery, while it is exciting to picture Muir as a celestial body riding out a windstorm swinging in a Douglas spruce, it is Burroughs who provides the steady light of the horizon toward which we must sail; he is the one who goes afoot in "A Snow-Storm" rather than riding a tree in the wind.[4] Burroughs is the one who writes of looking for a trail from the fishing campsite back to the farm, just as Austin writes of the trails of myriad small animals that lead a desert traveler toward lifesaving water in "Water Trails of the Cerisos."[5] In selecting Burroughs for study, then, I knew that I would want to emphasize the understated ways in which he criticizes but shows no contempt for contemporaneous society, and how he relies on the possibility of the reader's empathetic understanding for translating description into evaluation and judgment, and criticism into altered actions. But it was not until I prepared to have my students study Austin the week after Burroughs that I realized the key affinity between them and their distinction from Muir: inhabitation.

Both Burroughs and Austin are deeply and tirelessly concerned with how average human beings can and ought to live in nature, adapting themselves to the contours and the requirements of particular places, learning from the daily habits of the local flora and fauna, and critically considering the degree to which the places humans are already attempting to inhabit can adapt to the changes wrought by human cultures. Burroughs's and Austin's narratives contain other people, both those who belong and those who do not, but whose existence must be addressed. Austin's narrator is almost always an observer and relater and never a hero, and while Burroughs frequently narrates an adventure in which he is the main protagonist, he almost never single-handedly accomplishes his quest. Rather, he has help along the way, whether it be young boys giving directions on the river, farm women selling him milk, or Englishmen in the countryside directing and misdirecting him toward a nightingale. Students were quick to notice this humility but slow to consider its implications.

Birch Browsings proved to be a convenient Burroughs text, one that contrasted with and complemented the two western writers of this triumvirate. As the students noted, Austin frequently drew explicit philosophical conclusions from her vignettes and stories, but not Burroughs. Time and again he provides the basis for philosophical exclamations and ethical statements, but he seems to trust that the reader is a person of sufficiently good intentions, ethical integrity, and intellectual maturity to draw appropriate conclusions. Rarely if at all does he presume that the reader either agrees or disagrees, that he or she is already an ally or an enemy; rather, he keeps the possibility of understanding open through trying to step up alongside the reader and make comments worthy of consideration and meditation. Even in his moments of greatest apparent irritation, Burroughs's comments do not become polemical or didactic; they are not part of a confrontational shoving match, but rather a quiet and gentle nudge to someone walking beside him.

Students today, perhaps undergraduates more so than graduates, seem particularly prone to resist didactic texts through dismissal and refusal to engage rather than through direct disagreement. Particularly with environmental and multicultural issues, students become almost immediately defensive and tend to provide rationalizations for their lack of responsibility for the current state of affairs. Perhaps that is why addressing environmental themes and issues of inhabitation through bildungsromans like

Rudolfo Anaya's *Bless Me, Ultima* and Edna Escamill's *Daughter of the Mountain: Un Cuento* works so well with my undergraduate students, since they can identify with the protagonist's youthful situation even though they are not part of that ethnic group.

Although Burroughs is never a source of identification for students, they also do not become immediately defensive when he makes explicit or implicit environmental statements. Students in my class commented on his enthusiasm and passion for his subjects, noting that his remarks about human interaction with the land often shifted to less sanguine tones, as in the following from the title essay:

> Tanneries by the score have arisen and flourished upon the bark, and some of them still remain. Passing through that region the present season, I saw that the few patches of hemlock that lingered high up on the sides of the mountains were being felled and peeled, the fresh white boles of the trees, just stripped of their bark, being visible a long distance. . . .
>
> Wild pigeons, in immense numbers, used to breed regularly in the valley of the Big Ingin and about the head of the Neversink. . . . But the gunners soon got wind of it, and from far and near were wont to pour in during the spring, and to slaughter both old and young. This practice soon had the effect of driving the pigeons all away, and now only a few pairs breed in these woods. (*Browsings*, 2–3)

Clearly, these passages turn description into a powerful encouragement for critical self-reflection through the measured rhythm and tone of the sentences, the vivid images, and the evaluative word choice: "lingered," "visible a long distance," "gunners" (not "hunters," which he uses elsewhere), "slaughter" (not the euphemistic "harvest" that the Pennsylvania Game Commission uses for all types of hunting, including such practices as killing bears and other animals not for their meat but for the thrill of the hunt), and "soon." Part of the power here lies in Burroughs making his description historically comparative with the previous year and the very recent past, but he is careful not to make his expert knowledge an excuse for taking a smug position of authority that would distance him from the reader. Only two pages later he notes with humility a rather disastrous fishing trip, thereby maintaining the comic relationship between narrator and reader.

From there Burroughs tells of a later fishing trip, one taken in 1868, in which his small group fares better, but it reveals how little even these men—Burroughs included—know of the woods, the flora, the fauna, and the impact of their interaction. Of it he says, "I was taught how poor an Indian I should make, and what a ridiculous figure a party of men may cut in the woods when the way is uncertain and the mountains high" (*Browsings*, 5). While McKibben complains that Burroughs is too contented and too uncritical, I believe that here he is neither. Rather, he points out the limits of seasoned white sportsmen in comparison with the long-term inhabitants of these lands, and he sets up his party for negative critique by the reader, since the only groups of men previously cited in the essay are the hemlock-destroying bark peelers—whose consumptive practices are rapidly reducing their own numbers—and the species-extinguishing wanton "gunners." While Burroughs depicts himself as fully participating in the excessive taking of fish that this party achieves, he contrasts it with his far greater joy and deepened understanding of nature gained through the nonviolent, nondestructive sport of bird-watching. Burroughs's self-awareness of such a contrast remains a moot point; nevertheless, the descriptions afford the critical reader an opportunity for such comparison and consideration.

Burroughs creates such an opportunity for active rather than passive reading in part through his language, enthusiasm, and participation in the events and places depicted. Much of his writing is melodic if not poetic, as students noted, and he bridges the objective-subjective gap between science writing and personal writing by being friendly, familiar, and emotive, while also highly informative and very careful about the accuracy of his descriptions and claims, including his willingness to correct himself: "I had stated in print on two occasions that the wood thrush was not found in the higher lands of the Catskills. . . . It turns out this statement is only half true" (*Browsings*, 10). His role as a participant coupled with his willingness to include other people in his essays—something he does, like Austin, far more than many other nature writers—were also evaluated by the class as

strengths of his writing, ways by which narrator and reader are kept proximate despite the difference between the two in expertise.

There are four essays from *Birch Browsings* that I would like to focus on
briefly. The first was the favorite of the class, "A Snow-Storm," while the
next two, "Wildlife about My Cabin" and "The Art of Seeing Things,"
reinforced certain insights the students had expressed about earlier essays,
and the fourth is one that serves well my arguments for the benefits of
teaching Burroughs, "The Still Small Voice."

The first moment of enjoyment in "A Snow-Storm" comes immediately, with Burroughs's pleasant correction of Ralph Waldo Emerson, whose
grand poetics do not make up for his observational inaccuracy as far as Burroughs is concerned. Students appreciated throughout this brief piece the
way in which Burroughs wove poetry in and out of the observational prose,
intensifying the aesthetic affects of the essay while drawing attention to the
role poetry can play in developing nature awareness. This aesthetic emphasis renders more acceptable the anthropomorphizing of the snow and wind's
behavior, and, at the same time, sets the reader up for a surprise when
Burroughs, while still working within such poetic language, turns to the
accurate explanation of the beneficial, life-supporting qualities of a heavy
snowfall. Further, his appeal to the minute "Colorado valley" formations to
be found in the snowy countryside reminds readers that beauty is a perceptual phenomenon, one that does not require the magnitude or terror of
the sublime but only an observer's attentive eye—assuming that an individual is willing to venture forth in order to be attentive in such weather.
Finally, students and I found that part of the appeal of this essay comes with
its dual conclusion. The penultimate paragraph, building on the poetic language of the whole, establishes the wonder of geological crystallization and
identifies the two fundamental structures of matter: "Nature has but two
forms, the cell and the crystal—the crystal first, the cell last. All organic
nature is built up of the cell; all inorganic, of the crystal. Cell upon cell rises
the vegetable, rises the animal; crystal wedded to and compacted with crystal stretches the earth beneath them" (*Browsings*, 92). Having established
this dichotomy, Burroughs then dissolves it into a symbiotic relationship.
He furthers this reversal in the final paragraph, by also reversing human

perception of life and death: "We love the sight of the brown and ruddy earth; it is the color of life, while a snow-covered plain is the face of death; yet snow is but the mask of the life-giving rain; it, too, is the friend of man,—the tender, sculpturesque, immaculate, warming, fertilizing snow" (*Browsings*, 94). Rather than putting on the mask and claiming it as his own, or taking possession of the snowstorm through some heroic (or foolish) act of exposure, Burroughs steps aside and invites readers to step forward and reperceive what they think they have already seen.

"Wild Life about My Cabin" and "The Art of Seeing Things" work together to reinforce many of the points Burroughs raised in earlier essays. In the former, Burroughs makes explicit his previously implied humility by warning against always seeking the sublime, noting that "it is never wise to build your house on the most ambitious spot on the landscape" (*Browsings*, 95). Detailing his observations of birds, he also criticizes the sportsman who goes to the woods to kill and is unable to appreciate beauty without an effort at human mastery. The "gunner" ends up with only a "dead duck," while Burroughs has a vision of life in motion: "a live duck with whistling wings cleaving the air northward, where, in some lake or river of Maine or Canada, in late summer, I may meet him again with his brood" (*Browsings*, 109). At the end of this essay, Burroughs inveighs against Audubon and other naturalists who gain knowledge of another creature only through destroying it, and yet, rather than a polemic inflated with anger against a particular naturalist, Burroughs expresses a different emotion, one more in keeping with his encouragement for empathy with the rest of nature: "I felt ashamed for him" (*Browsings*, 115).

In "The Art of Seeing Things" he provides a rare commentary on his philosophy of observation. Noting the distinction between observation as a science and as an art, as well as various ways to cultivate "one's powers of observation," he makes a point in his conclusion that debunks the Kantian notion of disinterestedness and the scientific pretense of objectivity—a subject I take up in greater detail in the next chapter—"You must have the bird in your heart before you can find it in the bush" (*Browsings*, 133). This sentiment defines both the driving force behind his writing as well as the most important moral he would wish any reader to take from *Birch Browsings*.

If "The Art of Seeing Things" can be said to be Burroughs presenting his philosophy of observation, then "The Still Small Voice" may be identi-fied as a self-reflexive metanarrative, an essay about Burroughs's own essay writing. This self-reflexivity defines not only the tone and content of his essays, but also his overall strategy of relying on the quiet nudge rather than the polemical shove, on the slow accumulation of loving detail that may instill in others a similar empathy for the rest of nature. Burroughs is very much aware of the processes of inorganic and organic matter and of the dialectical change from quantitative increase to qualitative transformation, a distinction as applicable to cultural and political change as it is to geo-logical processes.

Commenting in several places about ecology, Burroughs also implicitly notes the role of his writing in American culture: "It is the slow insensible changes in the equipoise of the elements about us that, in the course of long periods of time, put a new face upon the aspect of the earth"; and "in the ordinary course of nature, the great beneficent changes come slowly and silently" (*Browsings*, 223). In case these remarks are too subtle for readers to apply them to their author, Burroughs becomes more explicit: "What a noise politics makes in the world, our politics especially! But some silent thinker in his study, or some inventor in his laboratory, is starting currents that will make or unmake politics for generations to come" (*Browsings*, 224–25). As if he were making a claim for a return to critical and public attention to his writings today, he concludes "The Still Small Voice" with these words: "In a time of noise and hurry and materialism like ours, the gospel of the still small voice is always seasonable" (*Browsings*, 227).

Burroughs as a Challenge to Expectations

In order for students in general to learn to hear, and for graduate stu-dents in particular to learn to teach, it is necessary for them to recognize and address directly the frequent limitations of their own educations up to the point at which a book like *Birch Browsings* is introduced. I am thinking here in terms of the mainstream American literary canon, the genre biases of most literature courses, and American popular culture's thirst for the quick, the terrifying, and the action packed. When I went around the room at the beginning of the class meeting devoted to Burroughs and Muir and asked for initial student responses, several of them began with "I don't know what to think." This remark was often followed by an expression of confusion over the genre of what we were reading (students had already informed me that most of them did not recognize the name of a single author on the reading list: Burroughs, Muir, Austin, Wendell Berry, Linda Hogan, Gretchen Legler, Dori Sanders, Terry Tempest Williams, and Karen Tei Yamashita).

The students who tried to read this material as American fiction were reading for the plot and not finding much of one, particularly when it came to identifying the moment of crisis. Students who recognized the need to take a different approach tended to veer toward rhetorical analysis, especially with anything labeled nonfiction, and then felt uncertain about attending to the aesthetic dimensions of *Birch Browsings*. In addition to their being unprepared for the literary nonfiction of nature writing, they also suffered, for the most part, from a lack of critical experience with biography, travel literature, diaries, and memoirs. As a result, they tended to see the authors as being confused about the genre in which they were writing, rather than seeing themselves as confused about the hybrid genre they were reading.

Exposure and patient clarification are the only remedies for these problems. Particularly for students already feeling uncertain about the prominence of plot in narrative, about the relationship of prose nature literature to the canon and to the familiar genres of poetry, fiction, and drama, as well as about the relationship of rhetorical argumentative persuasion and aesthetic emotive persuasion, Burroughs's quiet nudge can have tremendous power in helping them to comfortably and effectively reorient themselves toward the world in the literature.

12

Rudimentary Remarks on the Need for a Few New Words

Synthesis and the Limitations of Current Language

I N MY UPPER-DIVISION liberal studies synthesis course, "Other and Another: Ecology, Gender, and Culture," which I teach on a regular basis, I began the fall semester of 1996 with discussion focused largely on the very concept of synthesis that the university uses to define this type of interdisciplinary course required of all students to graduate. *Synthesis* was not a new word for students, but the application of its verb form to their own intellectual practice was new given the degree to which these seniors had been institutionalized by discipline.

Along the way, I introduced to them another word that was nouveau, like synthesis, but not *neue*, as in the French distinction between new-to-me and brand new. That word was *asymmetry*, and I was attempting to draw their attention to the asymmetry of the language and the asymmetry of cultural practices, as in the differences between the definitions of *mothering* and *fathering*, or as in the ubiquity of the word *hierarchy* and the rarity of the usage of its antonym, *heterarchy*—a key concept in dispute in environmental ethics and fundamental to much of ecological feminism.

Having made our way through all that, with varying degrees of attention and participation on the part of the twenty-five mostly female students, I assigned a majority of the chapters in Carolyn Merchant's *Earthcare*, with the readings spread over two weeks. Merchant labels the first three chapters of the book the theory section. The degree to which these students complained about Merchant's language, about their need to refer repeatedly to a dictionary, was striking. They did not complain about the quality or character of their education up to that point, nor did they note that it had not prepared most of them to read *Earthcare*. Rather, they complained that Merchant should have written the book more clearly using only language with which they were already familiar. Yet Merchant could not possibly have fulfilled that desire completely. While it is true that she could have defined more terms and presumed a lower level of knowledge on the part of her readers than she did, she could not have written *Earthcare* exclusively in the daily vocabulary of the students in this class.

Why? Because that language has failed them; it has proven inadequate for articulating the kinds of understanding that an ecological feminist philosophical orientation must enunciate; it lacks the terminology necessary for depicting the kinds of interdependencies that ground Merchant's culminating concept of partnership ethics. The language upon which most of these students rely is steeped in instrumental reason, American pragmatism, consumerist clichés, and the logic of domination. Over several years of teaching this course, I have come to realize that the difficulty students have in articulating their ideas in the context of Earthcare's subject matter arises from the inadequacy of the culture-bound language they employ.[1]

Merchant refers to "the obvious need for new symbols and a new language" in *Earthcare*.[2] When I hit that sentence, the conclusion of Annette Kolodny's *The Lay of the Land*, a now classic text of ecofeminist literary critique, flashed through my mind, as did the work of Suzette Haden Elgin. Kolodny writes about the American patriarchal metaphors of the domination of female nature and women, and of the need for new symbols and metaphors that challenge such cultural constructs. Part of Elgin's work in linguistics and science fiction is based on her determining that women's experiences could not be expressed in contemporary American English, and possibly not in any other language at the present time.[3] As she explains,

I had come across the hypothesis that existing human languages are not adequate to express the perceptions of women. . . . And I found the hypothesis especially interesting for its paradox [because] . . . then the only mechanism available to women for explaining this situation and for working with it was the very language that was inadequate! . . .

I then proposed that perhaps for any *language* there are certain perceptions that it cannot express. . . . for any culture there are certain languages that it cannot use because they would result in its self-destruction.[4]

Rather than just developing some new symbols and metaphors, or trying to invent a new word or two, like Marge Piercy's pronoun *per* in *Woman on the Edge of Time*, Elgin invented an entirely new language called Láadan, which accurately expresses women's perceptions, and then wrote a set of science fiction novels about the cultural transformation that the introduction of such a language into society would bring about.

We may very well need to go to the lengths Elgin suggests, but we will probably need to be much closer than we are now to a postpatriarchal society to do so. Using Bakhtinian dialogics and its emphasis on everyday living language as utterance, as process, as a simultaneity of breaking down and codifying movements, I will argue that in the meantime (or should that be *mean time*?) we can take smaller positive steps to alter American English right now, and that such language-building will move us a little closer to another type of society. We can facilitate ecofeminist, antianthropocentric thinking through revising the vocabulary to enable enunciation of other ways of thinking than those dictated by the dominant discourse structures and their attendant vocabularies.

To do so, we need to allow the generation of other symbols and metaphors, and even more so of other metonymies rather than metaphors, through providing some new words that foster a more user-friendly context for the deployment of new symbols and images, which are often the regeneration of very ancient and different cultural practices. Kristin Cashman, a research associate with the Center for Indigenous Knowledge for Agriculture and Rural Development, in "Systems of Knowledge as Systems of Domination: The Limitations of Established Meaning" noted that "Naming offers transformative powers, bringing into existence phenomena and experience previously denied. The act of naming, especially when words become part of the everyday language inclusive of a significant group, simultaneously affirms a changed consciousness of reality and contests existing Euramerican hegemony and authority."[5] What I am suggesting here, then, is the need to foray into alterations of word usage in everyday language in the same way that I have done in regard to genre and definitional analysis of nature writing and other forms of nature-oriented literature. Without new terminology it is just as difficult, or perhaps even impossible, to distinguish different forms of behavior and different modes of perceptions as it is to distinguish different types of representations of human–rest-of-nature relationships in literature.

Retooling Existing Words and Inventing Antonyms

One of our later readings in the course, *Ecofeminism and the Sacred*, edited by Carol J. Adams, reinforced this argument about the power of naming. While it did not contain very many brand new words, or neologisms, in various places it used existing words in different ways. It also demonstrated the need for privileging lesser known words to serve as antonyms, not simply to predominant words but more complexly to predominant paradigms. In the introduction, Adams discusses "false dualisms," noting that "the second part of the dualism is not only subordinate but *in service* to the first. . . . The voices of women of color and women from other philosophical traditions offer alternative metaphysical viewpoints in which the matter/spirit dualism evaporates."[6]

Subordinate and *subordination*, like *oppression*, are words commonly bandied about in critical work. But we need to hear not only those terms that depict oppression and hierarchy, but also the counter terms, such as *coordinate* and *dyad*, so that we can talk about night and day in some other way than as a hierarchical dichotomy in which day is always privileged and the good invariably associated with the light (a ready color hierarchy for white racism to naturalize its existence). If we think, rather, of night and day as a coordinate dyad, we can more easily recognize their mutually consti-

tutive, nonprivileging relationship, and realize that our privileging of day-
light results from the situated specific features of human eyesight. Our eyesight is only one particular kind of vision found among animal species; animals with other kinds view night and day differently or may even make little
distinction between the two. Some humans can, in fact, see quite well at
night if they learn how to utilize their own sensory perceptions to their
fullest potential—a potential inhibited by hierarchical dichotomies.

Additionally, I noted in thinking about this passage from Adams that
one always hears about subordinate relationships, but the word *superordinate*
seems to refer almost always only to factors in mathematical equations. The
suppression of the antonym serves to naturalize the position of the dominant category and imply that the subordinate is lacking something, is inferior, unnatural, and therefore fallen. What would happen in paradigmatic
thinking about political and social hierarchies if we suppressed *subordinate*
and privileged the use of *superordinate* in discussing dichotomous hierarchies? If newspapers began to discuss the superordinate character of U.S.
influence in the Middle East (a Eurocentric term itself), or the superordinate quality of Japanese automobiles, what happens to perceptions about
those relationships, their stability, and the nature of their occurrence? Like
the phrase "having the upper hand," *superordinate* would tend to imply the
temporary character of the hierarchy rather than its permanence, wouldn't it?

While in the former example I spun out alternative terms from Adams's
discussion, Stephanie Kaza in her chapter in *Ecofeminism and the Sacred* spins
out her own when she writes that "I outline here six areas of confluence."[7]
Confluence is used frequently with rivers and water flows, but rarely with
concepts, cultures, and societies, when *influence* is the privileged term, a
term that immediately institutes a hierarchy and a unidirectional flow. Yet,
one of the key points of the postcolonial theory of such writers as Homi K.
Bhabha and Trinh T. Min-ha is the impossibility of unidirectionality in the
case of cultural contact. Time and again the colonizers and their imperial-
ist descendants will attempt to deny the bidirectionality of colonialism, but
confluence emphasizes this mutuality, the bidirectionality of any encounter,
its character as a contact—the etymology of which means to touch together,
not Europeans touching Africans while remaining untouched in return.

Further, a term like *confluence* contradicts the cultural and linguistic tendencies toward the establishment of hierarchy through dichotomies by foregrounding dyads, triads, and multiplicities.

As a final example from *Ecofeminism and the Sacred*, there are the words *natural*, *supernatural*, and *ultranatural* from Charlene Spretnak. She critiques the dominant word usage and also offers an alternative usage—again from already existing language: "Revelation may be *extra*ordinary, but it is not *super*natural. It would more accurately be labeled *ultra*natural, a journey into the cosmic nature that lies within the world we tend to perceive as an aggregate of discrete fragment bound by such forces as gravity and electromagnetism."[8] When first reading this passage, I immediately thought of how dichotomy-minded Western science attempted to define photons as either waves or particles, which are conceptualized as mutually exclusive categories of existence. Photons finally had to be referred to as *wavicles*, since the properties they exhibit break the binary by being two things simultaneously—a category of existence long known to Eastern philosophies but only recently admitted by enlightened science.

My attention to these moments in Adams's collection came later in the semester, after a little exercise made me more attuned to their occurrence. I had built a small multiday group project for the class during its reading of *Earthcare*. The first day of this project required that I sit unobtrusively for about an hour while the groups got underway, and that is when I began jotting down some binaries and antonym dichotomies and thinking about alternative words. What first came to mind was the thought that even though I was sitting quietly, I was still observing and listening to the students at work, but then, reminding myself of such critiques of the Enlightenment as Merchant's, I realized that I was not observing the students at all. *Observation* has become very much entangled with the concept of objective, as in the fourth definition of *observation* in *Webster's New World Dictionary*: "the act or practice of noting and recording facts and events, as for some scientific study." Even when someone remarks, "let me make an observation on that point," they imply not a personal, subjective, interested, participatory position for their evaluative and persuasive remark, but imply that their viewpoint is informational and based on a detached form of objective study of phenomena external to the person speaking. Can anyone remember ever having actually stood in that kind of place when using that kind of phrase, rather than in a position of holding a subjective or partisan perspective?

Another example involves the practice of "faculty observations," which I attempted to make detached and impersonal, a sort of objective observation, when I first engaged in them. In order to do that I had to limit myself to description: "The teacher did this, and then did that, and the students responded in this way, and it appeared as such, and at the end of the hour five students approached the teacher with questions," and so on. Even in that selection process, however, the nonfiction description became fictionalized in the sense of having a thematically oriented plot that evaluatively shaped the arrangement, emphasis, inclusion, and omission of the details and events described. That is to say, I authored an ideologically based narrative of description that provided an evaluation of the teacher using the criteria of my subjective concept of effective pedagogy and appropriate class content. The more I revised such reports the more I tended to let the narrative and aesthetic dimensions of the formally finished text shape the representation of observed events. Even in a faculty observation, the gap between narrative-as-service and narrative-as-drive came into play. Eventually we were told that we should be making evaluations rather than observations. I would contend that in doing this we only moved from being implicit to being explicit—we were never making observations.

So, as I was meditating in the classroom on the inappropriateness and inaccuracy of the word *observation*, I asked why American English had no symmetrically structured antonym for it. Why was there no *subservation* or even *comservation* in the vocabulary? The former term would highlight the fundamentally personal and subjective character of any looking done on the basis that all such looking, describing, and analyzing is necessarily situated, partial, and ideologically, conceptually, and linguistically inflected and confluenced, if not overtly determined. The latter term, *comservation*, would highlight the degree to which the so-called object of attention, the observed of the observer during the observation, is a participant and mutual constructor of the experience to be seen, described, and evaluated. How rare is it for so-called observations to occur with the total lack of awareness of the person or entity being observed? How frequently do people sense that they are being watched when the individual watching is attempting to do so covertly and furtively? More often the watching is scheduled and structured through negotiation and agreement between the observer and the observed.

There is certainly a strong gender dimension to this issue, and the way that conceptualization is structured through language is similar, I believe, to the unidirectional myth of colonial influence. Historically, men have wished to imagine that they own the gaze, that whatever they look upon is the recipient of the look, and that there exists no reciprocity, confluence, or back-gazing that has an immanent power or transformative capability, as Susan Griffin's numerous quotations from the Western patriarchal tradition in *Woman and Nature* amply demonstrate. To "look someone in the eye" is to lay claim to a certain mutual power, a certain equality, a certain right to responsiveness, and all types of customs, regulations, and military procedures are designed to forestall such intergazing that might demonstrate fundamental intraspecies, and perhaps even interspecies, equality. The concept of observation fixes the location and position of only one participant in an interactive process. Alternative terms would encourage such an illusion to evaporate.

The observation-subservation-comserservation meditation led me back to *objective* and *subjective* on the one hand, and forward to *subservient* on the other. I stopped believing in the idea of objectivity a long time ago. What is most detrimental about the illusion of objectivity is that it discourages people from valuing their own experiences, opinions, and ideas. The anecdotal is classified as the inconsequential, which works particularly against women and the nonhuman.

For the former, the personal, the domestic, and the familial is relegated to the sphere of the anecdotal—the women's sphere of domestic experience and knowledge; the public sphere—that dominated by men—is perceived in contrast as the locus for the objective, the universal, and the factual. For the latter, the nonhuman, the experiences of individual animals and individual species, as witnessed by human beings and related to other human beings, are dismissed precisely because they can only be related in anecdotal forms. Perhaps because of this problem, there has been that tendency in analyses of nature writing to emphasize the genre's nonfiction status, to bring its depictions into line with the dominant scientific paradigm of observation and evidence. The result, then, is that the validity of the writing lies not in the record of human proximity with the rest of nature but in accuracy achievable only through distancing the experiences from one's self and one's situatedness—an alienation model.

To the degree that women engage in anecdotal acknowledgment of experience and situated implementation of ethics that reject the illusion of objectivity—the kind of female ethics-building and moral development analyzed by Carol Gilligan and others—their knowledge, experience, inferences, and conclusions can be disregarded, dismissed, and devalued within American patriarchal culture.[9] The subjective, which is defined as individual, is pitted against the objective, which is defined as universal. In the preface to *Mapping the Moral Domain*, Gilligan cites an example of the differences between boys' and girls' responses to an essay contest on the how to improve their city: "To the boys, improving the city meant urban renewal as we generally conceive it: more parks, new buildings, renovations, better streets, more lighting. Girls, however, wrote about improving the city in a way the reporter found surprising. They suggested strengthening relationships between people: responding to people in need and taking action to help them." Gilligan then raises these questions: "Whose meanings will prevail and be taken as 'right' or definitive? What are the implications of seeing or speaking in what is considered to be the 'right' language?"[10]

As long as binary oppositions between the objective and the subjective and the universal and the individual are used to answer Gilligan's questions, women's perspectives will not prevail. Instead, the possibility of a third term needs to be entertained here as well, that of *comjective*, which would refute the binary logic of mutual exclusion and posit a multiplicitous logic of inclusion. By comjective I mean an evaluation, decision, opinion, understanding, or depiction that is neither personal or universal, but that is the result of the group circulation of anecdotal information and the consideration of its frequency.

A comjective view would be established and maintained by a group even when enunciated by an individual. For example, many times when a student says that she is just expressing her personal opinion, further discussion reveals that she is expressing her concurrence with a comjective perspective developed among her peers, neighborhood residents, religious affiliates, family, or some other collective. When any group's values or beliefs are suppressed or isolated from the knowledge base articulated by the dominating culture, class, gender, race, or other structured hierarchy, then the group's members can never speak from the illusory, although powerful, position of universality and objectivity. Yet they must resist the disempowering illusion that their perspective is only personal because it is admittedly situated and partial.

Turning to the idea of *subservient*, I realized that it was much like *subordinate*. We hear all the time about subordinates and subservient behavior, but we never hear of superordinates and superservient behavior, and no one to my knowledge has ever referred to equiservient behavior. And yet, again, how can we have subservient behavior on the part of one person unless someone else is engaging in superservient behavior, that is, forcing or pressuring someone to act out a hierarchical relationship to the exclusive benefit of the one wielding the force.

Through the language, the culture in a sense blames the victim, rather than blaming the perpetrator by talking about superservience. What seems to be sorely missing here, as a result of the hierarchical dichotomy in which it is bad to be subservient but implicitly good to be the recipient of another's subservience, is the idea of equiservience, in which individuals engage in mutually beneficial relationships of service. Such a concept would reinforce the notion of multidirectional confluence and the possibility of equitable circuits of service among members of a community. It is likely that such circuits would work on the basis of consensus about skills, abilities, and needs—a determination based on power with rather than on a hierarchy of domination or power over.

Finally, I find myself wanting to move toward terms that break with the construction of binaries and dichotomies and the separations of categories into pseudoautonomous or independent structures of existence. Ecology for me is fundamentally an awareness of existence as interanimation, interdependency, and systemic process, which is always multifaceted and multi-variable. M.-Pierrette Malcuzynski, for instance, criticizes the term *alterity* as being based exclusively on a psychoanalytic model of literary interpreta-tion, which implies that there is only a B for any given A. He contrasts to it the term *heterogeneity*, which is based on a social model of interpretation and implies that for any given A there may be not only be B but also C, D, E, and so on. Malcuzynski's heterogeneity is developed from the terminol-ogy of Mikhail Bakhtin and is therefore implicitly dialogic.

Since Malcuzynski does not develop this point about heterogeneity's dialogic implication, I have concluded that being implicit about it is insuf-ficient. Both terms, *alterity* and *heterogeneity*, like *diversity* within the frame-work of multicultural analysis, can be perceived as nondialogic construc-tions of autonomous categories based on difference, in opposition to terminology that encourages the absorption of all experience into the self on the one hand and the absorption of all experience into a homogenizing universality on the other. Again, I think we need a third category of terms that emphasize interconnectedness and the relational character of differ-ence, suggested by the idea of *confluence* and the differential character of relationship already indicated by the distinction of confluence from the con-cept of *identity*.

Alterity tends to be too binary, based too much on the construct of self and other in psychoanalytic theory. Perhaps we need *polyterity*, which psy-choanalytically would at least include self, other, and another, which in turn could be socially related to such multipositionality as "I-for-myself," "I-for-another," "another-for-me," "another-for-itself," along with a "thing-in-itself," "thing-for-me," and "I-as-a-thing-for-others."[11] Such use of terms to reconceive our individual social situatedness might help us to see that *multipositionality* has a different emphasis from *heterogeneity*, the former more fluid, transitory, and processional than the latter's determined fixedness.

Just as we need terms like *confluence* to show the bidirectionality of con-tact and *comjective* to show the group constitution of individually held val-ues, perhaps we also need a term like *intervariating* as a more fluid, inter-active, mutually constitutive conception of relational difference than *diversity* can connote. Such new words and reconfigurations of conceptions could even serve to help the foregrounding of an ecology of language analysis that would begin to reveal all the roots, branches, and multiternatives that have been suppressed by dominant patriarchal discourses.

New Language and Ecological Literacy

Certainly such critiquing of language as a patriarchal system is nothing new. Barbara DiBernard and Sheila Reiter, for instance, demonstrate their application of such feminist linguistic critique in their essay "Two Women on the Verge of a Contextual Breakthrough: Using *A Feminist Dictionary* in the Literature Classroom." But their essay also demonstrates the difficulties in such an undertaking when they stumble over the subjective-objective dichotomy in several instances. For example, DiBernard, in one of her portions of this dialogic essay, admits that *A Feminist Dictionary* is subjective, but in order for that not to be cause for its dismissal she then must point out that male-authored dictionaries are "considerably less than objective," which defends the feminist agenda but leaves the dichotomy intact.[12] I do not mean this subservation to be a criticism of what these two have accomplished in their teaching and in their essay, but I want to emphasize the difficulty and complexity of what they are trying to do, and to suggest that we need multiternative definitions of existing words as well as new words, ones arising from and supporting other paradigms.

As with the rest of *Changing Classroom Practices*, edited by David B. Downing, in which the DiBernard and Reiter essay appears, no recognition exists of ecofeminist theory or analyses, no recognition of ecology or ecological criticism. Instead, Downing, Patricia Harkin, and James J. Sosnoski in an introductory essay, "Configurations of Lore," establish the basis for this omission by repeatedly discussing the idea of culture utterly divorced from any idea of nature but invariably married to the idea of technology. Perhaps most telling is their introduction of a redefined lore that utterly ignores the relationship of that concept to indigenous and inhabitory peoples, who develop their lore from constant interaction with the material world, not primarily as a series of humanly manipulated and culturally enfolded constructs but as a series of engagements with the rest of nature that boundaries human cultures and limits the extent of human manipulations.

Recall here Adams's words about the voices of women of color offering "alternative metaphysical viewpoints in which the matter/spirit dualism evaporates," and certainly along with it the nature-culture dualism.[13] By replicating the nature-culture dualism in their theoretical foundation, Downing, Harkin, and Sosnoski encourage the replication of other dualisms throughout, such as the objective-subjective dichotomy. This reduces concerns about oppression—and forms of resistance—to occurring only as reactions against dominant cultures and the discourses established by them, rather than advising proactively from the cultural agency of those who are oppressed.

When the issue of knowledge is limited to the concept of literacy as understanding culture, as it is in Downing, Harkin, and Sosnoski, then the wisdom, words, and languages of oral traditions focusing on human-non-human interaction at the edge of cultures are circumscribed. The focus remains on a negative critique aimed at dismantling "obsolete cultural standards" without enunciating a transformative agency based on building new paradigms for healthy cultural practices.[14] When the issue of women's oppression is treated as occurring only within the human contradictions arising from patriarchy and forms of feminism developed only in that context, then the recognition of the oppression of women as part of the domination of nature is ignored along with the forms of resistance to oppression and multiternative egalitarian culture-building practices inspired by ecofeminist analyses. We cannot afford the luxury of such ignorance and reliance on continuing negative critique, even in the rarified air of academic discourse, any more than we can afford to ignore the wisdom already available from other cultures and traditions.

As I hope I have demonstrated here, we cannot afford to work only with the words given us by a cultural system that continues to survive on the basis of a series of oppressions that are fundamentally contradictory to world nature, which includes human nature, even when those words are deployed in the form of negation. Rather, we must accept the responsibility of the potential for transformative agency upon which ecofeminism is

∾

based in order to engage in culture-building practices from theoretical articulations of deeply felt needs to modifications of basic mundane activities. The language in which we think and speak forms a part of such a spectrum. Carol Lee Sanchez has defined contemporary human duty in these terms: "Our duty to ourselves is to restore our own balance *within* the rest of creation."[15] Through recycling neglected words, redefining others, and inventing ones that help articulate and advance an ecofeminist practice, we can gain a more balanced language increasingly reflective of the multifaceted, intervariating world through which each of us will pass.

Conclusion

Direction and Intention

International Direction

T HE MAJORITY OF THE examples I have used in the previous chapters are taken from contemporary American literature, even though three chapters are devoted to the issue of internationalizing the study of nature-oriented literature. As with my previous book, *Literature, Nature, and Other,* I have made a conscious effort to emphasize the multicultural dimensions of contemporaneous writing by focusing on visibly ethnic authors. I have also emphasized women authors. While the situation is improving, it seems that critics and teachers still feel comfortable generating discussions and syllabi that exclude or nearly exclude women and that draw exclusively on Euro-American authors. Even when so-called minority writers and women are included, too often they are compared with and against the male writers.

For example, in the exchange on the Association for the Study of Literature and Environment Internet discussion group mentioned in chapter 2, over the differences between fiction and nonfiction, male examples predominated. Further, when some individuals sought to finely distinguish between the amount of imaginative reorganization or selective omission of facts and details allowed a work of nonfiction, it was almost always the case that women authors, such as Annie Dillard, were criticized, while male authors, such as Edward Abbey and Henry David Thoreau, were defended in their reorganizations, omissions, and imaginative embellishments.

I would like to see the day when more male critics can just admit that they prefer reading men because they themselves are men and want to read literature that speaks to their particular masculine inclinations, without the subsequent rationalizations that attempt to defend such preferred literature as better than literature by women. Such an admission would also require that men admit that they do not prefer reading literature by women because they do not understand it very well, or because they find it difficult to engage in cross-gender reading, which might sound to some of their own readers like an admission of weakness. Such an observation would, however, lead to the recognition of certain implications and issues in their classrooms, if they were teachers, regarding expectations that women students should joyfully, successfully, and unquestioningly engage in cross-gender reading for the majority of readings in their courses; or that northeastern Latinos should have no trouble identifying with southwestern Chicanos, let alone a bunch of white California mountain climbers.

The students in my upper-division synthesis course "Other and Another: Ecology, Gender, and Culture," who are mostly women, have concurred and elaborated on this point—in our culture women are expected to read, listen, and converse in cross-gender categories all the time, but men are expected to do so much less, if at all. Some women in the class felt obligated to apologize for their lack of interest in and knowledge of, say, the intricacies of hockey or football or arcane mechanics, but they had never seen a man apologize for being ignorant about the low quality and high expense of most women's clothing or group synchronization of menstrual cycles. The asymmetry of cross-gendered understanding in our culture is reflected in the asymmetry, and its attendant expectations, of both cross-gendered and cross-cultural reading and criticism.

While I would like to believe that I have made some headway toward correcting that score, I also recognize that I have not done much with international cross-cultural and cross-gendered reading and criticism. Certainly I am justified in limiting the range of my expertise and circumscribing the parameters of the literatures about which I will write and publish, but the field of ecological criticism as a whole cannot justify such circumscription, nor can it afford to remain as thoroughly ethnocentric as it is today. I do not think very many people want it to remain that way.

It is hard, though, being trained as Americanists or romanticists, to set our dinghy critical apparatuses afloat on international waters. We need the assistance of postcolonial theorists and critics, of comparativists, and of international-studies people to help us gain the minimum proficiency for such study and teaching. At the same time, it seems that in many cases we need to introduce such people to ecocriticism first, before they can help us with their knowledge of national literatures outside the Anglo-American tradition. To do that we need to know some examples that such people will recognize, which means we need to risk talking about and writing about international literature before we really know much about it. We will have to stand ready to be corrected for our oversights, omissions, and misinterpretations. Nevertheless, we need to get going and do our homework.

One part of that homework, as a part of the promotion of ecological criticism and nature-oriented literature for the reading public and college classrooms, is to collaborate on translating and editing international literature written in languages other than English. Translators are out there; American ecocritics have to help them determine what to translate and then help get it published.

Domestic Direction

At the same time that we need to look beyond our shores, around the Pacific Rim, across the Atlantic, and south past the Gulf, we also need to stare intently at the local, the domestic, and the familiar. I think here of the John Muir–John Burroughs kind of dichotomy. In my own life that dichotomy has not been California–New York, but California-Pennsylvania: the vast and towering western Sierra reaches and the proximate and tightly rippled eastern Appalachian ridges, the wilderness and the local valley, the redwoods and the willows, the eagle and the robin, Gary Snyder and Wendell Berry; or, in cross-gender and cross-ethnic terms: Gretel Ehrlich and Marcia Bonta, Octavia Butler and Pat Mora. The emphasis in ecocriticism has recently fallen on the Muir side, on the wilderness side, on the western slope, if you will. I do not want any of that attention lessened, but I think we need to increase the attention to the eastern slope.

While I do not want to see any national parks sold off to developers, or any national forests clear cut for more toilet paper and facial tissue, I would not mind if more people camped out in their own backyards and local parks rather than racing off to the government-run woods for the weekend. When I lived, or maybe just survived, in Los Angeles, people were always racing off to the mountains to go skiing or flying off to Cancún to go swimming. I never seemed to have the money to do either, but I could get on my motorcycle, or whatever else I was driving at a given time, and go up Angeles Crest Highway and in less than an hour some winter nights and see snow falling (perhaps because I grew up in Illinois, snow falling seemed even more important to me than the ocean roaring). Or I could drive a little farther in another direction toward Tejon Pass and get above the neon-incandescent glare of the city to see the stars. Like those who could afford to fly, ski, and swim somewhere else, I also often felt I had to get up and out of the city to see anything, to feel anything that was not synthetically structured by culture and machinery.

Today, living at the edge of the city of Indiana, Pennsylvania, I do not feel that way. A few weeks before drafting this conclusion I was painting a deck railing at the house near campus that we rent out to a family, and on one of the spindles clung a praying mantis. I introduced my daughter, Mariko, to it before moving it out of the line of work. Not more than a week or two before that, Mariko had also been introduced to the particularities of deer droppings deposited near our garden—they were proof of my contention regarding the loss of our lettuce. Gradually, I have come to look more and more for insights on such details in my reading, for lessons about the wildness we are always bordering that invigorates the wildness within us and helps balance out the ennatured cultural relationships of our human sociophysiological constructions. But such a local emphasis cannot apply only to my own national literature. When I go looking for that international literature and its translations, the domestic and the local, the proximate wildness of other places, will be part of what I am seeking to find.

Intention

Studying and critiquing nature-oriented literature should be something like setting out on a December night to go up the Angeles Crest highway to see snow. It ought to help us articulate our own understanding and feelings about humanity's relationship with the rest of the world, about our mind's relationship with our brain and nervous system, and about our molecules' relationships with the atoms of the universe. Articulating such understanding and feelings ought to help us make decisions about the degree to which we see the existence of an environmental crisis, looming or fully upon us, the degree to which we see a connection between that determination of crisis and our own work and careers, and the degree to which our theories and our thoughts square with the daily actions of our lives.

My intention has been to point out certain texts, authors, and groups that might have been overlooked or insufficiently represented and analyzed elsewhere, with the aim of helping readers with their understanding through articulating the theories that orient my representations and connecting the texts with others that are perhaps better known. To encourage further consideration, I have raised questions without answering them, or only partially answering them, and given readings geared to provoke more than to determine—or maybe here too we need a new word, like *intervoke*, to define a process of raising a challenging idea to get both the author and reader, speaker and listener, to contend with its implications. I hope that others will think about these works and these issues at least as much as I have, but not necessarily in the same ways.

Regarding some differences between a colleague and myself in pedagogy and advising of graduate students, my wife, Bonnie, recently commented that the other colleague acts like a parent, while I act like a therapist. In advising doctoral students about their comprehensive exam fields and then their dissertation topics, I try to help them figure out their desires, their interests, and their concepts through articulating what I hear them saying to me. The result usually is that they leave my office feeling that they have a better understanding of what they want to do and that at least one other person shares that understanding. My colleague is more likely to have students leaving the office knowing how the faculty member would pursue the topic and understanding the reasons why they should pursue it in the same way. I have not yet figured out how to practice such therapy in my writing, but I hope this book bears the marks of my attempts to resist playing the parent too extensively.

In my professional activities, I try to keep myself open to the idea that I am teaching, advising, and writing about ways to approach thinking about, drawing conclusions about, and resolving issues, problems, interpretations, and the application of interpretations to one's own life. With such an emphasis I accept and expect that students and readers will draw different conclusions from my own, but that we can share the process of learning. I firmly believe in the possibility of a multiplicity of positive, productive, and true answers to the same question, and I always suspect that today's answer may suffice only for today's version of the question, if even that.

Reading, studying, and writing about nature-oriented literature, then, should be like the summer's growth of poison ivy. It ought to be like a rhizome, free from dependence on a single tap root, with food for growth in every segment of the root system. Wild and multileafed, it ought to send out shoots in unexpected places, working its way in through cracks in the foundation, up between the bushes, out in the sun and deep in the shade. Unlike poison ivy, however, it should not choke the very trees around which it twines.

Notes

INTRODUCTION

1. Such a viewpoint is still reflected in the organization of so-called natural history museums, where allegedly primitive cultures are represented but contemporary cultures are not. This arrangement encourages a perception of a modern nature-culture split and implies that indigenous earth-oriented cultural practices belong to the past rather than to the present and future.

2. On the "nature fakers" controversy, see Lutts, *Nature Fakers*.

3. On this point, see the first chapter of Scheese, *Nature Writing*.

4. Dunne, *Before the Echo*, xii.

5. In what strikes me as a curious sleight of hand, Buell, in reading *Walden* "non-fictionally," to use his term, compares an early journal entry with the final version of the event in *Walden* and then remarks in *Environmental Imagination*: "These small changes ensured that the contact between mouse and man would *seem* more like an intimate, companionable interchange than the *Journal* version *imagined* it as being" (96; emphasis added). *Seem* means that something appears as if it were true, whether or not it actually is true or factual, which would imply that Thoreau is engaging in mimetic creativity, with mimesis being a type of artistic representation. In order to press his point, Buell closes by using the verb *imagined* rather than *represented* or *recorded* in order to make it *seem* as if the *Walden* passage is a more nonfictional account than the journal passage. And yet, which is more likely to be imagined? A journal entry written shortly after the event or a heavily reworked version written years later?

Buell's argument is about two different ways of reading, not about the degree of fiction and nonfiction in a specific work being read, since any work of fiction can draw heavily on past records of actual experience. That such is the case is evidenced by Buell moving from a discussion of how to read nonfiction to the benefits of applying the same reading approach to fiction and poetry (91–103). White's remarks about historical discourse in "The Real, the True" seem a pertinent reminder of the fictionality that can be found even in histories, much less in literary narratives:

Although historical discourse continually moves between the poles of the misrep-resentations of reality given in the historical record and its own reconstructions of "what really happened" (or what can be plausibly said really to have happened) in the past—and in the process provides reasons both for believing in these recon-structions and for understanding why reality was misrepresented in the way it is in the record—it remains blind to the extent to which its own reconstructions are, themselves, less defigurations than refigurations of the reality in question. This blindness sustains the ideology of realism that informs and authorizes history's claim to the status of a science in the modern age. (15)

Also, see "Ecology and American Literature," Kroeber's critique of Buell's book.

6. Ryden, "Landscape with Figures," 25–26n. 2.

7. Miner, *Comparative Poetics*, 51; see chapters 1 and 4 for pertinent discussions of the different types of poetics and the issues of mimesis and fact-fiction.

8. Duncan, *River Teeth*, 5.

9. Recent revelations about the life of John C. Van Dyke, for instance, raise ques-tions about how to classify his 1901 work *The Desert*, long considered a classic of non-fiction nature writing. *The Secret Life of John C. Van Dyke*, edited by Teague and Wild, re-veals that Van Dyke engaged in a significant amount of fictional self-representation in *The Desert*. Eric Gary Anderson writes in a review of *Secret Life that* Van Dyke "con-coct[ed] a fantasy travelogue" (168). If true, that would suggest to me that *The Desert* ought to be labeled fictional nature literature rather than nature writing. I suspect that future research will raise doubts over the nonfictionality of more such works.

1. When the Land Is More Than a Scape

1. Bryant, "Nature as Picture/Nature as Milieu," 29.

2. Ibid.; see also Cohen, "Literary Theory," 1099.

3. Marietta, *For People and the Planet*, 1–2.

4. Love, "*Et in Arcadia Ego*," 196, 197.

5. Meeker, *Comedy of Survival*, 4.

6. Branch, "Ecocriticism," 92.

7. Glotfelty, introduction to *Ecocriticism Reader*, Glotfelty and Fromm, xxii–xxiv.

8. Glotfelty, "Literary Studies," 1.

9. Rich, "Notes," 9.

10. Campbell, "Land and Language of Desire," 210–11.

11. Love, "*Et in Arcadia Ego*," 202.

12. Broder, *Sacred Hoop*, 9.

13. Ibid., 12.

14. Lorraine Anderson, *Sisters of the Earth*, xvi.

15. Wordsworth, "Preface to *Lyrical Ballads*," 288.

16. Lyon, *This Incomperable Lande*, xiv.

17. Ibid., xv.

18. Ibid.

19. Elder, introduction to *American Nature Writers*, 1:xvii.

20. Finch and Elder, *Norton Book of Nature Writing*, 19, 25. Scheese in *Nature Writing* also generates a definition of nature writing that emphasizes "first-person," "nonfiction," and "exploration" (6); Fritzell emphasizes even more strongly the "first-person singular" and "extensive, impersonal scientific description and explication" required of works to fit his definition of nature writing in *Nature Writing and America* (73).

21. Finch and Elder, *Norton Book of Nature Writing*, 25.

22. Siporin, "Terry Tempest Williams," 105, 106.

23. Duncan, "Nonfiction = Fiction," 55.

24. Finch and Elder, *Norton Book of Nature Writing*, 28.

25. An example of this tendency can be seen in Buell's *Environmental Imagination*, where he establishes the following dichotomy: "Nonfiction writers such as Thoreau, Austin, Berry, Dillard, and Janovy—and poets like Wordsworth, Frost, and Snyder" (108), even though he discusses Berry's poetry elsewhere in the book.

26. Slovic and Dixon, *Being in the World*, 545.

27. Glotfelty and Fromm, *Ecocriticism Reader*, xxvi.

28. Cohen, "Literary Theory," 1101–2.

29. Flores, "Place," 2–3.

30. Don D. Elgin, *Comedy*, 22.

31. Cashman, "Systems of Knowledge," 55.

32. Don D. Elgin, *Comedy*, 23.

33. See Dwyer's *Earth Works* for an amazingly extensive list of nature-oriented fiction by diverse authors across a variety of modes.

34. Westling takes a positive step in this direction in *Green Breast of the New World* when she rereads American canonical writers Willa Cather, Ernest Hemingway, William Faulkner, and Eudora Welty from an ecocritical perspective in terms of their nature orientations. Westling, however, finds all of them wanting: "None of the writers examined so far has succeeded in breaking out of the archaic gendered sense of the human relations to the landscape and its life" (148). She points to Octavia Butler and Louise Erdrich as contemporary fiction writers who succeed in this task.

Writing the Environment, edited by Kerridge and Sammells, contains a mix of ecocritical essays on theory, fiction, nonfiction, poetry, and drama, rather than privileging any single literary genre. See also Raglon and Scholtmeijer, "Shifting Ground," for a discussion of international postmodern stories that challenge "the metanarrative of nature" (22).

2. Environmental Literature

1. Scheese, *Nature Writing*, 6.

2. Branch, "Early Romantic," 1060.

3. Wennerstrom, *Soldiers Delight Journal*, xiii–xiv.

4. Ibid., 44.

5. Dunne, *Before the Echo*, 6–7.

6. Bonta, *Appalachian Autumn*, ix.

7. Ibid., x.

8. Scheese, *Nature Writing* (127), interestingly enough, uses this same passage from *Pilgrim*. He does so in making his point that Dillard is more concerned that she "celebrates a mental terrain more than a physical terrain, the invisible over the visible landscape," 130.

9. Scheese, ibid., 126.

10. Buell, *Environmental Imagination*, 94. Buell derives the term from Barry Lopez but provides his own definition.

11. I am not contending that these studies are invalid or that what they say about these small number of writers ought to be disregarded, but that I think the fiction of nonfictionality has contributed to a surprisingly narrow range of study examples in full-length critical works. For instance, Fritzell in *Nature Writing and America* focuses on Thoreau, Leopold, and Dillard; McClintock in *Nature's Kindred Spirits* treats Leopold, Krutch, Abbey, Dillard, and Snyder; O'Grady in *Pilgrims to the Wild* treats Ruess, Thoreau, Muir, King, and Austin; Scheese in *Nature Writing* treats Thoreau, Muir, Austin, Leopold, Abbey, and Dillard; Slovic in *Seeking Awareness* treats Thoreau, Dillard, Abbey, Berry, and Lopez. Some of these books were originally written as doctoral dissertations, which may be a factor in the apparently conservative selection of study examples.

12. Such study, however, will largely depend on the degree to which ecocritics involve themselves in translation and writing about works that have been translated or need to be translated. Up to now, there has been little in ecocritical studies focused on nature writing, as narrowly defined, that would encourage such attention to translation and international reading.

3. Refining through Redefining Our Sensibilities

1. Welch, *Ring of Bone*, 73.

2. Yu Kwang-chung, *Night Watchman*, 116. Following Chinese practice, I have arranged the family name (Yu) first, followed by the personal name.

3. Harjo, *Spiral*, 136.

4. Allen, *Sacred Hoop*, 243.

5. See Jose, "Reflections on the Politics," for a discussion of this feature of Le Guin's fiction; see also Murphy, "Pivots Instead of Centers: Postmodern Spirituality of Gary Snyder and Ursula K. Le Guin," in *Literature, Nature, and Other*, 111–21.

6. Buell, *Environmental Imagination*, 6–8, and "Representing the Environment," 83–114.

7. Harjo, *Spiral*, 79.

8. Owens, "'The Song Is Very Short,'" 53, 54.

9. Dozier, *Codes*, 184.

10. Quoted in Owens, "'The Song Is Very Short,'" 51.

11. Harjo, *Spiral*, 127.

12. On Scott and Stevenson, see MacLachlan, "Nature in Scottish Literature," 184–86. On Kavanagh, see Gifford, "The Anti-Pastoral Tradition and Patrick Kavanagh's *The Great Hunger*," in *Green Voices*, 55–71. On Kavanagh and Lawless, see Mc Elroy, "Na-

ture Writing in Irish Literature," 178–80. On Lawless, see Cahalan, "Forging a Tradition." On Jeffers, see Murphy, "Beyond Humanism" and "Reclaiming the Power"; Karman, *Robinson Jeffers*. On Wordsworth, see Choi, "Ecological Vision." On Wordsworth and Coleridge, see Kroeber, *Ecological Literary Criticism*; Roberts and Gifford, "Nature in English Poetry," 167–69.

13. See Deena, "Caribbean," for a detailed discussion of Caribbean literature in English.

14. See Haynes, "Australian Desert"; Drayson, "Early Perceptions"; and Norden, "Ecological Restoration" on Australian and New Zealand literature, both Aboriginal and settler writings.

15. See Platt, "Two Centuries," for a discussion of Chipko and other Indian environmental literature.

16. On Devi, see Platt, "Two Centuries"; Jia-yi Cheng-Levine's doctoral dissertation, "Neo-Colonialism, Post-Colonial Ecology, and Ecofeminism."

17. See Ombaka, "War and Environment."

18. On the version of *Shan-hai ching chiao-chu* (Guideways through mountains and seas), anonymously written in the third or fourth century B.C.E. and edited by Yüan K'o, which apparently has not been translated in its entirety into English and is therefore far less widely known in the United States than *Epic of Gilgamesh*, see Strassberg, *Inscribed Landscapes*, 16–17.

19. Walls, "Science and Shaping," 20. See also her comments on the influence of the Humboldts (21).

20. See Snyder's *He Who Hunted Birds*, the published version of his Reed College undergraduate honor's thesis, for evidence of these influences.

21. See Toohey, "Dialogic Abundance," for a thorough discussion of Hildegard of Bingen.

22. Burroughs, "Wild Life about My Cabin," in *Birch Browsings*, 95–97.

23. For Muir's and Burroughs's Alaska writings, see Burroughs, "Narrative of the Expedition"; Muir, *Cruise of the Corwin*, "Pacific Coast Glaciers," *Stickeen*, and *Travels in Alaska*.

4. ECOFEMINISM AND POSTMODERNISM

1. Parpart and Marchand, "Exploding the Canon," 1–2, 3.

2. Ibid., 4.

3. Parpart and Marchand, *Feminism/Postmodernism/Development*, 127, 128.

4. Nzomo, "Women and Democratization Struggles," 141.

5. hooks, "Postmodern Blackness," 28.

6. Ibid., 29.

7. Cornell, *Philosophy of the Limit*, 11–12. Hereafter cited in the text as *Limit*.

8. In my definition of *paramodern*, *modern* comes from modernity and postmodernity as conditions of being, with modernism and postmodernism as their related ideological formations. The prefix *para-* means beside, near, or alongside; it also means beyond or, according to *The American Heritage College Dictionary* (3d ed.) definition: "a

diatomic molecule in which the nuclei have opposite spin directions." *Paramodernity*, then, would be a condition of being that has existed and exists alongside modernity and postmodernity but is beyond both, and that is spinning in the opposite direction, in competition for the space of existence. *Paramodernism*, in turn, might then be defined as an ideological formation in which beliefs and cultural practices run alongside modernity or postmodernity in the contemporary world, and as an aesthetic movement in which such practices are represented by means of literary strategies and techniques not found in either modernist or postmodernist works.

9. For a viewpoint in contrast to Cornell's formulations, see Mora's argument for the relationship of cultural conservation and environmental conservation in *Nepantla*, which I discuss in chapter 7.

10. Hutcheon, *Politics*, 3.

11. Gelpi, "Genealogy," 523.

12. Hutcheon, *Politics*, 142.

13. Ibid., 168.

14. Merchant, "Ecofeminism," 100.

15. Diamond and Orenstein, *Reweaving*, xi.

16. Starhawk, "Power," 77, 83.

17. King, "Healing," 117.

18. King, "Ecology," 19–20.

19. Spretnak, "Ecofeminism," 9.

20. Haraway, *Symians*, 199.

21. Murphy, *Literature, Nature, and Other*, 35, 152–53.

22. Hartsock, "Foucault," 171.

23. D'Souza, "A New Movement," 36, 38–39.

24. See Curtin's "Making Peace with the Earth" in regard to this point.

25. Ruether, "First and Third World Women," 31.

26. See Gaard and Murphy, *Ecofeminist Literary Criticism*.

27. See Legler, *All the Powerful Invisible Things*, and "Toward a Postmodern Pastoral."

5. ANOTHERNESS AND INHABITATION IN RECENT MULTICULTURAL AMERICAN LITERATURE

1. Bakhtin, *Toward a Philosophy of the Act*, 54. Hereafter cited in the text as *Toward*.

2. Bakhtin, *Problems of Dostoevsky's Poetics*, 302n. 15.

3. On this point, see Ortner.

4. Voloshinov, *Freudianism*, 15.

5. Rolston, *Philosophy*, 59.

6. Cajete, *Look to the Mountain*, 84.

7. Gifford, "The Anti-Pastoral Tradition and Patrick Kavanagh's *The Great Hunger*," in *Green Voices*, 55–71.

8. Hogan, *Dwellings*, 11. Hereafter cited in the text as *Dwellings*.

9. Williams, *Pieces of White Shell*, 3. Hereafter cited in the text as *White Shell*.

10. Snyder, *No Nature*, 369–70.

11. Ibid., 373–74.

12. Ibid., 381.

13. *Diamond Sutra*, 60.

14. Cajete, *Look to the Mountain*, 68.

15. Ortiz, *Woven Stone*, 63.

16. Smith, "Coyote Ortiz," 209.

17. Ortiz, *Woven Stone*, 108.

18. Ibid., 202.

19. Platt, "Ecocritical Chicana Literature," 139, 146.

6. THE WORLDLY DIVERSITY OF NATURE-ORIENTED PROSE LITERATURE

1. Olafson, "B. Traven's Six-Novel Epic," 141.

2. Zogbaum, *B. Traven*, 200.

3. Ibid., 208.

4. Murphy, "B. Traven"; Barry Carr in his foreword to Zogbaum's book claims that in *Land*, Traven produced "a piece of barely disguised propaganda presenting President Plutarco Elías Calles (1924–1928) as the architect of working-class power and the progenitor of a new nationalist synthesis of indigenous and proletarian culture. Traven did not take long to realize how mistaken his conclusions were, and he refused to allow *Land des Frühlings* to be republished or translated into Spanish or English" (x). Zogbaum provides a detailed examination of *Land*'s sources and contents, however.

5. Baumann, "B. Traven's *Land*," 246.

6. Ibid., 247.

7. Traven, *Government*, 12–13.

8. Ibid., *General*, 4. Zogbaum in *B. Traven* draws a very different conclusion about the end of *General*, seeing Traven's Caoba cycle as deeply pessimistic because his heroes in the last novel do not continue the revolution but settle down to build an independent village: "This was the bleakest and most unjust commentary Traven could have produced on the outcome of the Mexican Revolution. . . . Traven's commentary, however, no longer reflected the state of Mexican politics but rather his own inflexible perception of the rights and wrong's of Mexico's postrevolutionary development" (208). Obviously I disagree with her interpretation of the Caoba cycle, but it is important to note that our approaches are fundamentally different. Zogbaum insists on reading these novels "as a valuable and highly individual contribution to Mexican historiography" (xx); I read them as works of fiction, as literature, in terms of what they might say to readers today about living in the present rather than the degree to which they conform to nonfiction standards and what they say about the history of Mexico. In other words, because Zogbaum's study is historical, she necessarily invokes a nonfictional prejudice.

9. See Cobos, "Testimonies and Rites from Home."

10. Griffiths, introduction to *Green Days*, by Anthony, xv–xviii.

11. Anthony, *Green Days*, 175.

12. Ibid., 180.

13. Ibid., 192.

14. See Deena, "Caribbean," for brief remarks on another novel by Anthony as well

as discussion of other Caribbean writers who emphasize an agrarian alternative to post-colonial maldevelopment.

15. Head, *When Rain Clouds Gather,* 3. Hereafter cited in the text as *Rain Clouds.*

16. Nfah-Abbenyi, *Gender in African Women's Writing,* 146.

17. See Ibid., "Ecological Postcolonialism," 347. My entire discussion of *When Rain Clouds Gather* is heavily indebted to Nfah-Abbenyi's concise analysis.

18. Dayton, foreword to *Countryside of Níjar,* by Goytisolo.

19. Ibid.

20. Pratt and Gordon, "Environment," 254.

21. Goytisolo, *Countryside of Níjar,* 6, 7. Hereafter cited in the text as *Countryside.*

22. The arrangement of Japanese names here follows the cultural practice of that country, with the family name followed by the personal name.

23. Gerbert, introduction to *Love of Mountains,* 20, and preface to *Love of Mountains,* ix.

24. Shiga, "At Kinosaki," 272, 277.

25. Gerbert, introduction, 21.

26. Uno, "Love of Mountains," 202; Shinano is the name of an old province of Japan, which is now Nagano prefecture, according to Gerbert's place-name notes at the end of the book (224).

7. Conserving Natural and Cultural Diversity

1. Mora, *Nepantla,* 19, 18.

2. Ibid., 9. Hereafter these four books will be cited in the text by title.

3. Rebolledo and Rivero, *Infinite Divisions,* 32.

4. See Fast, "Nature and Creative Power," 30.

5. See Murphy, "Grandmother Borderland."

6. See Fast, "Nature and Creative Power," 31.

7. See Rebolledo, "Tradition and Mythology," 122–23.

8. See Rosaldo, *Culture and Truth,* "Border Crossings," 196–217.

9. Rebolledo and Rivero, *Infinite Divisions,* 160.

10. Rebolledo, "Tradition and Mythology," 96–97.

8. Ishimure Michiko

1. Hereafter these works will be cited in the text as *Paradise* and *Story,* respectively. Following Japanese practice, the family name (Ishimure) is given first and is followed by the personal name (Michiko). This is also the case for the names of characters in the two books, when both family name and personal name are given.

2. Ishimure, *Paradise,* inside back dust jacket. Also, Monnet states: "Far from being merely a journalistic account of the early history of Minamata Disease, it is an extremely complex work, employing such diverse techniques as flashback, stream-of-consciousness, and inner monologue; documentary evidence such as minutes, newspaper articles and medical reports; journal notations, prose poems, lyrical prose and poetic dialect. . . . [It]

may be regarded as Ishimure's ambitious attempt to reform the language of contemporary Japanese fiction, which she regards as degraded and unsatisfactory, and to create a new literary genre, a mixture of authentic autobiography, fiction and journalism that seems to point to the literature of the future" (translator's introduction to *Paradise*, v).

3. See Platt, "Ecocritical Chicana Literature," and "Two Centuries"; and Killingsworth and Palmer, "Ecopolitics and the Literature of the Borderlands," for examples of such environmental-justice literary criticism.

4. See the following poems by Ortiz: "We Have Been Told Many Things but We Know This to Be True" and "Our Homeland, a National Sacrifice Area" (*Woven Stone*, 324–25, 337–63).

5. Sarane Spence Boocock points out that "the proverb 'Until seven, children are with the gods,' refers both to the divine nature of infants and young children and to the folk belief that infants and young children exist in a kind of limbo between the spirit world and the human world, a particularly vulnerable position in that they are always at risk of being 'called back'" ("Social Construction of Childhood," 168).

6. Although many of these animistic religious practices appear to me to be Shinto in origin, Ishimure nowhere identifies them as such in *Story*, and so I refrain from so labeling them here. There are many possible explanations, such as the idea that they were once but in the time of *Story* are no longer associated with any official Shinto shrines in the area. The period about which Ishimure writes is one following the government consolidation-of-shrines movement in the late Meiji period, so many of the local religious practices Ishimure identifies may have been officially abolished by the central government but maintained by local villagers. Or, since Shinto is an official religion, Ishimure may have wanted to distance local practices from government-associated ones. But these are just my own speculations. On the consolidation-of-shrines movement and environmentalist reactions against it, see Kato's essay on Minikata Kumagusu.

9. "The Women Are Speaking"

The title for this chapter comes from Le Guin's quoting of Hogan's poem "The Women Are Speaking" in "Woman/Wilderness," a talk Le Guin gave at the University of California, Davis, in 1986, and published in *Dancing at the Edge of the World*, 161–64.

1. Tisdale, *Stepping Westward*, 32. Hereafter cited in the text as *Stepping*.

2. Brox, *Here and Nowhere Else*, 142–43.

3. Ibid., 138.

4. Vance, "Politics of Reality," 137.

5. Ibid., 139–40.

6. Theses categories are addressed by many of the critics I cited in the chapters 1 and 2, either with acceptance or reservation. For reservations, see, for example, Gifford, *Green Voices*; Hay, "Nature Writer's Dilemma." For an example of criticism of a poet for breaking out of the meditative, observational mode, see Altieri, "Gary Snyder's *Turtle Island*."

7. Legler, review of *Cultivating Excess*, 190.

8. The following interpretation of "Fish in Air" is the result of a collaboration with

Greta Gaard and is in part based on the ideas represented in her essay "Toward a Queer Ecofeminism."

9. Lori Anderson, *Cultivating Excess*, 9. Hereafter cited in the text as *Excess*.

10. See Legler, review of *Cultivating Excess*, 191.

11. Ibid., 192.

12. Naranjo-Morse, *Mud Woman*, 9. Hereafter cited in the text as *Mud Woman*.

13. *Towa* is the word for people in the Tewa language. The Tewa is a tribe of the Santa Clara Pueblo. Naranjo-Morse's use of *Towa* emphasizes a sense of community, while her use of the Tewa language emphasizes formal tribal affiliation and lineage.

14. Gaard, "Ecofeminism and Native American Cultures," 309–10.

10. COMMODIFICATION, RESISTANCE, INHABITATION, AND IDENTITY

1. Hogan, *Mean Spirit*, 14.

2. Ibid., 375.

3. Escamill, *Daughter of the Mountain*, 170.

4. Rogers, "Mora Valley," 132–33, 139.

5. Yamashita, *Through the Arc*, 212.

11. THE TREMENDOUS POWER OF A QUIET NUDGE

1. Platt and I are coediting an international anthology of contemporary environmental drama, which we hope will both educate us and provide impetus for critical studies of this genre, one that has been almost entirely neglected in ecocriticism.

2. McKibben, introduction to *Birch Browsings*, by Burroughs, xi.

3. Ibid., xii.

4. Muir, *Mountains of California*, 176–79; Burroughs, *Birch Browsings*, 87–94. Hereafter cited in the text as *Browsings*.

5. Austin, *Stories from the Country*, 19–29.

12. RUDIMENTARY REMARKS ON THE NEED FOR A FEW NEW WORDS

1. For this synthesis course I used the following texts in 1996: Adams, *Ecofeminism and the Sacred*; Escamill, *Daughter of the Mountain*; Kingsolver, *Animal Dreams*; Merchant, *Earthcare*; Plant and Plant, *Turtle Talk*; Smiley, *A Thousand Acres*; Weisman, *Discrimination by Design*. In previous years, I have used some of the preceding along with Anzaldúa, *Borderlands/La Frontera*; Diamond and Orenstein, *Reweaving the World*; Ehrlich, *Islands, the Universe, Home*; Griffin, *Woman and Nature*; Haraway, *Simians, Cyborgs, and Women*; Le Guin, *The Dispossessed*; Merchant, *The Death of Nature*; Plant, *Healing the Wounds*.

2. Merchant, *Earthcare*, 142.

3. Works by Suzette Haden Elgin pertinent to this discussion are *Native Tongue, Native Tongue II: The Judas Rose, Earthsong: Native Tongue Three*, and *A First Dictionary and Grammar of Láadan*. It should also be noted that Elgin, who taught at the university level as a linguist, is the author of *Genderspeak: Men, Women, and the Gentle Art of Verbal Self*

Defense and other books that explicitly address gender issues in language and the possibilities of self-empowerment for women working through a patriarchal tongue.

4. Suzette Haden Elgin, "Women's Language," 177.
5. Cashman, "Systems of Knowledge," 55.
6. Adams, introduction to *Ecofeminism*, 2.
7. Kaza, "Acting with Compassion," 53.
8. Spretnak, "Earthbound and Personal Body as Sacred," 264.
9. See Gilligan, *In a Different Voice*; Gilligan et al., *Mapping the Moral Domain*.
10. Gilligan, preface to *Mapping the Moral Domain*, i.
11. See Bakhtin, *Toward a Philosophy of the Act*; Murphy, *Literature, Nature, and Other*.
12. DiBernard and Reiter, "Two Women on the Verge," 107.
13. Adams, introduction to *Ecofeminism*, 2.
14. Downing, Harkin, and Sosnoski, "Configurations of Lore," 11–12.
15. Sanchez, "Animal, Vegetable, and Mineral," 220.

Bibliography

Abbey, Edward. *Desert Solitaire: A Season in the Wilderness.* 1968. New York: Ballantine, 1991.

———. *The Monkey Wrench Gang.* New York: Avon, 1975.

Adams, Carol J. *The Sexual Politics of Meat: A Feminist-Vegetarian Critical Theory.* New York: Continuum, 1990.

———, ed. *Ecofeminism and the Sacred.* New York: Continuum, 1993.

Adamson, Joni. *The Middle Place: Native American Literature, Environmental Justice, and Ecocriticism.* Tucson: Univ. of Arizona Press, in press.

Allen, Paula Gunn. *The Sacred Hoop: Recovering the Feminine in American Indian Traditions.* Boston: Beacon, 1986.

Altieri, Charles. "Gary Snyder's *Turtle Island*: The Problem of Reconciling the Roles of Seer and Prophet." *Boundary Two* 4, no. 3 (1976): 761–77.

Anaya, Rudolfo. *Bless Me, Ultima.* 1972. New York: Warner Books, 1994.

Anderson, Eric Gary. Review of *The Secret Life of John C. Van Dyke: Selected Letters,* ed. David W. Teague and Peter Wild. *ISLE: Interdisciplinary Studies in Literature and Environment* 5, no. 2 (summer 1998): 167–68.

Anderson, Lori. *Cultivating Excess.* Portland: Eighth Mountain Press, 1992.

Anderson, Lorraine, ed. *Sisters of the Earth: Women's Prose and Poetry About Nature.* New York: Vintage, 1991.

Anthony, Michael. *Green Days by the River.* 1967. Oxford: Heinemann, 1973.

Anzaldúa, Gloria. *Borderlands/La Frontera.* San Francisco: Spinsters/aunt lute books, 1987.

Atwood, Margaret. *Surfacing.* 1972. New York: Fawcett Crest, 1987.

Austin, Mary. *Stories from the Country of Lost Borders.* Ed. Marjorie Pryse. New Brunswick, NJ: Rutgers Univ. Press, 1987.

Bailey, Robert G., comp. *Description of the Ecoregions of the United States*, 2d ed. Misc. pub. 1391. Washington, DC: U.S. Department of Agriculture, 1995.

Bakhtin, Mikhail. *Art and Answerability: Early Philosophical Essays*. Ed. Michael Holquist and Vadim Liapunov. Trans. Vadim Liapunov. Austin: Univ. of Texas Press, 1992.

———. *Problems of Dostoevsky's Poetics*. Trans. and ed. Caryl Emerson. Minneapolis: Univ. of Minnesota Press, 1984.

———. *Toward a Philosophy of the Act*. Ed. Vadim Liapunov and Michael Holquist. Trans. Vadim Liapunov. Austin: Univ. of Texas Press, 1993.

Baumann, Friederike. "B. Traven's *Land des Frühlings* and the Caoba Cycle as a Source for the Study of Agrarian Society." In *B. Traven*, ed. Schürer and Jenkins, 245–57.

Berry, Wendell. *The Gift of Good Land: Further Essays Cultural and Agricultural*. San Francisco: North Point Press, 1981.

———. *The Memory of Old Jack*. San Diego: Harcourt Brace, 1974.

———. *A Place on Earth, a Revision*. San Francisco: North Point Press, 1983.

———. *Remembering, a Novel*. San Francisco: North Point Press, 1988.

———. *A Timbered Choir: The Sabbath Poems 1979–1997*. Washington, DC: Counterpoint, 1998.

Bhabha, Homi K. "Postcolonial Criticism." In *Redrawing the Boundaries: The Transformation of English and American Literary Studies*, ed. Stephen Greenblatt and Giles Gunn, 437–65. New York: Modern Language Association, 1992.

Bohjalian, Chris. *Water Witches*. Hanover, NH: Univ. Press of New England, 1995.

Bonta, Marcia. *Appalachian Autumn*. Pittsburgh: Univ. of Pittsburgh Press, 1994.

———. *Appalachian Spring*. Pittsburgh: Univ. of Pittsburgh Press, 1991.

Boocock, Sarane Spence. "The Social Construction of Childhood in Contemporary Japan." In *Constructions of the Self*, ed. George Levine, 165–88. New Brunswick, NJ: Rutgers Univ. Press, 1992.

Branch, Michael. "Early Romantic Natural History Literature (1782–1836)." In *American Nature Writers*, ed. Elder, 2:1059–77.

———. "Ecocriticism: Surviving Institutionalization in the Academic Environment." *ISLE: Interdisciplinary Studies in Literature and Environment* 2, no. 1 (1994): 91–99.

Broder, Bill. *The Sacred Hoop: A Cycle of Earth Tales*. 1979. San Francisco: Sierra Club Books, 1992.

Brox, Jane. *Here and Nowhere Else: Late Seasons of a Farm and Its Family*. Boston: Beacon, 1995.

Bruner, John. *The Sheep Look Up*. 1972. New York: Del Rey, 1982.

Bryant, Paul T. "Nature as Picture/Nature as Milieu." *CEA Critic*, "The Literature of Nature" special issue, 54, no. 1 (fall 1991): 22–34.

Buell, Lawrence. *The Environmental Imagination: Thoreau, Nature Writing, and the Foundation of American Culture.* Cambridge: Belknap Press of Harvard Univ. Press, 1995.

Burroughs, John. *Birch Browsings: A John Burroughs Reader.* Ed. and with an introduction by Bill McKibben. New York: Penguin, 1992.

———. "Narrative of the Expedition." In *Harriman Alaska Expedition*, ed. C. Hart Merriam, 1:1–118. New York: Doubleday, Page, 1901.

Cahalan, James M. "Forging a Tradition: Emily Lawless and the Irish Literary Canon." *Colby Quarterly* 27, no. 1 (Mar. 1991): 27–39.

Cajete, Gregory. *Look to the Mountain: An Ecology of Indigenous Education.* Durango, CO: Kivakí Press, 1994.

Campbell, SueEllen. "The Land and Language of Desire: Where Deep Ecology and Post-Structuralism Meet." *Western American Literature* 24, no. 3 (1989): 199–211.

Carson, Rachel. *Silent Spring.* 1962. Boston: Houghton Mifflin, 1994.

Cashman, Kristin. "Systems of Knowledge as Systems of Domination: The Limitations of Established Meaning." *Agriculture and Human Values* 8, no. 1–2 (1991): 49–58.

Castillo, Ana. *So Far from God.* New York: Norton, 1993.

Cheng-Levine, Jia-yi. "Neo-Colonialism, Post-Colonial Ecology, and Ecofeminism in the Works of Native American, Chicano/a, and International Writers." Ph.D. diss., Indiana University of Pennsylvania, 1997.

Choi, Dong-oh. "Ecological Vision in Selected Poems of William Wordsworth, 1797–1800." Ph.D. diss., Indiana University of Pennsylvania, 1998.

Cobos, Andres King. "Testimonies and Rites from Home." *Studies in the Humanities*, "Gary Snyder: An International Perspective" special issue, guest ed. Patrick D. Murphy, 26, no. 1–2 (1999): 57–66.

Cohen, Michael P. "Literary Theory and Nature Writing." In *American Nature Writers*, ed. Elder, 2:1099–113.

Cornell, Drucilla. *The Philosophy of the Limit.* New York: Routledge, 1992.

Curtin, Deane. "Making Peace with the Earth: Indigenous Agriculture and the Green Revolution." *Environmental Ethics* 17, no. 1 (1995): 59–73.

Davenport, Kiana. *Shark Dialogues.* New York: Plume, 1995.

Deena, Seodial, "The Caribbean: Colonial and Postcolonial Representations of the Land and the People's Relationships to Their Environment." In *Literature of Nature*, ed. Murphy, 366–73.

Diamond, Irene, and Gloria Feman Orenstein, eds. *Reweaving the World: The Emergence of Ecofeminism.* San Francisco: Sierra Club Books, 1990.

The Diamond Sutra and the Sutra of Hui Neng. Trans. A. F. Price and Wong Mou-Lam. Berkeley: Shambala, 1969.

DiBernard, Barbara, and Sheila Reiter. "Two Women on the Verge of a Contextual Breakthrough: Using *A Feminist Dictionary* in the Literature Classroom." In *Changing Classroom Practices*, ed. Downing, 104–21.

Downing, David B., ed. *Changing Classroom Practices: Resources for Literary and Cultural Studies*. Urbana, IL: National Councils of Teachers of English, 1994.

———, Patricia Harkin, and James J. Sosnoski. "Configurations of Lore: The Changing Relations of Theory, Research, and Pedagogy." In *Changing Classroom Practices*, ed. Downing, 3–34.

Dozier, Rush W., Jr. *Codes of Evolution*. New York: Crown, 1992.

Drayson, Nick. "Early Perceptions of the Natural History of Australia in Popular Literature." In *Literature of Nature*, ed. Murphy, 264–69.

D'Souza, Corinne Kumar. "A New Movement, a New Hope: East Wind, West Wind, and the Wind from the South." In *Healing the Wounds*, ed. Plant, 29–39.

Duncan, David James. "Nonfiction = Fiction." *Orion* 15, no. 3 (summer 1996): 55–57.

———. *River Teeth: Stories and Writings*. New York: Doubleday, 1995.

Dunne, Pete. *Before the Echo: Essays on Nature*. Austin: Univ. of Texas Press, 1995.

Dwyer, Jim. *Earth Works: Recommended Fiction and Nonfiction about Nature and the Environment for Adults and Young Adults*. New York: Neal Schuman, 1996.

"Ecofeminism/Ecocriticism I." Special issue of *Phoebe: Journal of Feminist Scholarship, Theory and Aesthetics* 9, no. 1 (1997).

Ehrlich, Gretel. *Islands, the Universe, Home*. 1991. New York: Penguin, 1992.

Elder, John, ed. *American Nature Writers*. 2 vols. New York: Scribner's, 1996.

Elgin, Don D. *The Comedy of the Fantastic: Ecological Perspectives on the Fantasy Novel*. Westport, CT: Greenwood, 1985.

Elgin, Suzette Haden. *Earthsong: Native Tongue Three*. New York: DAW, 1994.

———. *A First Dictionary and Grammar of Láadan*, 2d ed. Ed. Diane Martin. Madison, WI: SF³, 1988.

———. *Genderspeak: Men, Women, and the Gentle Art of Verbal Self Defense*. New York: Wiley, 1993.

———. *Native Tongue*. New York: DAW, 1984.

———. *Native Tongue II: The Judas Rose*. New York: DAW, 1987.

———. "Women's Language and Near Future Science Fiction: A Reply." *Women's Studies*, "Feminism Faces the Fantastic," special issue, guest eds. Marleen Barr and Patrick D. Murphy, 14, no. 2 (1987): 175–81.

Emecheta, Buchi. *The Rape of Shavi*. 1983. New York: George Braziller, 1985.

The Epic of Gilgamesh. Trans. Nancy K. Sandars. Harmondsworth, UK: Penguin, 1960.

Escamill, Edna. *Daughter of the Mountain: Un Cuento*. San Francisco: aunt lute books, 1991.

Evers, Larry, and Felipe S. Molina. *Yaqui Deer Songs/Maso Bwikam: A Native American Poetry.* Tucson: Univ. of Arizona Press, 1987.

Fast, Robin Riley. "Nature and Creative Power: Pat Mora and Patricia Hampl." *San Jose Studies* 15, no. 2 (1989): 29–40.

Finch, Robert, and John Elder, eds. *The Norton Book of Nature Writing.* New York: Norton, 1990.

Flores, Dan. "Place: An Argument for Bioregional History." *Environmental History Review* 18, no. 4 (1994): 1–18.

Fritzell, Peter A. *Nature Writing and America: Essays upon a Cultural Type.* Ames: Iowa State Univ. Press, 1990.

Gaard, Greta. "Ecofeminism and Native American Cultures: Pushing the Limits of Cultural Imperialism." In *Ecofeminism: Women, Animals, Nature,* ed. Gaard, 295–314. Philadelphia: Temple Univ. Press, 1993.

———. "Toward a Queer Ecofeminism." *Hypatia* 12, no. 1 (1997): 114–37.

Gaard, Greta, and Patrick D. Murphy, eds. "Ecofeminist Literary Criticism," special issue of *ISLE: Interdisciplinary Studies in Literature and Environment* 3, no. 1 (1996).

———, eds. *Ecofeminist Literary Criticism: Theory, Criticism, Pedagogy.* Urbana: Univ. of Illinois Press, 1998.

Gelpi, Albert. "The Genealogy of Postmodernism: Contemporary American Poetry." *Southern Review* 26, no. 4 (1990): 517–41.

Gerbert, Elaine. Preface and introduction to *Love of Mountains: Two Stories by Uno Kōji,* by Kōji, ed. and trans. Gerbert, ix–x and 1–38.

Gibson, William. *Neuromancer.* New York: Ace, 1984.

Gifford, Terry. *Green Voices: Understanding Contemporary Nature Poetry.* Manchester, UK: Manchester Univ. Press, 1995.

Gilligan, Carol. *In a Different Voice: Psychological Theory and Women's Development.* Cambridge: Harvard Univ. Press, 1982.

———. Preface to *Mapping the Moral Domain,* ed. Gilligan et al., i–v.

——— et al., eds. *Mapping the Moral Domain: A Contribution of Women's Thinking to Psychological Theory and Education.* Cambridge: Harvard Univ. Press, 1988.

Gish, Robert Franklin. *When Coyote Howls: A Lavaland Fable.* Albuquerque: Univ. of New Mexico Press, 1994.

Glotfelty, Cheryll (Burgess). "Literary Studies and Environmental Issues: An Introduction to Ecocriticism." Paper presented at the annual Modern Language Association conference, Dec. 1991.

Glotfelty, Cheryll (Burgess), and Harold Fromm, eds. *The Ecocriticism Reader: Landmarks in Literary Ecology.* Athens: Univ. of Georgia Press, 1996.

Goytisolo, Juan. *The Countryside of Níjar* (1960). In *The Countryside of Níjar and La Chanca.* Trans. Luigi Luccarelli. Foreword by David Dayton. Plainfield, IN: Alembic Press, 1987. 1–79.

Graves, Robert. *The White Goddess.* 1948. Amended and enl. ed. New York: Farrar, Straus & Giroux, 1966.

Griffin, Susan. *Woman and Nature: The Roaring inside Her.* New York: Harper & Row, 1978.

Griffiths, Gareth. Introduction to *Green Days by the River,* by Anthony, vii–xviii.

Haraway, Donna. *Primate Visions: Gender, Race, and Nature in the World of Modern Science.* New York: Routledge, 1989.

———. *Symians, Cyborgs, and Women: The Reinvention of Nature.* New York: Routledge, 1991.

Harding, Sandra. *The Science Question in Feminism.* Ithaca: Cornell Univ. Press, 1986.

Harjo, Joy. *The Spiral of Memory: Interviews.* Ed. Laura Coltelli. Ann Arbor: Univ. of Michigan Press, 1996.

Hartsock, Nancy. "Foucault on Power: A Theory for Women?" In *Feminism/Postmodernism,* ed. Linda J. Nicholson, 157–75. New York: Routledge, 1990.

Hasselstrom, Linda. *Going over East: Reflections of a Woman Rancher.* Golden, CO: Fulcrum Publishing, 1987.

Hay, John. "The Nature Writer's Dilemma." In *On Nature,* ed. Daniel Halpern, 7–10. San Francisco: North Point Press, 1987.

Hayles, N. Katherine. "Searching for Common Ground." In *Reinventing Nature? Responses to Postmodern Deconstruction,* ed. Michael E. Soulé and Gary Lease, 47–63. Washington, DC: Island Press, 1995.

Haynes, Roslynn D. "Two Hundred Years of the Australian Desert in Literature." In *Literature of Nature,* ed. Murphy, 259–63.

Head, Bessie. *Maru.* 1971. Portsmouth, NH: Heinemann, 1995.

———. *When Rain Clouds Gather.* 1969. Portsmouth, NH: Heinemann, 1995.

Hildegard of Bingen. *Hildegard of Bingen: Mystical Writings.* Ed. Fiona Bowie and Oliver Davies. Trans. Robert Carver. New York: Crossroad, 1993.

———. *Hildegard of Bingen's Book of Divine Works.* Ed. Matthew Fox. Santa Fe: Bear, 1987.

———. *Hildegard of Bingen's Scivias.* Trans. Bruce Hozeski. Santa Fe: Bear, 1986.

———. *Hildegard von Bingen's Physica: The Complete English Translation of Her Classic Work on Health and Healing.* Trans. Priscilla Throop. Rochester, VT: Healing Arts, 1998.

Hogan, Linda. *Dwellings: A Spiritual History of the Living World.* New York: Norton, 1995.

———. *Mean Spirit.* 1990. New York: Ivy Books, 1992.

———. *Solar Storms.* New York: Scribner, 1995.

———. "The Women Are Speaking." In *That's What She Said: Contemporary Poetry and Fiction by Native American Women,* ed. Rayna Green, 172. Bloomington: Indiana Univ. Press, 1984.

hooks, bell. "Postmodern Blackness." In *Yearning: Race, Gender, and Cultural Politics*, 23–31. Boston: South End Press, 1990.

Hutcheon, Linda. *The Politics of Postmodernism*. New York: Routledge, 1989.

Ishimure Michiko. *Paradise in the Sea of Sorrow: Our Minimata Disease (Kugai jōdo: Waga Minamata-byō*, 1972). Trans. and with a preface by Livia Monnet. Kyōto: Yamaguchi Publishing House, 1990.

———. *Story of the Sea of Camellias (Tsubaki no umi no ki*, 1976). Trans. and with a preface by Livia Monnet. Kyōto: Yamaguchi Publishing House, 1983.

Jose, Jim. "Reflections on the Politics of Le Guin's Narrative Shifts." *Science-Fiction Studies* 18, no. 2 (1991): 180–97.

Karman, James. *Robinson Jeffers, Poet of California*. Brownsville, OR: Story Line Press, 1994.

Kato, Sadamichi. "Minikata Kumagusu." *Organization and Environment* 12, no. 1 (1999): 85–98.

Kaza, Stephanie. "Acting with Compassion: Buddhism, Feminism, and the Environmental Crisis." In *Ecofeminism and the Sacred*, ed. Adams, 50–69.

Kazin, Alfred. *On Native Grounds: An Interpretation of Modern American Prose Literature*. New York: Harcourt, Brace & World, 1942.

Kerridge, Richard, and Neil Sammells, eds. *Writing the Environment: Ecocriticism and Literature*. London: Zed, 1998.

Killingsworth, M. Jimmie, and Jacqueline S. Palmer. "Ecopolitics and the Literature of the Borderlands: The Frontiers of Environmental Justice in Latina and Native American Writing." In *Writing the Environment*, ed. Kerridge and Sammells, 196–207.

King, Ynestra. "The Ecology of Feminism and the Feminism of Ecology." In *Healing the Wounds*, ed. Plant, 18–28.

———. "Healing the Wounds: Feminism, Ecology, and the Nature/Culture Dualism." In *Reweaving the World*, ed. Diamond and Orenstein, 106–21.

———. "Toward an Ecological Feminism and a Feminist Ecology." In *Machina Ex Dea: Feminist Perspectives on Technology*, ed. Joan Rothschild, 118–29. New York: Pergamon Press, 1983.

Kingsolver, Barbara. *Animal Dreams*. New York: Harper, 1991.

Kolodny, Annette. *The Lay of the Land: Metaphor as Experience and History in American Life and Letters*. Chapel Hill: Univ. of North Carolina Press, 1975.

Kroeber, Karl. *Ecological Literary Criticism: Romantic Imagining and the Biology of Mind*. New York: Columbia Univ. Press, 1994.

———. "Ecology and American Literature: Thoreau and Un-Thoreau." *American Literary History* 9, no. 2 (1997): 309–28.

Legler, Gretchen. *All the Powerful Invisible Things: A Sportswaman's Notebook*. Seattle: Seal Press, 1995.

———. Review of *Cultivating Excess*, by Lori Anderson. *ISLE: Interdisciplinary Studies in Literature and Environment* 1, no. 1 (spring 1993): 190–92.

———. "Toward a Postmodern Pastoral: The Erotic Landscape in Gretel Ehrlich." *ISLE: Interdisciplinary Studies in Literature and Environment* 1, no. 2 (fall 1993): 45–56.

Le Guin, Ursula K. *Buffalo Gals and Other Animal Presences.* Santa Barbara, CA: Capra, 1987.

———. *Dancing at the Edge of the World: Thoughts on Words, Women, Places.* New York: Harper Perennial, 1990.

———. *The Dispossessed.* New York: Avon, 1975.

Leopold, Aldo. *A Sand County Almanac and Sketches Here and There.* 1949. New York: Oxford Univ. Press, 1987.

Love, Glen A. "*Et in Arcadia Ego*: Pastoral Theory Meets Ecocriticism." *Western American Literature* 27, no. 3 (1992): 195–207.

Lutts, Ralph. *The Nature Fakers: Wildlife, Science and Sentiment.* Golden, CO: Fulcrum, 1990.

Lyon, Thomas J. "A History." In *This Incomperable Lande*, by Lyon, 3–91.

———, ed. *This Incomperable Lande: A Book of American Nature Writing.* 1989. New York: Penguin, 1991.

MacLachlan, Christopher. "Nature in Scottish Literature." In *The Literature of Nature*, ed. Murphy, 184–90.

Malcuzynski, M.-Pierrette. "The Sociocritical Perspective and Cultural Studies." *Critical Studies* 1, no. 1 (1989): 1–22.

Marietta, Don E., Jr. *For People and the Planet: Holism and Humanism in Environmental Ethics.* Philadelphia: Temple Univ. Press, 1995.

Matthiessen, F. O. *American Renaissance: Art and Expression in the Age of Emerson and Whitman.* New York: Oxford Univ. Press, 1941.

McClintock, James I. *Nature's Kindred Spirits: Aldo Leopold, Joseph Wood Krutch, Edward Abbey, Annie Dillard, and Gary Snyder.* Madison: Univ. of Wisconsin Press, 1994.

Mc Elroy, James. "Nature Writing in Irish Literature." In *Literature of Nature*, ed. Murphy, 177–83.

McKibben, Bill. Introduction to *Birch Browsings*, by Burroughs, ix–xix.

McKillip, Patricia. *The Riddle-Master of Hed.* 3 vols. Vol. 1, *The Riddle-Master of Hed*, New York: Del Rey, 1976. Vol. 2, *Heir of Sea and Fire*, New York: Del Rey, 1977. Vol. 3, *Harpist in the Wind*, New York: Del Rey, 1979.

Meeker, Joseph W. *The Comedy of Survival: Literary Ecology and a Play Ethic*, 3d ed. Tucson: Univ. of Arizona Press, 1997.

Merchant, Carolyn. *The Death of Nature: Women, Ecology, and the Scientific Revolution.* 1980. New York: Harper Collins, 1990.

————. *Earthcare: Women and the Environment.* New York: Routledge, 1995.

————. "Ecofeminism and Feminist Theory." In *Reweaving the World,* ed. Diamond and Orenstein, 100–105.

Mezo, Richard E. *A Study of B. Traven's Fiction: The Journey to Solipaz.* San Francisco: Mellen Research Univ. Press, 1993.

Miner, Earl. *Comparative Poetic: An Intercultural Essay on Theories of Literature.* Princeton: Princeton Univ. Press, 1990.

Mora, Pat. *Borders.* Houston: Arte Público, 1986.

————. *Chants.* Houston: Arte Público, 1985.

————. *Communion.* Houston: Arte Público, 1991.

————. *Nepantla: Essays from the Land in the Middle.* Albuquerque: Univ. of New Mexico Press, 1993.

Mudrooroo (Colin Johnson). *Dr. Wooreddy's Prescription for Enduring the Ending of the World.* New York: Ballantine, 1983.

Mueller, Marnie. *Green Fires, Assault on Eden: A Novel of the Ecuadorian Rainforest.* Willimantic, CT: Curbstone Press, 1994.

Muir, John. *The Cruise of the Corwin.* 1917. San Francisco: Sierra Club Books, 1993.

————. *The Mountains of California.* New York: Penguin, 1985.

————. "Notes on the Pacific Coast Glaciers." In *Harriman Alaska Expedition,* ed. C. Hart Merriam, 1:119–35. New York: Doubleday, Page, 1901.

————. *Stickeen: The Story of a Dog.* Boston: Houghton Mifflin, 1909. Berkeley, CA: Heyday Books, 1990.

————. *Travels in Alaska.* 1915. Boston: Houghton Mifflin, 1998.

Murphy, Patrick D. "Beyond Humanism: Mythic Fantasy and Inhumanist Philosophy in the Long Poems of Robinson Jeffers and Gary Snyder." *American Studies* 30, no. 1 (1989): 53–71.

————. "B. Traven: Anarchist from the Jungle. Anarcho-Primitivism in the Jungle Novels." In *B. Traven,* ed. Schürer and Jenkins, 216–25.

————. "Grandmother Borderland: Placing Identity and Ethnicity." *ISLE: Interdisciplinary Studies in Literature and Environment* 1, no. 1 (1993): 35–41.

————. *Literature, Nature, and Other: Ecofeminist Critiques.* Albany: State Univ. of New York Press, 1995.

————. "Reclaiming the Power: Robinson Jeffers's Verse Novels." *Western American Literature* 22, no. 2 (1987): 125–48.

————, ed. *The Literature of Nature: An International Sourcebook.* Chicago: Fitzroy Dearborn, 1998.

Naranjo-Morse, Nora. *Mud Woman: Poems from the Clay.* Tucson: Univ. of Arizona Press, 1992.

Nfah-Abbenyi, Juliana Makuchi. "Ecological Postcolonialism in African Women's Literature." In *Literature of Nature,* ed. Murphy, 344–49.

———. *Gender in African Women's Writing: Identity, Sexuality, and Difference.* Bloomington: Indiana Univ. Press, 1997.

Ngugi wa Thiong'o. *Petals of Blood.* London: Heinemann, 1977. New York: E. P. Dutton, 1978.

Norden, C. Christopher. "Ecological Restoration and the Evolution of Postcolonial National Identity in the Maori and Australian Aboriginal Novel." In *Literature of Nature,* ed. Murphy, 270–76.

Nzomo, Maria. "Women and Democratization Struggles in Africa, What Relevance to Postmodernist Discourse?" In *Feminism/Postmodernism/Development,* ed. Parpart and Marchand, 131–41.

Ombaka, Christine. "War and Environment in African Literature." In *Literature of Nature,* ed. Murphy, 327–36.

O'Grady, John P. *Pilgrims to the Wild: Everett Ruess, Henry David Thoreau, John Muir, Clarence King, Mary Austin.* Salt Lake City: Univ. of Utah Press, 1993.

Olafson, Robert B. "B. Traven's Six-Novel Epic of the Mexican Revolution: An Overview." In *B. Traven,* ed. Schürer and Jenkins, 141–47.

Ortiz, Simon J. "The Language We Know." In *I Tell You Now: Autobiographical Essays by Native American Writers,* ed. Brian Swann and Arnold Krupat, 185–94. Lincoln: Univ. of Nebraska Press, 1987.

———. *Woven Stone.* Tucson: Univ. of Arizona Press, 1992.

Ortner, Sherry B. "Is Female to Male as Nature Is to Culture?" In *Woman, Culture, and Society,* ed. Michelle Rosaldo and Louise Lamphere, 67–87. Stanford, CA: Stanford Univ. Press, 1974.

Owens, Louis. "'The Song Is Very Short': Native American Literature and Literary Theory." *Weber Studies* 12, no. 3 (1995): 51–62.

———. *Wolfsong.* Albuquerque: West End Press, 1991.

Parpart, Jane L., and Marianne H. Marchand, "Exploding the Canon: An Introduction/Conclusion." In *Feminism/Postmodernism/Development,* ed. Parpart and Marchand, 1–22.

———, eds. *Feminism/Postmodernism/Development.* London: Routledge, 1995.

Piercy, Marge. *Woman on the Edge of Time.* New York: Fawcett Crest, 1977.

Plant, Judith, ed. *Healing the Wounds: The Promise of Ecofeminism.* Philadelphia: New Society, 1990.

Plant, Judith, and Christopher Plant, eds. *Turtle Talk: Voices for a Sustainable Future.* Philadelphia: New Society, 1990.

Platt, Kamala. "Ecocritical Chicana Literature: Ana Castillo's 'Virtual Realism.'" In *Ecofeminist Literary Criticism,* ed. Gaard and Murphy, 139–57.

———. "Two Centuries of Environmental Writing in India." In *Literature of Nature,* ed. Murphy, 315–24.

Poe, Edgar Allan. *The Narrative of Arthur Gordon Pym.* 1838. New York: Hill and Wang, 1960.

Pratt, Dale, and Barbara Gordon. "The Environment and Nineteenth- and Twentieth-Century Spanish Literature." In *Literature of Nature*, ed. Murphy, 248–56.

Raglon, Rebecca, and Marian Scholtmeijer. "Shifting Ground: Metanarratives, Epistemology, and the Stories of Nature." *Environmental Ethics* 18, no. 1 (spring 1996): 19–38.

Rebolledo, Tey Diana. "Tradition and Mythology: Signatures of Landscape in Chicana Literature." In *The Desert Is No Lady: Southwestern Landscapes in Women's Writing and Art*, ed. Vera Norwood and Janice Monk, 96–124. New Haven, CT: Yale Univ. Press, 1987.

Rebolledo, Tey Diana, and Eliana S. Rivero. Introduction to *Infinite Divisions: An Anthology of Chicana Literature*, ed. Rebolledo and Rivero, 1–33. Tucson: Univ. of Arizona Press, 1993.

Rhys, Jean. *Wide Sargasso Sea*. 1966. New York: Norton, 1982.

Rich, Adrienne. "Notes toward a Politics of Location." In *Women, Feminist Identity and Society in the 1980s: Selected Papers*, ed. Myriam Díaz-Diocaretz and Iris M. Zavala, 7–22. Philadelphia: John Benjamins, 1985.

Roberts, Neil, and Terry Gifford. "The Idea of Nature in English Poetry." In Murphy, *Literature of Nature*, 166–76.

Rocheleau, Dianne, Barbara Thomas-Slayter, and Esther Wangari, eds. *Feminist Political Ecology: Global Issues and Local Experiences*. New York: Routledge, 1996.

Rogers, Gary W. "The Mora Valley and Frank Waters's *People of the Valley*." *South Dakota Review* 31 (spring 1993): 132–41.

Rolston, Holmes, III. *Philosophy Gone Wild: Essays in Environmental Ethics*. Buffalo, NY: Prometheus Books, 1986.

Rosaldo, Renato. *Culture and Truth: The Remaking of Social Analysis*. Boston: Beacon, 1989.

Ruether, Rosemary Radford. "First and Third World Women: Spirituality and Ecology." *Vox Feminarum: The Canadian Journal of Feminist Spirituality* 1, no. 2 (Sept. 1996): 28–33.

Russ, Joanna. *We Who Are about To. . . .* 1977. London: The Women's Press, 1987.

Ryden, Kent S. "Landscape with Figures: Nature, Folk, Culture, and the Human Ecology of American Environmental Writing." *ISLE: Interdisciplinary Studies in Literature and Environment* 4, no. 1 (spring 1997): 1–28.

Salleh, Ariel. "Second Thoughts on *Rethinking Ecofeminist Politics*: A Dialectical Critique." *ISLE: Interdisciplinary Studies in Literature and Environment* 1, no. 2 (fall 1993): 93–106.

Sanchez, Carol Lee. "Animal, Vegetable, and Mineral: The Sacred Connection." In Adams, *Ecofeminism and the Sacred*, 207–28.

Scheese, Don. *Nature Writing: The Pastoral Impulse in America*. New York: Twayne, 1996.

Schürer, Ernst, and Philip Jenkins, eds. *B. Traven: Life and Work*. University Park: Pennsylvania State Univ. Press, 1987.

Shiga Naoya. "At Kinosaki" ("Kinosaki ni te," 1917). Trans. Edward Seidensticker. In *Modern Japanese Literature*, comp. and ed. Donald Keene, 272–77. New York: Grove Press, 1956.

Shiva, Vandana. *Staying Alive: Women, Ecology, and Development*. London: Zed Books, 1988.

Silko, Leslie Marmon. *Almanac of the Dead*. New York: Penguin, 1991.

Siporin, Ona. "Terry Tempest Williams and Ona Siporin: A Conversation." *Western American Literature* 31, no. 2 (1996): 99–113.

Slovic, Scott H. *Seeking Awareness in American Nature Writing: Henry Thoreau, Annie Dillard, Edward Abbey, Wendell Berry, Barry Lopez*. Salt Lake City: Univ. of Utah Press, 1992.

Slovic, Scott H., and Terrell F. Dixon, eds. *Being in the World: An Environmental Reader for Writers*. New York: Macmillan, 1993.

Smiley, Jane. *A Thousand Acres*. New York: Fawcett Columbine, 1992.

Smith, Patricia Clark. "Coyote Ortiz: *Canis Iatrans Iatrans* in the Poetry of Simon Ortiz." In *Studies in American Indian Literature*, ed. Paula Gunn Allen, 192–210. New York: Modern Language Association, 1983.

Snyder, Gary. *He Who Hunted Birds in His Father's Village: The Dimensons of a Haida Myth*. Bolinas, CA: Grey Fox Press, 1979.

———. *No Nature: New and Selected Poems*. New York: Pantheon, 1992.

Spiller, Robert E., et al. *Literary History of the United States*. 3 vols. 1946–48. 4th rev. ed., 2 vols. New York: Macmillan, 1974.

Spretnak, Charlene. "Earthbound and Personal Body as Sacred." In *Ecofeminism and the Sacred*, ed. Adams, 261–80.

———. "Ecofeminism: Our Roots and Flowering." In *Reweaving the World*, ed. Diamond and Orenstein, 3–14.

Starhawk. *The Fifth Sacred Thing*. New York: Bantam, 1993.

———. "Power, Authority, and Mystery: Ecofeminism and Earth-Based Spirituality." In *Reweaving the World*, ed. Diamond and Orenstein, 73–86.

Strassberg, Richard E., ed. and trans. *Inscribed Landscapes: Travel Writing from Imperial China*. Berkeley and Los Angeles: Univ. of California Press, 1994.

Teague, David W., and Peter Wild, eds. *The Secret Life of John C. Van Dyke: Selected Letters*. Reno: Univ. of Nevada Press, 1997.

Tepper, Sherri. *Grass*. New York: Bantam, 1990.

Thomas, Lewis. "Death in the Open." In *The Lives of a Cell: Notes of a Biology Watcher*, 96–99. New York: Viking, 1974.

Thoreau, Henry David. *Walden*. 1854. With an introduction and annotations by Bill McKibben. Boston: Beacon, 1997.

Tisdale, Sallie. *Stepping Westward: The Long Search for Home in the Pacific Northwest.* New York: Henry Holt, 1991.

Toohey, Michell Campbell. "Dialogic Abundance: Hildegard of Bingen, Francis Ellen Watkins Harper, and Paula Gunn Allen." Ph.D. diss., Indiana University of Pennsylvania, 1996.

Traherne, Thomas. *Centuries of Meditations.* In *Centuries, Poems, and Thanksgivings,* ed. H. M. Margoliouth, 1:3–225. 2 vols. Oxford: Clarendon Press, 1958.

Traven, B. *The Carreta (Der Karren,* 1931). New York: Hill and Wang, 1970.

———. *The Death Ship (Das Totenschiff,* 1926). 1934. New York: Collier, 1979.

———. *General from the Jungle (Ein General kommt aus dem Dschungel,* 1939). New York: Hill and Wang, 1974.

———. *Government (Regierung,* 1931). London: Allison & Busby, 1983.

———. *Land des Frühlings.* Berlin: Büchergilde Gutenberg, 1928.

———. *March to the Montería (Der Marsch ins Reich der Caoba,* 1933). New York: Hill and Wang, 1971.

———. *The Rebellion of the Hanged (Die Rebellion der Gehenkten,* 1936). New York: Hill and Wang, 1974.

———. *The Treasure of the Sierra Madre (Der Schatz der Sierra Madre,* 1927). 1935. New York: Signet, 1968.

———. *Trozas (Die Troza,* 1936). Trans. Hugh Young. Chicago: Ivan R. Dee, 1998.

Trinh, T. Min-ha. *Woman, Native, Other: Writing Postcoloniality and Feminism.* Bloomington: Indiana Univ. Press, 1989.

Uno Kōji. "Love of Mountains" ("Yamagoi," 1922). In *Love of Mountains: Two Stories by Uno Kōji,* trans. Elaine Gerbert, 85–226. Honolulu: Univ. of Hawai'i Press, 1997.

Vance, Linda. "Ecofeminism and the Politics of Reality." In *Ecofeminism: Women, Animals, Nature,* ed. Greta Gaard, 118–45. Philadelphia: Temple Univ. Press, 1993.

Vizenor, Gerald. *Bearheart: The Heirship Chronicles.* 1978. Reprint, Minneapolis: Univ. of Minnesota Press, 1990.

Voloshinov, V. N. *Freudianism: A Marxist Critique.* Ed. I. R. Titunik and Neal H. Bruss. Trans. I. R. Titunik. New York: Academic Press, 1976.

Walker, Alice. *In Search of Our Mother's Gardens.* New York: Harcourt Brace Jovanovich, 1983.

———. *Living by the Word: Selected Writings, 1973–1987.* New York: Harcourt Brace Jovanovich, 1988.

———. *The Temple of My Familiar.* New York: Pocket Books, 1990.

Walls, Laura Dassow. "Science and the Shaping of Nineteenth-Century American Nature Literature." In *Literature of Nature,* ed. Murphy, 18–25.

Warren, Karen J. "Feminism and Ecology: Making Connections." *Environmental Ethics* 9, no. 1 (1987): 3–20.

———, ed. *Ecological Feminist Philosophies.* Bloomington: Indiana Univ. Press, 1996.

Weisman, Leslie Kanes. *Discrimination by Design: A Feminist Critique of the Man-Made Environment.* Urbana: Univ. of Illinois Press, 1992.

Welch, Lew. *Ring of Bone: Collected Poems 1950–1971.* Bolinas, CA: Grey Fox Press, 1979.

Wennerstrom, Jack. *Soldiers Delight Journal: Exploring a Globally Rare Ecosystem.* Pittsburgh: Univ. of Pittsburgh Press, 1995.

Westling, Louise H. *The Green Breast of the New World: Landscape, Gender, and American Fiction.* Athens: Univ. of Georgia Press, 1996.

White, Hayden. "The Real, the True, and the Figurative in the Human Sciences." *Profession* 92 (1992): 15–17.

Williams, Terry Tempest. *Pieces of White Shell: A Journey to Navajoland.* Albuquerque: Univ. of New Mexico Press, 1994.

Woolf, Virginia. "The Death of the Moth." In *The Death of the Moth and Other Essays,* ed. Leonard Woolf, 3–6. New York: Harcourt Brace Jovanovich, 1974.

Wordsworth, William. "Preface to *Lyrical Ballads.*" In *The Critical Tradition: Classic Texts and Contemporary Trends,* ed. David H. Richter, 285–98. New York: St. Martin's, 1989.

Yamashita, Karen Tei. *Through the Arc of the Rain Forest.* Minneapolis: Coffee House Press, 1990.

———. *Tropic of Orange.* Minneapolis: Coffee House Press, 1997.

Yu, Kwang-chung. *The Night Watchman.* Taipei: Chiu Ko Publishing, 1992.

Yüan K'o, ed. *Shan-hai ching chiao-chu* (Guideways through mountains and seas). Shanghai: Shanghai ku-chi ch'u-pan-she, 1980.

Zogbaum, Heidi. *B. Traven: A Vision of Mexico.* Foreword by Barry Carr. Wilmington, DE: Scholarly Resources, 1992.

Index

Abbey, Edward, 21, 27, 28, 29, 50, 177, 216; *Desert Solitaire*, 21, 50; *The Monkey Wrench Gang*, 27
Aboriginal epic songs, 55, 67
Achebe, Chinua, 68
Acoma Pueblo, 106
Adams, Carol J., 175, 204, 205, 213; *Ecofeminism and the Sacred*, 204, 205, 206
Adamson, Joni, 64; *The Middle Place*, 64
African Americans, 79, 180. *See also* hooks, bell
African literature. *See* Emecheta, Buchi; Head, Bessie
agency, 75–76, 77, 82–84, 87
agrarianism, 30, 163–66
AIDS, 171
alienation, 53, 88, 97, 172, 209
Allen, Paula Gunn, 61, 62, 93
Almanac of the Dead (Silko), 37, 64
American Nature Writers (Elder), 23
anarcho-primitivism, 115. *See also* Traven, B.
Anderson, Lori, 93, 94, 160, 167–72; *Cultivating Excess*, 167–72
Anderson, Lorraine, 20; *Sisters of the Earth*, 20
Angle of Repose (Stegner), 108
Animal Dreams (Kingsolver), 29–30, 41
animal fable stories, 34–35
animism/animist, 156

"another," 88, 95–98, 104, 111. *See also* "other"
anotherness, 99–100, 103, 111
answerability, 96–98, 101. *See also* Bakhtin, Mikhail
Anthony, Michael, 67, 117–19, 130; *Green Days by the River*, 67, 117–19, 121
Anzaldúa, Gloria, 92, 94, 144
Appalachian Autumn (Bonta), 48, 49
Appalachian Spring (Bonta), 49
architectonics, 62
Armah, Ayi Kwei, 68
Arnold, Mary Ellicott, 162
Art and Answerability (Bakhtin), 96
Association for the Study of Literature and Environment (ASLE), 50, 215
Atwood, Margaret, 32, 34; *Surfacing*, 32, 34
Austin, Mary, 3, 17, 28, 66, 92, 193, 194, 196, 200
autobiography, 28

B. Traven (Zogbaum), 227 n. 8
Bakhtin, Mikhail, xii, 96–98, 203, 211; *Art and Answerability*, 96; *Problems of Dostoevsky's Poetics*, 96; *Toward a Philosophy of the Act*, 96, 97
Barth, John, 37
"Bear, The" (Faulkner), 45
Bearheart (Vizenor), 37
Before the Echo (Dunne), 6–7, 48, 49

247